KANTFLY

A Paraplegic's Story

Bobby DePalo

Kantfly: A Paraplegic's Story
Copyright © 2022 Bobby DePalo

Visit our website at
www.StillwaterPress.com
for more information.

First Stillwater River Publications Edition

ISBN: 978-1-955123-61-7

1 2 3 4 5 6 7 8 9 10
Written by Bobby DePalo
Cover design by Lindsay Whelan
Cover photo by Shelby Sprague
Interior book design by Matthew St. Jean
Published by Stillwater River Publications,
Pawtucket, RI, USA.

Publisher's Cataloging-In-Publication Data
(Prepared by The Donohue Group, Inc.)

Names: DePalo, Bobby, author.
Title: Kantfly : a paraplegic's story / Bobby DePalo.
Description: First Stillwater River Publications edition. |
Pawtucket, RI, USA : Stillwater River Publications, [2021]
Identifiers: ISBN 9781955123617
Subjects: LCSH: DePalo, Bobby. | Paraplegics--Biography. |
Paraplegia--Rehabilitation. | LCGFT: Autobiographies. |
Self-help publications.
Classification: LCC RC406.P3 D46 2021 |
DDC 362.43092--dc23

The views and opinions expressed
in this book are solely those of the author(s)
and do not necessarily reflect the views
and opinions of the publisher.

KANTFLY

A Paraplegic's Story

PROLOGUE

I DEDICATE THIS BOOK to my beautiful cousin and best friend, Carolyn Sonstroem Forest. She inspired me like no other and was truly the bravest person I have ever known. It is Carolyn's words that I try to remember, especially when I am feeling a little down or itching for a pity party. I have learned so much from her.

While battling cancer, she shared this poem with me and taught me never to give up. It was her favorite.

"Hope is the thing with feathers that perches in the soul and sings the tune without the words and never stops at all." *Emily Dickinson*

I am not a writer, but I wanted to tell my story—and I knew that in doing so, I needed to do it in proper book form. However, I couldn't write a proper book; I didn't know how. So, I did a little online research, changed some of the names to protect the innocent, borrowed some writing books, and got lots of help from my godmother..., Aunt Norma. Her relentless encouragement to get this book done pushed me in my goal to help others. "Thank you, Auntie. I could not have done it without you."

It has taken me twenty years to throw all my notes together and get it down on paper. I'm ashamed of that. My initial goal was to help someone that needed it. I think two reasons prolonged me from finishing it from start to finish. The first, my life got in the way. That's the ashamed part. It's no excuse. The second? It hurts to do it. It really sucks. Reliving that time in my life, time and time again, going over every sentence, looking for grammar errors, stuff like that—was really hard.

But thank God for bladder infections. I would have to guess that seventy-five percent of this book/journal thing was written while I had a urinary tract infection—up late at night and trying to keep my mind off the neuropathic pain it caused me. Lying on my right side, pressing my p.t. cane in my "spot" on my back to block pain signals from getting out and typing the only way I know how. With one finger. I must have the strongest middle finger in the world. It poked 95,663 keys plus the mistakes and changes along the way.

Anyway, it's done. I hope to God that it helps someone find a little inspiration—and a lot of hope.

I also want to thank the brave men and women of the Foster Police, Fire and Rescue Depts. Also, the dedicated staff at Rhode Island Hospital and the tireless, devoted and unsung heroes at Kent Hospital in Warwick, Rhode Island.

Lastly, I want to thank author, C. K. Sholly. She is an amazing writer, editor and friend. I have learned so much from her as we sat by my fireplace and worked on each other's books together. I still don't know if I should be calling mine a journal or a memoir. I guess I'll find out though. I'm still learning.

If I come across as ungrateful for any of the care I have received, please know that my perception of things was that of a wounded soul. People like "Nurse Ratchet," or anyone else I may have poked fun at, continue to have my utmost respect and appreciation for what they did for me. I will never forget.

Maybe I don't belong writing a book, but that's okay; I just wanted someone to know my story. Someone that needs hope. Someone like me.

To the Moms,

If you, your spouse, child, family member or friend has experienced sudden paralysis, at whatever level and you are searching for hope, please go right to Chapter 69, and skip some of the heartache. That part of the story you already know. I hope you will see that there really is a bright light at the end of your dark tunnel.

And if I ever get this story published, then maybe someday, someone will say, "Hey, I just read a journal from another person with paralysis. He says that it really does get better! He wants you to know that!"

If it helps just one person, just a little, then it's worth writing, because the initial fear and anguish of experiencing paralysis is something no one should ever have to go through alone.

1

THE THUNDEROUS *"CRACK!"* sounded so final—even after I hit the ground, its echo lingered in my mind, mimicking the solid snap of a cleanup batter connecting with a fastball.

From my heaving chest, a low-pitched *"crunch"* instantly followed, and although my mind worked frantically to process the data, my heart already sensed a loss and began to sadden.

A kaleidoscope of colors swirled vividly before my eyes, blurring my vision with dots of reds, yellows and blues—forcing my eyelids to blink crazily while trying to make sense of it all. I was suddenly on the cold, hard and prickly ground, but wasn't sure why.

Snowflakes blew sideways and added to my confusion,—and a sense of bewilderment, just sort of hovered there, like a thick fog over a rocky sea shoal. *When did it start snowing?* I thought, and shook my head twice, stunned by the sudden change before me.

And between long blinks, I caught glimpses of orangey-colored leaves but wasn't sure if they were real or not. I wasn't sure if anything was.

Primal instincts triggered involuntary movements as I raced frantically to get to my feet. I jumped upwards, about a foot or so, and then fell clumsily back to the ground, panting with short and rapid half-breaths.

What just happened to me? I asked myself, as a pit began to form in the bottom of my stomach, making me instantly nauseated. *Get up!* I told myself. *Why can't I get up? Get up! What is..., what is happening to me?* I lay motionless for a few seconds before jumping up again, this time with more determination and force. Again, I fell back to the ground, fast and hard in a puff of dry and stifling dirt, shutting my eyes tightly to it all, hoping it would all go away.

Among the snowflakes, dusty leave particles squalled from my sudden impact, and I detected a fresh scent of pine needles, trailed by an evanescent hint of garden loam.

At first, my heart beat fast, redlining to a dangerous rev, and then slowed to a steady pound, low and deep like a tribal drum, bellowing mournfully in a sacrificial ceremony. It was all so surreal...

Why can't I get up? Why? I don't understand!

The maddening ring in my head made it hard to think, and it pierced my eardrums along with sharp jabs that gave birth to an instant migraine that hammered my head on every heartbeat. I still kept trying, though. I still kept trying to get up. My upper body flopped around like a fish out of water, yet my lower half never moved, as if it were a suction cup that stuck flatly and firmly to the cold, hard ground.

"No...!" I screamed, through tightly clenched teeth, looking in all directions but seeing nothing recognizable except slanted twigs and thick underbrush that looked to be cold to the touch.

With my back to the ground, I propped my top half up on one elbow and threw my throbbing head back to think. That's when I noticed my back and front ribs were killing me beyond belief. I couldn't make sense of that either.

"Oh, shhhhit—this is bad!" I said aloud, while grasping and searching the ground with widespread fingers as if I had lost something dear,—then I dug my fingers into the forest floor and held on tight.

Calm down and don't panic..., just think! I repeated the same thought over and over. *Calm down and don't panic, think!* And in time, eventually I was able to slow my thrashing down to a quivering stall.

There I stayed, shaking like a leaf, trying to get my wits about me. Instinctively, I began to use the martial arts breathing exercises I had been so used to. *That's it..., slow it down. Remember your training. Breathe in through your nose and out through your mouth. Just breathe.*

After a few moments, things were clearer, and my heart rate slowed. I could think. I shut my eyes tight, continued my breathing, and then slowly tested my legs and feet by commanding them to move—but they didn't obey. Quickly, I tried to move them again. Nothing. Nothing!

Devastated—I screamed in my head! *There's no connection to my legs!* I thought it but didn't fully believe it. *What did I do? Did I just break my back?* I asked myself, looking up to the heavens but only in my mind as my eyes were still shut tight. *That loud crack, was that my spine breaking? Did I really just break my spine? Oh, come on..., please..., you've got to be kidding me! Don't tell me that, please, it can't be!*

Again, I commanded my legs and feet to move but there was no response—nothing at all. The sensation was so weird and all so..., I can't explain it..., it was all just so weird.

Besides my head and spine, another intense ache emerged and gripped me like a boa. The front, the back and even the sides of my torso were hurting me. I needed to deal with it, so, holding back tears and with a silent whine, I blinked hard—twice, I think. Then, gritted my teeth and breathed anxiously—this time through my mouth—fast, just like a pissed off Brahma Bull, snorting in rhythmic pants, seconds before the gate opens to a taunting rodeo crowd.

I tried to get up again but slumped back to the rock-hard ground, lifelessly, feeling like a rag doll being tossed aside by an uninterested three-year-old.

"No...! Don't!" I whispered. "Come on, please don't. Don't do this to me!" I begged and pleaded louder. "No!"

Propped up by my left quivering elbow and choreographed by emotions, my right arm flailed about hysterically, as the Scarecrow's did in the land of Oz. I remembered those winged monkeys—and how they paralyzed the Scarecrow by tearing him in two at the waist, leaving him feebly searching for his lower half as he tried frantically to get up. The frightened soul pointed in crisscrossed directions and went on and on about his sudden plight.

"They threw one leg over here! And another one over there!" He complained in frustration and confusion, just like me. I remember watching that movie as a kid and imagined how creepy it would feel if I couldn't feel *my* lower half.

The thought of the Scarecrow made me begin to move more erratically. So, without thinking, I reached down to find my butt and quickly latched onto it too, except it felt as though I was holding onto someone else's!

Then, without warning and as if touching a red-hot stove, my hand retreated right back up to where it felt safe again. Did I not want to know? I paused. Then tried again.

Once more, my hand probed bravely downward. But much, much slower this time. Inch by inch my fingers crept, then reached and latched onto a thigh, or at least where and what I thought was a thigh. I squeezed the slab-of-meat-like limb and waited. I squeezed again, and again I waited. I felt nothing though, nothing at all.

Burning chest pain prevented me from tilting my head forward to look, so I tried to use my mind's eye to see.

Am I paralyzed? Again, I squeezed. *Don't think it! Don't think it or it may come true!* I squeezed the slab tighter—again nothing. That's when I began to think of my daughter, Lauren.

Will I be able to walk her down the aisle on her wedding day? Oh my God! I relaxed my grip. *Am I grabbing the wrong thing? Are my legs even there?* One more squeeze. Still nothing. That result triggered a frantic squirm, which must have looked as though a thousand leggy spiders covered me, and I needed to get them off right away.

I had to get up, get out of my body and run away from it all. My body couldn't do it but my mind could. So, instead, I closed my eyes and tilted my head back between my shoulders to escape.

The thought of Lauren's wedding day was foremost on my mind. With my mind's eye, I imagined the interior of St. Rocco's Church, with all its saintly statues and magnificent stained-glass windows.

Lauren stood nervously posed in an old fashioned, white-laced wedding gown made just for her. She was waiting in the foyer, looking so beautiful by the lighted, red-glassed prayer candles and the full-sized marble likeness of the Virgin Mary. She was waiting for me.

I will never get to walk her down the aisle, I thought. *I just know it.* I squeezed my eye lids tighter together, tighter, in order to see. And, although she was just thirteen and still far from that day, a deep sense of disappointment set in. It was like getting the wind knocked out of me from a sucker punch to the gut. Only there was no one there to punch back. I was powerless and it sickened me.

Of all the worries that troubled me, under that tree, the thought of disappointing my daughter on her wedding day bothered me the most. More than I can speak about, so I'll leave it there.

Once again and without being able to see downward, my hand searched aimlessly below my waist, trying to locate some-thing familiar..., anything—anything at all that resembled a body part. *Keep searching,* I told myself. *Something has to be there that I recognize—anything!*

My head still hurt and my back and ribs ached beyond words. As my eyes darted across the wintry sky above, my right hand searched down a little lower, groping and slapping lifeless objects that I still didn't recognize as my own. I couldn't tell if I was slapping my thigh or a dead log. But I slapped, and I slapped, and I slapped.

Dry, crackly leaves crumbled through my stiff, icy fingers, while random ground scratching unearthed foliage from seasons past. Churning them up released the musty old smell of mold and decay. It made me think of death.

Where the hell are my legs? I asked again, searching for an answer but receiving none. *I can't feel them! I really can't feel them! Were my limbs separated from me? Were they torn off and thrown away somewhere in another direction? Like the Scarecrow's?*

I felt sad for myself. I felt bad for the Scarecrow. And, in a long moment of stillness— in awe, snippets of a familiar scene began to play out in my mind's watery eye...

2

I REMEMBERED WATCHING A World War II movie depicting an unsuspecting soldier suddenly finding himself in a predicament not unlike my own.

The year was 1944. He was an American GI from an Italian neighborhood in the Bronx of New York, on patrol in the South of France just days after the D-Day invasion of Normandy. He and his buddies had survived the beach landing together, only to encounter even fiercer enemy fighting in the occupied townships ahead.

To the side of his helmet, the young soldier took a rubber band and fastened to it a picture card of Saint Christopher, the patron saint of good luck. Tucked safely underneath and inside the helmet was a picture of his childhood sweetheart, Catherine. Deeply in love, he took the photograph out to gaze at her so often that his coarse and grimy thumbprints began to wear her angelic image away.

He and his pals fought for their country and for the girls they left behind, but most of all, they fought for each other.

I remembered the look on the young soldier's face as he gawked downward just moments after stepping on a German land mine.

He just sat there, quietly, unable to move, gazing at the blood-soaked stumps that were once his legs, while his buddies helplessly looked on through hopeless eyes.

The handsome young private had been the tough guy, the cool

one in the squad, and in the blink of an eye—along with his legs, it was all just whisked away.

He was no longer the same man he once was. I could identify with his sudden transformation. As he sat in silence, the shock of it all remained imbedded in his face,—and I envisioned that same expression on mine...

I've ruined Debbie's life, I thought, waving my hands conversationally to no one in particular. *How am I going to protect my wife and kids now? How are they going to handle this? They will hate me and I don't blame them. I've ruined their lives. I've ruined everything.*

A wimpy sigh jump-started a sickening rage and made me contemplate things, all sorts of things. The more I added up my losses, the more enraged I became. I was becoming blindly furious.

In sports, fury had often fueled my will, and in a pinch, it produced adrenaline to help me persevere. This time I knew I was in more than just a pinch.

I had always believed that a brush with death could summon your life to pass before your eyes, and either you give in and accept your fate, or you search for another way.

So, as faces and events scrolled past my shut-tight eyes, I searched hard for that other way...

3

M<small>Y MIND WAS</small> on overdrive but my body felt half dead. The two halves didn't match up! I was out of sync! I laid there, motionless, squeezing my eyelids together in hope that it would all go away, but I knew it wouldn't. And it didn't.

What am I gonna do? Just..., what..., am I..., gonna do? It's getting cold out here and I'm in trouble. Big trouble. Someone even said that we may be getting a small snowstorm. Great. Like a movie reel, my life continued to pass before my eyes. More emotions arose and flooded my bloodstream with adrenaline, churning out horrible thoughts and fears.

Think! I kept saying to myself. *Keep on thinking!*

Snowflakes stuck to my eyelashes like caked on mascara, so I blinked like a nervous wreck and sifted through the voices in my screaming head. As moments passed, the voices seemed to scream louder and all at once. There had to be scores of them! One stood out, though. One clear and soul-stirring voice stood out above all. The voice that screamed the words, "never surrender!"

Never surrender, I said to myself in a whisper. *No matter what, don't give up. Never surrender, ever!*

I always thought the term "Never Surrender" was the ultimate saying and had valued its meaning since reading about Winston Churchill, my all-time hero, in history class as a young boy. Some sayings just stick with you, and I was glad because giving up was not an option for me, and I needed a label to put on my feelings of action. Besides, I knew the secret. I knew the secret of the Rain Dance and why it rained for the Indians when they danced. (It was because they danced until it did.) They never gave up.

Never surrender! I told myself. *Don't give up! You know the secret!* So once more, I threw my torso upward, upward toward the sky and away from it all, only to clumsily flop back down, down to where I began. I clenched my teeth even tighter and tried again. I did it again and again and again, only to fall back harder on my broken back and my throbbing head.

"You mother fucker!" I said aloud, with total surprise in my tone. "You piece of fuckin' shit." This time I said it with sarcasm and disgust.

"Don't you fuckin' do this to me! Don't you fuckin' do it, you fuckin' mother fucker!" *Whoa! Did I just say that? Did I say those words to Him?* I pictured His face as I confronted Him. I pictured it while calling Him on. I was talking to God.

I had never spoken to God like that before, never, and maybe my punishment had already begun because a chilling emotion started to emerge that really unnerved me. I couldn't quite put my finger on it at the time but it was terrifying. It was an overwhelming feeling of being smothered. A feeling of being suffocated. A feeling of being buried alive!

The walls in my mind were closing in on me, and I couldn't get out. I pushed my legs and feet again, wanting to get up and run away, yet felt nothing. It was the most horrifying feeling. *I feel panicky, panicky in a way I have never felt before. Is this what they call, anxiety?*

I had heard of anxiety but never actually experienced it. But that smothering feeling? Now that was a little more familiar...

4

I HAVE A MEMORY as a kid while playing with my friends at Galilee, our favorite family beach down at Point Judith, Rhode Island. I was probably about eight. It was my turn. My turn to be buried from the neck down beneath the cool, wet, beach sand. I secretly dreaded the weighted feeling on my chest but didn't show any fear to the rest of the boys. Showing fear was a sign of weakness, and I didn't want that. I knew that everyone else felt the same way I did but would never admit it.

As the sand pails of heavy mud began to cover my legs and torso, a sense of panic flirted with my mind, and then the weight of it all pushed down on my chest like a ton of bricks!

I gasped for air and began to get up, but while trying, a dreadful feeling overwhelmed me. And, the more I tried to move under that heavy sand, the more I felt like I was suffocating. Suffocating and being buried alive!

That was a long time ago, I thought. *But I'll never forget that feeling. Was that anxiety?*

Again, I cursed at God, and again I saw His face. With clenched fists and closed eyes, I visualized God in that gold-framed picture, the one that most Roman Catholics hang over their marriage beds. I knew and remembered that picture very well.

I remember He had a nice face. His long, straight hair was parted in the middle, and His thin beard and mustache kind of reminded me of a hippy but more like Clint Eastwood from his nineteen six-ties spaghetti westerns. That's how I imagined God.

I grew up around that picture yet never thought much about it at the time. It was a part of my childhood. I remember once asking my mother if that was a picture of God or Jesus. "Both," she said, and I just accepted that without question.

I liked that particular portrait of God, mostly because of the fond childhood memories associated with it. Like Sundays, after church, when I would be in charge of piling the old-timer's fox fur overcoats and gangster-looking fedora hats on my grandmother's bed. I would glance at the face of God on the wall above the headboard after each family member arrived. The oldest boy always had the job of the coat check. It was a proud job to have.

Gazing up from under that picture, I remember the smell of chopped garlic, fresh onion and basil and the clinking sounds of the thick milk glasses and flowery dinner plates skimming the soapy sides of the ever-busy, white porcelain sink.

Voices multiplied, as more and more family members arrived at the Providence tenement, always entering the house through the gas-warmed kitchen, the heart of the home.

The bubbling sound of boiling water told me that Grandma Dena's macaroni and meatballs were coming soon. She made the best meatballs. Sometimes she served sweet sausage with her ziti. Other times we found twine-tied braccioli (pronounced bra-shole), buried in the slow-cooked tomato sauce that we called "gravy."

The silver cheese grater and fresh Italian bread from the bakery were on the table minutes before the meal, which signaled us to go wash our hands and get ready to sit.

I couldn't wait to get back out to the kitchen, so I threw coats and jackets on the bottom, pocketbooks on top and wrapped the knitted scarves around the bedposts. I tried to keep everyone's things together as a set so I could easily find them later.

Then I made a parting glance at God's face as I left the bedroom.

Coming in, I always had to look at Him and then again going out. I don't know why. Maybe because unlike the bloody crucifix that hung morbidly over our church's altar, that picture of Him made me feel safe.

———————

AS I LAY PARALYZED FROM the waist down, I thought of that face until intense chest pain got my attention again. I breathed inward but had to stop short. I had bruised enough ribs in karate to know that this time they were probably broken. My lower rib cage ached with every breath too, so I tried to reposition myself for some relief.

I thought I could just flip over onto my side, so I tried. Big mistake. The burning back pain stopped me from moving another inch and left me lying halfway between my side and my back. I was stuck in an awkward position and now it hurt more than before.

With my left elbow planted in the dirt, I held my shattered back slightly off the cold ground, but it was becoming unbearable. I dropped my eyelids in order to deal with it, but I must have passed out because I never heard it coming.

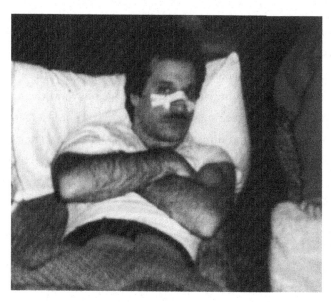

Broken nose and ribs after kickboxing.

5

I NEVER HEARD IT coming. Startled by the growl of the approaching bear, I quickly came to alertness, hunkered down and got myself ready for the big bruin's massive pounce. I waited. I waited but it never came! *What the hell was that? Was that a dream? Was that a real growl I heard? Was that a bear?*

Still, I waited and listened with all senses.

It could not have been a bear! I told myself. *This is Rhode Island, not Maine. It can't be a bear, can it?* I closed my eyes and listened for more.

There it is again! The rumble was hair-raising this time and sounded like it was right behind me!

My crooked neck barred my head from turning, so my eyes took over and although it hurt to do, scanned well beyond their normal reach. I spotted my tree stand for the very first time. There it was. It was all twisted up and flipped upside down, leaning where it landed against the tree trunk at the base of the tree. The broken chain dangled from it, slowly swinging in the breeze like a silent pendulum inside a grandfather clock.

My deer hunting tree stand looks a lot different from this angle, especially it being on the ground. Unfamiliar, I thought.

Again, the grizzly groan hummed in a drawn out and deliberate rhythm, totally scaring the living crap out of me! Pursing my eyebrows together, I listened, held my breath and listened again.

I began to notice that when I held my breath, the growling stopped. And, when I breathed, it began again. I repeated the exercise a few more times, and it didn't take me long to figure it out after that.

How stupid. I thought. *Man, how stupid!* It was me doing it! It was me all along!

Every time I exhaled, a gruff purr rattled from my diaphragm, like a wheeze of a sleeping dragon. It sounded so foreign to me, yet I embraced it, because it seemed to release some of the pain from my body.

As I growled like a wounded animal, I realized that a survival mechanism was kicking in. My body was fighting back.

Still stuck halfway on my side, my left elbow was holding up my torso just inches off the wintery ground, while my triceps' muscle quivered uncontrollably nonstop.

The snow had stopped falling, but I hadn't noticed when. I was covered in it though. Without planning, I slapped my right hand to the forest floor and panned for a stick, any stick, and on my first try, I found the perfect one.

Stripped of its bark and dark in color, white oak I think, it looked to be about 1 inch in diameter and around 4 inches long, about the size of a child's big pencil. Crispy and cold to the touch, it had moisture stains on it, more so on one side than the other. Without bothering to blow on it or brush it off, I placed the thick twig between my teeth in the left side of my mouth and bit down hard.

Bite the bullet, I told myself, and like a moth to a flame, my tongue found the stick right away. It tasted bitter, with a metallic-like tang to it. Like the way tabletops smell after you dust them down with Old English Furniture Polish. It reminded me of stale rain.

I bit down harder and set my jaw like a locked vise grip. Immediately, I felt some relief in taking charge of the situation, and for the first time, I was able to take back some control and combat the awful hurt.

I guessed that I might be bleeding internally and worried that a broken rib might splinter and pierce an organ or something. I didn't want to think about what a broken spine could do. So, with my arm shaking like a trembling tree leaf in a wind storm, I carefully tried to reposition myself, but any effort to move, further increased my agony. I just kept thinking—*never surrender. Just, never surrender.* The intense ache was becoming unbearable. So, again, I shut my eyes tight and dealt with it...

6

AFTER A TIME, I opened my tired eyes to the densely-wooded scene around me, not sure how much time had passed. I tried to gage it by the snowfall but couldn't think that clearly. By then, I was really tired and convinced that I couldn't hold my back off the ground for another second.

My arm wants to give in and rest so badly, I thought. *Don't give in! You can't let your broken back touch the ground or you'll never be able to stand it. I* was aggravated and needed to vent, so again, and only in my mind, I roared at God in defiance. *I won't let you beat me, I won't!* He let this happen to me, so I held Him personally responsible.

Sunday school had taught me that God was all caring, and He'd look after me forever if I were a good person, and I *was* a good person! I couldn't understand it. I was offended, and I wanted Him to know it. Never before had I disrespected Him, or cursed at Him like that, ever! However, never before had He done such an unforgivable thing to me. I hated Him for that. *Had I committed a mortal sin for cursing at Him? Was I going to Hell?* I didn't care.

My mind was shooting off in all directions. I was desperate and needed to take back what I did that day along with all the events that led up to my nightmare. I needed to change what I did.

Change it, I thought. *Change what you did!*

Crazily, I closed my eyes and willed it to change. I willed it with all I had.

This shouldn't have happened, I told myself. *I need another chance to make it right. Take it back, take back what you did and do it again, but this time do it right! I'll put my safety strap on this time. I'll do it right. Take it all back, all of it! Turn the clock back and do it again. Turn back time and get another chance. Superman did it, and I can do it too! Turn it back God damn it!* I talked myself right into it and dove into the fantasy headfirst.

Superman did it! He circled the planet from outer space and slowed its rotation down to a complete stop! Then, he reversed the earth's direction and then stopped it at a point in time just before the events that led up to the death of Lois Lane. He turned back time! He then did things differently to create an alternative outcome!

Although sensing my mind was bordering on delirium, I continued to try to make it happen. I lay there *willing* the foolish fantasy with all that I had.

I imagined planet Earth like a swirling blue and white marble, spinning cumbersomely in pitch-black outer space. I then willed it to slow its rotation to a complete stop.

Then I willed it to reverse its direction by spinning it clockwise and slowed it down again to the point in time just moments before my fall.

I put my safety strap on this time and then willed the earth to begin spinning in its normal rotation again.

Nothing is impossible, I thought. *I can do this!*

I think as desperation prevailed, reality slipped away and assigned fantasy to search for a way out.

I truly believed it could work, until shaken from the delusion by the chill from an icy wind gust, which bit at my exposed neck like the ghostliest draft. My legs weren't cold, though. My legs *weren't* cold.

Holding a constant pressure on the stick caused my jaw to throb and my teeth to wobble in their sockets, but I bit down hard just the same.

Stay focused and don't drift off again, I told myself. *That was ridiculous, you cannot stop the earth from spinning, you cannot turn back time, and you cannot have another chance. You're becoming delirious. Stay awake and think of another way...*

7

JUST AS SOON as I told myself not to slip into a daydream, I would fall back into another one. It was like one trance after another. My eyelids were heavy, yet my mind still raced. I was sleepy, so sleepy—it felt good to close my watery eyes, so I let them fall and gave in to another dream.

I began to see the haunting image of a high school student, Kyle C, lying on his back, stiff, like a slab-laden corpse in an all-night coroner's lab. But Kyle wasn't dead. Kyle was paralyzed. I visualized that image of the boy, back when it happened to him as a sophomore, all those years ago.

I was probably twelve or thirteen when the local news reported that Kyle, a Cranston High School football player, had broken his neck during the East/West homecoming game. Even though we were from the rival West, the horrific tale shook us to the core.

The Kyle C tragedy grew to seismic proportions as it passed from family to family throughout the early seventies.

"Kyle is paralyzed for life," the grownups would tell us and threaten us with his plight if we played too rough.

"Do you guys want to end up like that paralyzed boy? Then knock it off, and don't play so hard or that will happen to you!" I was petrified of it.

I pictured him then, not in a wheelchair, not in a therapeutic pool and certainly not in a rehabilitation center, but flat on his back, helplessly looking up at the ceiling, 24 hours a day, 7 days a week and 365 days a year.

I imagined him battling insanity minute by minute and wearing baby diapers, with matronly-looking nurses spoon-feeding him like an infant.

Yet, as I remembered Kyle's plight, and although I could still move my neck and arms, I imagined *myself* living that way, like him. And the thought of it frightened me.

Again, I looked to the sky and this time changed strategy. I tried pleading my case instead.

God, please don't do this to me, I don't deserve it. And why me? Why are you doing this to me? I'm a good person, aren't I? With all the rotten people in this world, with people who hurt others, why would you pick me to suffer like this? Why me? I pleaded. *Why?*

Then it dawned on me! *Was God punishing me for the deer I killed the day before? The one I crippled. Was that it? Was that why?*

The way that buck died had bothered me and left me with a guilty conscience. I was now beginning to understand what I had done wrong.

Just one day before, I was bow hunting on Prudence Island when a buck and a doe made their way up a well-used deer run trail that I was waiting by.

Sitting camouflaged and undetected about eighteen feet high up a dormant oak tree, November's morning sun warmed my face as it floated up over my tree stand and the island's eastern crest. The raven-sized crows were sounding their noisy alarms from their strategic locations, drowning out the distant foghorns from the returning fishing fleet. I could just make out the bell's ding from the buoy off Bullock's Wharf, so I knew that the bay was a little rough.

At about twenty-five yards and closing, I had a good shot at the buck's heart and lungs. With the animal walking broadside to me, I felt it was a perfect shot for a quick kill.

I drew back my bow and blew a short whistle between my teeth.

The six-pointer halted and expanded his stature. My twenty-yard sight pin locked in on its target, and I elevated the bow just a hair to compensate for the extra distance.

As the arrow left the bow, the shot felt good, and it flew straight and flat, as it should have. My bow shoots at 296 feet per second and the arrow usually gets there before the sound from the string is detected. However, this time the buck heard and "jumped the string," then ducked when he sensed the arrow's flight. This rarely happens, but it can and it did.

The arrow landed high and pierced its spine, crippling the deer in its tracks. His hindquarters dropped to the ground in a spread-eagle stance, while his front legs stayed up in a lock kneed position. Using its front hooves, the buck peeled out in place and desperately tried to find traction for a frantic escape. It too reminded me of the Scarecrow.

I cringed and prayed for it to have a quick and painless death. Although it was just seconds, it seemed like an eternity before it finally fell over at about three yards from where I had hit it. The arrowheads are made of super thin surgical steel for a painless kill, with most animals being unaware that they were even shot, but I didn't like it just the same. There he lay, slowly kicking his front legs until he went into shock and took his last few breaths seconds later. It was heart-wrenching to watch, and I felt a deep sense of remorse as I watched from high up in that tree.

I had always justified my hunting by my ability to find the kill zone each and every time and to put the animal down respectfully, ethically and humanely. And, of course, to shoot only what I eat.

With my fellow hunters and myself, marksmanship was paramount and proficiency was mandatory. A biannual, state competency test is required prior to purchasing an island hunting license, so one really has to practice in order to pass the shooting test. This weeded out the guys who didn't care.

I had hunted on the island with the same guys for more than

twenty years and carefully chose my friends with the same hunting
ethics that I had.

My brother Ricky brought me to Prudence Island in the seventies, when bow hunting was still a primitive sport and game wardens
hadn't discovered the island yet.

My friend Vinnie had hunted the island from the dilapidated
house that we called Barr's shack and invited Ricky and me to rent it
with him. Our kids grew up hunting out of that old shack and shared
with us countless, unforgettable and treasured memories.

I watched as Vinnie beamed with pride when his son shot his
first deer at the age of fourteen. Vinnie couldn't wait to rub the
deer's blood on Marc's blissful face, handing down a tradition that
goes back thousands of years. I remember my son Derek and my
nephew Michael looking on with wide eyes, listening to the story
of the young Indian brave, fulfilling his rite of passage after downing
his first stag.

The Indians believed that when a hunter stalks and kills his first
prey, he acquires the skills and knowledge that the animal possesses.

When this great feat was accomplished, the young warrior was
given an eagle or turkey feather to wear proudly in his headband.
This is where the white man's term, "adding another feather to his
cap," derived.

In the ritual of harvesting his first deer, an elder hunter would
wipe a small smudge of the animal's blood to both sides of the young
brave's face. Agility, speed, and stamina are then acquired from the
deer, and both the spirit of the deer and the brave become one.

My nephew Brandon, Ricky's youngest son, looked up to his
cousins and waited impatiently for his turn, and when he turned
twelve, he received the same bow that was handed down from one
hunter to the next. We are all of the same mindset, that to allow an
animal to suffer is unacceptable.

I kept picturing that deer trying to get up from the ground that
day and it tormented me.

Was this it? I asked. *Was this the reason for my death sentence?* Inside my head, I could hear God saying, *"How do you like it, Bobby? Huh? How do you like it now? How does it feel to have* your *spine broken?"*

I was being punished for what I did and was beginning to feel as though I deserved it. I replayed that event repeatedly in my mind and gradually stopped believing that God would reverse his decision. So eventually, I quit asking.

8

I LAY THERE FEELING sorry for all the people I loved as Lauren's future wedding day played out in my mind again. I could see her in that wedding dress looking more beautiful than the stars. By now, the pain had stepped up another notch, and the thought of my spine being broken was giving me the willies. I was cold and it started snowing again.

Dry leaves from the underbrush began annoying me by tickling my face on my left cheek, but because I was on one elbow and my other arm was behind me, I couldn't reach to scratch the itch. I spent the next few minutes living through the most annoying, torturous, nonstop itch.

Is this how it's going to be? I asked. *Not being able to scratch an itch on my own face? Like Kyle C?*

I tried to figure out how much time had passed but couldn't. It was overcast, and there was no sun to tell time with, only a snowy, gray and uninviting sky.

This much is certain, I thought. *I will not be found here.* I had no reason to be in that area because I had not hunted in those woods in quite some time, so that would be the last place that they'd look for me. I also knew I was a long way from home and definitely out of shouting range. No one knew those woods as I did and finding me would be like finding a needle in a haystack. Far off the beaten path, the underbrush was thick with walls of bull briars and there were

Birthday celebration.

no trails for someone to wander by on, so if I weren't tripped over, I wouldn't be found.

Stupid, I thought. *Just stupid. How did I let this happen?*

I had been such a safety-minded hunter and preached safety to the kids until I was blue in the face. My son Derek and I had practiced safe hunting and took every precaution to make each and every hunt a safe one.

Oh my God, what about Derek? What about my son? He will be crushed. I knew my son, and I knew that he would suffer with me. It would be as if this had happened to him. Derek is one of the strongest boys there is but also the most caring. My heart was breaking from the thought of it.

How did I get into this mess? I sighed, while looking over at the broken tree stand and dangling chain. *How did I let this happen?* I tilted my head back to reflect.

Derek and me at Galilee.

I had many things on my mind that morning and was in deep thought making my way through the thicket and around the soggy swamp, layered with deep muck and stinky skunk cabbage. Debbie and I were having marital problems, so I was in deep thought as I hoofed it up a small hill, ducking under low-hanging branches until I reached a small opening within the white pines and red and white oaks. The annoying briars were knee high and made it hard to walk naturally.

I looked up as I approached the tall oak and admired my partially concealed tree stand on that tall tree without many branches. So I wouldn't lose it and to lighten my load, I removed my Buck Knife from my pocket and dropped it to the ground but not before looking for a landmark to find it later. I placed it next to a Signorina Mushroom that had a rabbit bite taken out of it. That's how we were taught to distinguish between the good mushrooms and the poisonous ones. Never eat a perfect mushroom. The animals know.

I stopped briefly, looking up to the tree stand. *Awe jeez—I forgot my safety strap. Damn it. I should go back and get it.* With both hands on my hips, I took in a long and slow breath as my chest inflated with cool country air. *Well, I'm only taking the tree stand down. I won't be sitting in it. I'll be okay.*

Nearing the oak tree, I looked up again and had to tilt my head quite a way back to view the stand because of its height. Again, it made me reconsider hiking back to the house to get the nylon-webbed safety belt I left behind.

Nah, I thought. *It's too far. I'll be careful going up. Plus, I just cut all that wood this morning, and I'm still winded from running the chainsaw all morning, let me do this and get out of here. I'll be okay.*

I talked myself right out of it.

I swapped the wrenches from my front pocket to my back and looked up to calculate the difficulty of the climb. Screwed into and staggered up the smooth-barked tree, were eighteen steel spike steps. They were like the spike steps you used to see on telephone poles before linemen started using bucket trucks for safety. Yeah, I know.

I'm sure glad I screwed those spikes into that tree last year and don't have to monkey up there on those uneven branches. It looks very high.

The metal spikes screwed into the tree all the way up to the tree stand and were spread out at about two-foot intervals. Rigid, narrow points made each step razor sharp at the ends and as deadly as a bayonet. I was always afraid of missing a step, slipping and falling, and opening myself up like a gutted fish on the way down. I knew of someone that it happened to, and he bled to death before reaching his truck for help.

Tipping my head back farther, I viewed the camouflaged deer stand sitting high up above the last step. It looked to be in good shape, but the chain that secured it to the tree appeared to be rusty. Rust was common.

Whilst climbing, I formulated a plan to outsmart that elusive whitetail buck I had previously seen and was after.

I'll take this tree stand down and chain it up into another tree about a mile away in that buck's territory. I know just the tree too. The buck will never suspect my presence because no one has hunted in that area this season yet, it's near the reservoir, and it is virtually free of human scent. I couldn't wait to get it out there.

Slowly climbing higher, I was mindful of the sharp ends of each pointy step and was again surprised at the height of the perch. *It's more than two stories up*, I thought. *I don't remember hanging it up so high.* With my right pointer finger, I reached out and pushed on the end of one of the step spikes. *Yow!* I thought. *Why would they make these things so sharp at the ends? What if someone falls off their tree stand? They'll die just from these things before they hit the ground! They should put rubber or something on the ends.*

When I finally reached the top step, I paused to take a swig of the cool fresh air, admire the view and reminisce about earlier hunts up there.

I could see quite a distance at that height, so with both feet still on the spike steps, I grabbed a branch and stretched my neck out to catch a glimpse of the stone wall which guarded the old cattle field in the distance. *Boy, if that wall could talk,* I thought. *What a story it could tell.* I thought briefly of the six bulls that jumped over it when I was a younger man. *That was one heck of a story.* I thought.

I didn't have permission to be on that property and found that exhilarating. I always found excitement in doing things that I wasn't supposed to be doing, ever since I was a kid.

I had spent many cold mornings shivering up here, I thought. *It's cold up here, even now! But I really don't mind, because being up here like this is like revisiting an old friend.*

Tightening my grip onto the branch, I was reminded of the elusive fisher cat that I watched one season while sitting high up there, concealed and totally undetected. Fisher cats, sometimes called polecats, are nasty critters. They will tear up a raccoon, evict it from its den, and take up residency like a third world occupying force.

And, I once watched a chipmunk gathering acorns for the winter, who never did notice that red fox sneaking up on it just before pouncing on the busy rodent with deadly precision. I hadn't seen the fox either until the very last second. We were *both* surprised.

Hunting was my passion and soothed me like nothing else. The sights, smells and sounds that I've observed will be etched in my mind forever.

At the very top, I pulled on the tree stand and it felt solid, so I threw my right knee up onto the bottom platform and kept my left foot planted securely on the top spiked step. The tree swayed a little from a small gust of wind. While spookily holding onto the tree with my left hand, I unhinged the tiny seat above the small platform with my right—then unfolded it by pulling it down and open. Because the seat had been folded shut for so long, I cautiously leaned back, expecting a furry mouse to come scurrying out. That was the case more times than not, especially if the tree stand hadn't been used in a while. No one was home but the telltale signs were evident. Caught between the seat's webbing were acorn shells, wood shavings and scraps of bark. I also caught a whiff of mouse or squirrel urine as I brushed off the debris, then I leaned back to inhale some fresh air but refused to look down.

I was afraid of heights—no, correction—I was petrified of falling. I could look out, but I couldn't look down. Most of my nightmares involved some type of falling scenario, and I wanted to sleep well that night, so I tightened my grip on the tree and pushed the thought far from my mind. Since I was a kid, I could monkey up any tree, branched or not, or climb up onto a house or barn roof better and faster than anyone I knew. But once I got to the top, I could never look straight down.

As a teenager I worked from staging, many stories up, swinging from one metal staging to the other, like Tarzan, too hurried to climb down from one and then up the other like you are supposed to. But again, if I looked straight down, I would freak myself right out.

Everything looks so different from up here. It's so peaceful, I thought, as the oak tree slowly swayed in the wind again. The tree was slippery from the falling snow, so I squeezed my grip on it tighter. Then, with my right hand and arm, I pulled myself up and swung my other knee onto the base. Rising up a bit, I got that spooky feeling in the pit of my stomach, like having nothing but air and infinite distance under your feet, or, like the tingles that you get when you imagine the nothingness under your elevator's floor, as it ascends past the skyscraper's highest levels. I didn't like it at all.

The hairs on the back of my neck stood up straight and my butt cheeks began to twitch. I maneuvered both feet onto the platform and stood up ever so slowly, hugging the tree bark with my face and neck, scraping some skin off my nose in the process. It stung and probably drew some blood, but the stomach butterflies bothered me more.

Then, suddenly, and without warning, a muffled 'Pop!' exploded from beneath me! It was the kind of pop something makes when it's stretched to its limits and decides to finally let go. I knew instantly what it was and what it meant for me. My worst nightmare had just come true!

The platform I was standing on left my feet and plunged down beneath me to the infinite distance below. While time slowed to an eerie crawl, I floated downward on a puffy cloud that softly carried me toward earth and away from the overcast, gray sky.

This is how it feels to fly, I briefly thought, confused, as time inched forward ever so slowly. I instinctively pulled myself from the stupor and pushed myself out and away from the tree, as not to impale myself by the pointy, spiked steps on the way down. But that sent me away from the branches with nothing to grab onto!

As I fell to my demise, I threw my right hand out to the side and turned my head in the same direction. Somehow, I knew there was a needle-covered pine branch reaching out to me from a young evergreen standing about five feet from my tree. The needles felt soft and exceptionally green for that time of year, and I strangely focused on that.

Clutching at a clump of green, I watched as the limp needles slowly slipped through my fingers and passed me by. It was so surreal. Time had nearly stopped, and I marveled at the weirdness of it all. I thought to myself, *push away from the spikes and take the fall, don't risk impalement. Push away and take the fall.*

The feeling of falling was terrifying as well as calming... almost euphoric. I wanted to accept it and make it easy, even enjoy it in some way.

My belly did flip-flops and tickled inside. I think everyone has experienced those butterflies, as most dads have thrived on goosing the family car over hilly, back road "whoop-de-dos," while the kids screamed in terror, only to beg for more. "Go faster over the hill, Daddy!"

Floated downward, I remember thinking how long it was taking to reach the ground. It took forever, and I wanted to react somehow and brace myself for impact but didn't know how. Instead, a soothing calmness came over me and prepared me for what laid ahead.

I don't remember exactly how I hit the ground, but memory of the loud *crack* that followed will never leave me.

All right, I thought. *Forget about that now. That's how I got here, now how do I get home?*

9

B Y NOW, THE stick was flattening out between my teeth and not nearly as effective as before. I guessed that I was on the ground for at least two hours, maybe even three or four. The scent of decaying leaves was all around and seemed to envelope me. It was an odor that had once pleased me.

I must have nodded out for a few minutes, only to jump awakened and feel as though my belly was full of butterflies again.

God, I thought. *I don't want to be paralyzed. I want to go home. I don't want to die here. I won't!* I told myself. *I won't! I'll crawl out of this place on my belly if I need to.* I began thinking of the mountain man Hugh Glass and how he crawled out of the wilderness after being left for dead. He crawled on his belly, on and off for 200 miles and over the course of 3 months, so the story goes. *If he did it, I can surely do it!* I thought, with defiance.

Hugh Glass was a trapper and a scout in the Dakota Territory in the 1800s. He was scouting out ahead of his group when he got between a mother grizzly bear and her two cubs. It happened so fast he couldn't get a shot off and dropped his rifle in the surprise attack. With just his knife and bare hands, he managed to kill the bear, but it left him critically mauled with horrific wounds and unable to walk. At the moment, I identified with him and what he must have felt at the time of *his* quandary.

When members of his party found the lifeless bruin lying on top of Glass's maimed body, it had torn the top of his scalp off and ripped flesh from the back of his neck, all the way down to the bottom of his thighs. It even broke his leg. He lost so much blood, that the party didn't expect him to last through the night. I was worried that *I* wouldn't make it through the night as well.

They carried Glass along on a makeshift stretcher for two days waiting for him to die, but when they entered hostile Indian Territory, Major Henry didn't want to risk the safety of the rest of the company with their sluggish pace, so he asked for two volunteers to stay behind and bury Glass when he died. The volunteers gave up when they heard a band of hostile Indians and left him to die. They took his knife and rifle, placed him in a shallow grave, and laid a bearskin hide over him before covering his body with dirt and leaves. The two men left him there, alive, and never looked back.

Glass still refused to die. *I refuse to die, too!* I thought, as I fought to recall his act of survival. Alone and defenseless, he managed to crawl out of the open grave, pack his wounds with strips of clothing, and even set and braced his broken leg.

He dragged himself along by gripping two pointed sticks, jabbing them into the ground and pulling himself ahead on his belly with just his arms.

I can do that, I convinced myself. *There must be sticks here! I can pull myself along with them like he did!*

Eventually, Glass was able to walk upright with the aid of a crudely made crutch and painfully pushed ahead to Fort Kiowa, which was almost 200 miles away. Revenge was his motivation. *Survival is mine! I can do this!*

The legend of the man who crawled out of the wilderness spread among mountain men, as well as Indian tribes.

I too envisioned myself clutching two sticks, crawling on my stomach through the swampy muck and stinky skunk cabbage, and then on through the prickly bull briars. *If Hugh Glass did it, I can do it! I'll crawl to the stone wall at the end of the cow pasture. I'll go over that wall like the bulls did. Just like the bulls! It seems like a long way to crawl, especially with a broken back. But, if I need be, I'll do it. I'll do it if it's my last chance to live. Try to remember the overall direction in case I need to do it in the dark tonight. And, most of all, Never surrender.*

10

Snow was forming on my face. I hadn't noticed it accumulating. In turning my eyeballs sideways, which even that hurt to do, I noticed one promising stick to pull myself along the ground. It was about five feet away, but after contemplating the pain I was in, even to move one inch, the long distance I would have to travel over countless obstacles and the fact that I needed two sticks not just one, I realized that Hugh Glass's method was impossible for me. It would take me over a month to crawl home.

My arm and shoulder were becoming numb like so much of my body was. My bottom half was painless while my top half was screaming in agony.

Maybe if I yell for help someone will hear me. I thought it without really believing it. I rested my head back between my shoulder blades and gazed at the treetops, testing the acoustics with a holler for help that literally brought tears to my eyes. The slightest chest movement made yelling almost torturous. My voice didn't project very high anyway, because the treetops formed a canopy of leaves and branches that bounced my plea right back down to me on the forest floor.

Even so, and once again, I hollered. It was a weak and pitiful, *"Help!"* It hurt so bad to do and my head was still pounding, only worse.

It was late November, and I knew that the frigid air would force my neighbors' windows shut tight, further dampening my already muted cry. The closest home was a half-mile away as the crow flies, over a mile if you meander through the thickets.

My mouth was so dry. *Shock? Am I in shock?* I swallowed several times to lubricate my throat but again only mustered up another weak and muffled cry.

I ordered my tongue to gather as much saliva as possible, and this time I swallowed slowly and evenly, savoring every drop of moisture possible.

I'm definitely in shock, I told myself and continued to gather saliva several times while contemplating spending the night on the ground in the frigid cold and snow.

Just then, I remembered Shadow! I passed by her doghouse on the way into the woods and even spoke to her on the way by!

She knows I'm in here! She saw me go in! Maybe when Derek unties her tonight, she'll run from them and head in my direction to be with me! Maybe she will follow my scent trail and find me.

Shadow was a smart German shepherd who I knew would remember that I went into the woods but never came out. It was

Shadow.

definitely worth a try, so I used the last drop of spit I licked off the inside of my cheeks and prepared for a final attempt to yell for my dog. My cottony mouth foiled any more attempts to swallow, so I ran my tongue across the front of my teeth too, but it got stuck halfway across, sticking to the enamel and finding no moisture there at all. I tried to swallow again but could not, so I held my ribs and meekly called out her name to help her to locate my position.

"Shadow!" I hollered meekly again, this time for my dog. I was relying on her keen sense of hearing and her overwhelming urge to be with me. She was good and loyal. I hollered her name again.

"Shadow!"

After four or five attempts, my voice was faint and I was getting weaker, dizzier and losing hope. I called out her name in my mind, too. I screamed it in my head louder than I did out loud! The discomfort was overtaking me, and I was exhausted. It all just hurt so bad.

At the same time and unbeknownst to me, a new neighbor from the city living on Foster Center Road had just returned home from the graveyard shift. Bob Monroe lived about a half-mile away in the old one-room schoolhouse. He had just decided to bring in some firewood before the forecasted snowstorm came.

The wind blew steadily in a westerly direction, carrying with it my faint cry of what Bob thought was an owner calling his dog to come home. He made his way across his backyard and toward the barn where he stored his cordwood.

Rushing through the barn door and out of the swirling wind, Bob quickly reached back to push closed the resistant door behind him. At that instant, I shut my eyes very tight, took a deep breath and let it out in a slow and deliberate exhale. I tried to use my breath to help carry my weak cry out and away from my parched throat. With the flattened stick still between my teeth, I unclenched my jaw and prepared to give it my all, for I knew it was my last shot. It would be the last call for my dog or for anybody in fact, and for some reason, this time and without thinking about it, I ended with the words, "help me!"

"Shadow!" I cried out to her, "help me!"

My blood pressure must have dropped, or maybe exhaustion overcame me because I passed out.

Monroe paused, raised an ear to the wind's gust and held the door open with his shoulder, using his weight to offset the air's heaviness, which surprisingly was equal to his own strength. He heard the words "help me" this time and instinctively backed out from the doorway in an attempt to latch onto the curious plea.

Dreaming of Shadow when she was a playful puppy, I awoke to the sounds of rustling leaves, snapping twigs, and the accumulated snow that told me lots of time had passed. The ruckus echoed from a distance and I couldn't quite put a bearing on it.

Bob Monroe was like a bull in a china closet as he plowed through the thicket in the direction of my cry. Suddenly, I got glimpses of him staggering through pockets of light, off-balance and unsure footed, before disappearing again in the shadows. I sensed he was way out of his element and could see him but knew he couldn't see me.

As he came into view, I saw that he was carrying a huge log on his shoulder. I felt that was so odd at the time. *What is he doing with that thing?* I tried to yell out to him but found no voice left at all, so I rolled my desiccated tongue around the inside of my cheeks again and tried to collect any renewed saliva I could find. Some new spit had formed under my tongue, which stuck to the roof of my mouth like plaster when I repositioned it, and I made soft smacking sounds while testing it.

My level of pain was off the charts, and I knew that was my only chance to get help before I fell unconscious again, so I swallowed that small pool of spittle coating my throat, for one last, pleading, half-assed holler. I took a short breath and went for it.

"Hey!" I bellowed, with nothing but air emanating between the stick and my cheek. I sounded more like a flat tire losing its air. He was moving away from me in a diagonal direction so, I shut my eyes tight and took a long and meaningful gulp. Then I gave it all I had.

"Hey!" I screeched out again, with a laryngitis-like squeal.

The good neighbor, stopped, turned in my direction and called out to me while trying to catch his breath and balance at the same time. He was panting hard and looking up to the trees for a sign.

"Hey, who's out there?" he yelled, almost falling over with exertion, yet staggering my way with that big log still teetering on his shoulder. I caught his eye and directed him to my location by using my right arm and shirtsleeve as a signal flag. It hurt so much to do it but it worked. He saw me!

As he approached, I announced my condition in a soft and measured whisper.

"My back is broken, man. I need a rescue." With my whole body shaking, I wondered what he was making of the odd sight before him.

"What?" he said nervously, still reeling from his slog through the bull briars and underbrush.

"My back is broken and I need a rescue!" *Please don't make me repeat it,* I thought.

His eyes opened wide as he got a closer peek at me, while bobbing and weaving his head through pockets of open spots in the thickets. He looked more frightened than I did.

This guy doesn't belong here, I thought. *He is way out of his element and I need to calm him down.*

"I thought someone was being murdered out here!" he declared, still not looking directly at me. "Are you okay, buddy?" he said, as he positioned his head through a wall of twigs with his outstretched neck.

"I'm fine. I just need a rescue, okay?"

"I'll—I'll get some help!" He looked right, then left. "I'm—I'm not sure if I can..., I'll be back, hang on!" Then he dropped the heavy log—just missing his foot by inches. He grunted a small sigh of frustration and began running off in a zigzag direction—the wrong way at first and then correcting his course a little at a time as he went. I couldn't see him anymore, so I tilted my head back, repositioned an inch or so and bit down harder on my stick.

Did I just dream of that guy or was he real? I laid there replaying it all, sometimes doubting that it happened. I really wasn't sure.

11

My face still itched like crazy, so I made horrendous expressions to stretch my facial skin to try to relieve it. It helped a little but not much.

More time passed and a sense of relief came over me when I heard the sirens miles off in the distance. I dropped my guard, alpha zoned out, and began falling into more confusing thoughts.

I have to make it to that stone wall, I thought, *and go over it like the bulls did all those years ago. When I was younger. That's the only way out of here. Go over the wall like the bulls...just like the bulls did.*

I lay there remembering the story of the bulls I used to tell my kids. I wanted to forget my plight and forget about *this* day, so I thought about *that* day instead. I closed my eyes and heard more sirens blaring faintly in the distance and recalled what happened twenty years in the past. It seemed like yesterday...

12

I DRIFTED BACK TO the past, twenty years before. The memory of the bulls was still fresh in my mind, especially with the stone wall just one hundred or so yards away.

Drifting deeper, I dreamed of my horse snorting frantically with his head raised high. He shook it from side to side, as if he had stepped on a hornet's nest and had bees in his bonnet.

First, there were long and deliberate snorts and then there were faster, shorter and more uncontrolled pants. He whinnied deeply as he ran back and forth inside the freshly-painted, red-fenced corral. His tangled black mane stood up high on his curved, brawny neck, giving him the appearance of a mighty steed that a colorful Roman Centurion should sit upon.

Something was really spooking him! I never saw him so panicked! His tailbone fought hard to keep his lush tail horizontal, adding length to his already massive structure. I called him Tuffy, short for some Latin word that he was registered under. The American Quarter Horse Association called him, *Tufacas Maximus* or something like that, I can't remember exactly.

At fifteen-three hands at the withers, the five-year-old bay gelding was an exceptionally handsome quarter horse. A little headstrong and spirited but that's what I liked about him. No one but I could ride him. He would rear up and try to buck off anyone else who tried.

He was a cool horse to own, too. On hot summer evenings at

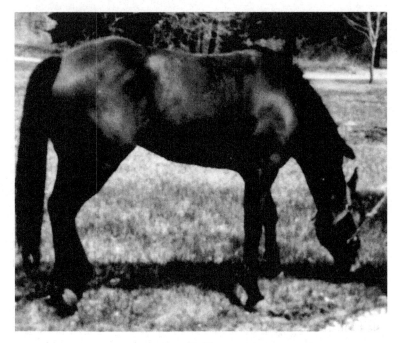

Tuffy.

age nineteen, I would ride him through the woods and down to the Westconnaug Reservoir just before sundown. That is when the environmental police went off duty. I would uncinch the western saddle and lay it on the pine needles by the water's edge. Then I would transform him into an Indian pony by hopping up on his bare back and guiding him into the still waters by just his long, loose and tangled mane. Nothing compares to riding a horse as it swims through the water. Nothing at all. The suspension is incredible.

Tuffy continued sprinting to both ends of the corral, still in a full-blown panic with foam dripping from the corners of his wide-stretched mouth. The dust cloud he kicked up made it hard to see what was scaring him, but I squinted through it anyway. I could barely make them out but saw several dark figures moving out from the wood line and into view. I had never seen my horse's nostrils spread so wide, as he blew puffs of steam out of each blowhole.

I became worried that he would go into cardiac arrest or break right through the fence boards and run right into the road! I had to act fast, so I ran toward the figures just as the dust settled in front of them to get a clearer view. Luckily, the last of the fading sun shined a little light on the intruders as they advanced their march toward us.

There they were. At about sixty feet and closing fast, I counted two, then four, then six! Yes, six of them! It was a small herd of black, burly bulls! Real bulls! With horns! I could not believe my eyes!

They trotted by the barn, past the corral, and right through a patch of wild Lady Slippers that only came up every seven years— if we were lucky. Then they stomped right through our vegetable garden, trampling the entire plot in seconds.

The intruders headed toward the hay field that I had just culti-vated. I spent hours encircling that field with electric fence wire, post by post and strand by stand. There must have been an acre's worth of fence line that I put up, that's why I flipped out when I watched those bulls walk right through that fence wire as if it were mere sewing thread. They didn't even flinch when the electric current zapped a good amount of voltage across their muscular and massive chests! They just plowed right through, making popping and ping-ing sounds as they went. It sounded like an electric guitar string sud-denly snapping in the middle of a high note.

One bull got his leg caught in the bottom wire strand, then coiled himself up in the top row, becoming wound up in a snarled spool. The other bulls got tripped up in the mess and tangled them-selves up as well.

In a nervous frenzy, the herd stampeded through the rest of the field with their trampling feet tugging on any remaining wire still connected to the fence posts. Before I could react, the metal posts bent over like man-made crop circles, only to be pulled out by the stretched-out wire, still tangled around the bulls' legs. I watched, and I was angry! They then turned their attention to Tuffy's corral. I think they smelled the fresh alfalfa hay that lay strewn around his water and feeding trough.

I ran to the barn where I kept the oats. Grabbing a galvanized pail by its handle, I scooped a half bucket of molasses-rich grain and headed for those bulls. I don't think I made it twenty steps before they spotted me, smelled the sweet oats I was now flashing before them, and ran at me like they had no intention of ever stopping once they reached me.

With the grain bucket in hand, I sprinted toward the woods from which they came, trying to remember if there was a path or trail there that they might have followed. I knew there was a farm on the next road—way out back and abutting my property—so I figured that's where they came from, but I couldn't remember ever seeing a trail there.

Navigating the darkening woods, I think my body hit every branch, sapling, and twig imaginable on the way. There was no path to run on and no light to guide me, yet those damn bulls just plowed through the woods the same way they did through my yard. I couldn't believe it!

I thought I should slow down and let them get another whiff of the grain before they lost interest. That was a mistake. When I turned to see how far back they were, I was shocked to see that they were right on my butt and knocking down everything in their path to get to me! It must have scared the heck out of me because as I turned back to run again, my legs were running faster than my body and totally out of sync with the rest of me. I tripped over my own feet and down I went, keeping the bucket raised up and managing not to spill a kernel. Those bulls were on me in no time. I was back running again before I even stood all the way up, sensing their presence just steps behind me. All I could picture was those sharp horns piercing through my back and into my gut-filled ribcage. So, I kept running and running and running!

A thick branch caught me across my nose bridge and forehead, but I fought to keep my bearings through my watery eyes. Deeper in the woods it was nearly dark now, but the sky above the trees was moonlit so I used that to guide me as best I could.

Another good-sized branch landed hard on my nose, watering up my eyes again and pissing me off even more. Then came the briars. They ripped at me as though I was a victim running a gauntlet. Some of the pointy prickers broke off from their vines and embedded their pointy tips in my neck, then, other vines latched onto those and tore *them* away, ripping my skin with them.

I could feel the ground rising before me so I knew I was running up hill. This slowed me down and showed me just how tired I really was.

Then, all at once, I stopped. I stopped with a thud as if I had hit a brick wall. A wide tree trunk had decided to stand its ground before me and I ran right into it. It was a pine tree so wide that I couldn't put my arms around it if I wanted to. And, unfortunately for me, there was a wall of brush, full of bull briars on each side of it, preventing me from escaping around it for a shorter route.

Something told me to turn around quickly and protect myself with the metal bucket. So, I did. Then, "*clang!*" The first bull hit the pail like a Mac Truck! "Clang, clang!" The next one nuzzled his giant head in for his prize! "Clang!—Thud!" The third one came in even harder than the first two, with the other three pushing on him from the rear, making the ones in front lean in farther against me.

With my back to the massive tree trunk, they thought they could all get their noses in the bucket at the same time, but all they were really doing was crushing it against my chest! That is when I smelled them. They had a putrid stench that I'd never smelled before. It smelled a little like sulfur and a little like a wet dog, only much worse. And although they were huge, I sensed that they were young. Maybe even yearlings but enormous just the same!

The lead three pushed against the metal bucket so hard that they almost folded it in half against my stomach and chest. This caused me to lose my breath and prevented me from taking in much needed oxygen. And to make matters worse, they were stepping on my toes with their narrow hooves. No, not stepping, stomping! It really hurt!

I was once told that if a horse steps on your foot, it hurts. However, if a cow does it, the pain is immense because the hoof is so narrow and the entire animal's weight is concentrated on that small spot rather than being spread out in a wider area. I'm a firm believer in that because it hurt big time.

With my back still to the tree trunk and my body now in distress, I went into survival mode and began punching those bulls with all I had. Rapid down-blows to the snout, followed by a barrage of undercuts to the jaw, yielded no let up on their end, only moist hands on my end from smashing their warm and wet snouts, which caused spews of boogers to bridge between their noses and my hand. I even elbowed one of them straight down between the eyes! He didn't even blink! That bull just kept pushing forward against the grain bucket, squishing me in the middle like a jelly sandwich. At one point, I hit the same bull with about four shots to the eyes! He didn't care about that either!

The stink, the hurt, and the sheer exasperation were overwhelming. My arms were getting tired of swinging and the tops of my feet were stinging. A few morsels of oats spilled out from atop the pail and bounced off both my shoes. Two of the bulls lowered their heads to beat the others to the crumbs. This gave me a chance to spin to the left of the tree and circle round the bulk of the briars, still clutching the only bait I had to lure them away from my property.

Pushing on through, I could see some light up ahead and above the tree line. This told me that the cow pasture wasn't far ahead of us. When a fallen tree tripped me and skinned my knees, I looked back quickly at the dark figures closing in on me, and I gave it all I had in a race for the cow pasture.

The dark woods opened to a small clearing as I neared the field's edge, allowing me to increase my speed without the threat of unseen obstacles. The bulls took full advantage of that, too, and really began gaining on me. I hadn't been out in that area in years, and I tried to remember what kept the animals confined in that farm pasture but could only picture a low-lying stone wall with a crude barbed wire fence strung out on top of it. I was right. Quickly coming into view was just that, only worse. It hadn't been attended to in quite some time, and fallen trees had flattened some of the barbed wire which is what let the bulls climb over the stones for their initial escape.

I was running like the dickens, the stone wall was coming up fast, and I still didn't have a plan. Then I was there. I was at the wall.

I waited an extra second for the bulls to close the distance on me, and then I swung the bucket by its mangled handle, up and over my right shoulder. I put a lot of oomph into it and watched it fly through the air and over the rocky wall. I didn't realize just how close those bulls were to me because the first two flew past me even before the pail hit the ground on the other side!

I hit the ground, too, imagining a thousand-pounder impaling my butt with those pointy horns because it thought I still had that bucket in my possession. With one eye open, I watched as the remaining four chased the bait and ran past me. Then six massive bovines jumped that stone wall one by one with the grace of a gazelle! The scene reminded me of the cow jumping over the moon.

Still laying there, panting, I could hear the metal bucket being kicked across the dark field on the other side. I was afraid that once they slopped up the grain, they'd be back over the wall for another go-around. So, I jumped to my feet, ran toward the dim and shadowy cow pasture, and leaped over the stone wall the same way they did. From the other side, I quickly propped up what I could of the downed barbed wire and fence post that lay atop of the stones but without much confidence in its staying power.

With probably only a handful of feed left in the upset pail, I could barely make out one of the bulls already looking back at me. I knew what he was thinking. Beyond their silhouette, a wooden fence line divided the cow pasture in half. It had an opened gate about halfway across, and I knew I needed to get them into that next field and lock the gate!

Another bull had already lifted his head from the spilled bucket and was looking back at me too. His brighter horns glowed against the night sky. I prayed that the opened gate beyond had a way to latch it shut. I lowered my stature, took a deep breath, and ran full speed at them. You would think that they would disperse, even a little, wouldn't you? Wrong. Those things were fearless! I whizzed by the first one's big square head. His snotty nostrils glistened and reflected the moon's dim beam. Then I sidestepped another one and went in for the upset bucket on the ground. The handle was squashed, but I caught the pail's rim and scooped up the last remaining crumbs along with some torn up field grass and topsoil. I pivoted past the others like a nervous quarterback about to be sacked. The pivot twisted my ankle, and I found myself with a serious limp as I headed full throttle to the gate. One last show of the bucket got them running after me again, and I was glad, but worried about my ankle slowing me down. I worried, too, about squeezing through that gate, all of us, all at the same time. I was there in no time and so were they. I stopped at the gate opening, and like before, I lobbed the pail over my head like a hand grenade, then faked to the right and darted to the left. I don't know why I faked. It was a useless move.

They ran through the opened gate and went for the bucket as soon as it left my hand. What gluttons they were! The gate was held open by a looped piece of rope, which I quickly popped off its post. In all the excitement, I hadn't noticed the moon's wane, and it was now hard to see just what held the gate shut as I pulled it closed. I almost forgot to get on the right side of the gate before I closed it, too. Imagining myself closed in on the wrong side of the fence with those creatures, gave me a shiver, especially now that it was so dark.

I stared at the galvanized locking mechanism on the fence post. It was quickly fading away in the darkness, so I commanded my pupils to grow to a "see in the dark mode," by staring at the dark gate latch.

By now, I couldn't see anything on the other side of the gate, although the clanging sound from the bulls pawing and gorging the pail told me just where they were. I fumbled with that lock way too long. The air was colder than before, I couldn't see much at all, and my nose and ankle hurt. I wanted to go home.

I thought the gate lock felt rusty and probably didn't work anyway, so I unbuckled my pants belt in a fast and impatient motion. By feeling my way along, I tied my belt to the gate and began to do the same to the gatepost. Wrapping it around, I began to replay the events that led up to that moment, and I wondered, *Did I count the bulls as they ran through the gate? Were there six of them that went through? I should have made sure.*

The sky was pitch black by now, and I had to keep my face just inches away from the belt as I tied its last cinch. My breathing was still quick as I tried to adjust my eyes and lean in even closer. Then—something was wrong! Something was warm! Something was bad!

The skin on the back of my naked neck tingled and the hairs on it began to stand up straight! It tingled even more intensely as something cast a steady stream of hot mist on my bare neck and down the back of my shirt. My knees buckled as the warmth cooled for a split second. Then, straightening my stance, a heated fog touched my skin again in a deliberate and faithful rhythm! It was breathing! It was breathing on my neck! Now I could hear it! Or, at least I imagined I could hear it with each deep breath it took! It all happened so fast!

A tingle ran from the base of my spine to the top of my head! It was dark in front of me and terrifying behind me, and I think I froze in those one or two seconds! But my ankle didn't hurt anymore.

With both hands out toward the darkness, I spun around in a stupor, seeming to look wherever it wasn't, until I finally locked onto it! I must have scared the culprit as much as it scared me because it jumped back two or three feet and its knees seemed to buckle as well! I couldn't make it out even though it was so close! My eyes couldn't adjust; I could see the outline but not the details! We just stood there, motionless, staring at each other in utter disbelief and darkness! My heart pounded hard, and I thought we both could hear

it through my rising chest. My pupils finally began to dilate, probably more in response to primal fear.

Slowly, the image began to materialize like vapor turning to a
solid. It was amazing! It was awesome! It was—it was a white horse!
A white horse with one eye and a flowing white mane. I know it
sounds fantastical, but it was real!

It was like a magical, mystical white horse with a long flowing
mane that nearly reached its knees! Like something you'd see on a
merry-go-round or a carousel at a country fair. I could see that it
wore no horseshoes and had overgrown and untrimmed hooves.
And, yup, it had just one eye! Well, it had two eyes, but just one
pupil. The other one had only the white of the eye and remnants of a
glazed over, pale blue pupil where one once was. I just knew she was
a mare even without looking at her genitalia. She was surely magical
and mystical. The only things missing were Pegasus wings and a spiraled unicorn horn!

Just three steps toward her brought us nose to nose. She put her
head down and let me run my fingers between her eyes and under
her long and uneven bangs. She was beautiful. The both of us just
stood there in that field, head-to-head and in total darkness. Did I
mention my ankle didn't hurt anymore?

After a time, I talked to her and gained her trust. I then left
the closed gate and walked back toward the stone wall, hoping she
would follow. Yup, she walked behind me with her chin touching
my back all the way. I wondered if she was lonely and why her owner
let her lead such a wild life with no shoes, untrimmed hooves, an
overgrown tail and an unkempt mane hanging in her one good eye.
I couldn't figure it out.

I scratched her neck and said goodbye to her in a soothing voice
that seemed to calm the both of us.

Before I turned to leave, I had an overwhelming desire to climb
up on her just to see if she'd let me. I thought about it for a moment
and then went for it! Talking to her in an assuring tone, I grabbed

hold of her tangled mane and pulled myself up, over, and onto her soft bare back.

She danced sideways which gave me the thrill I was seeking but never reared up or tried to buck me off. It was wonderful! My butt fit her seat like we were made for each other. She even let me steer her by her mane without a bridle. I quickly dismounted, though, when I remembered that her feet were untrimmed and she had no shoes.

I leaned my forehead against hers and closed my eyes. A deep breath took in one of my favorite animal smells, horse, and I said the word *goodbye* to her in my mind. Over the stone wall I went and headed for home.

The journey back was a little difficult because of the dark and cold, but the night's recollections lit my spirits and warmed my soul, and my ankle definitely didn't bother me anymore...

13

I BROKE FROM THE daydream when the memory ended and opened my eyes. I hadn't thought of those bulls in years. It was nice to recall those days gone by. But as the wonderful memory of the white mare faded, a sad realization overcame me. *I can't move my legs, I cannot feel my lower half, I'm cold and I want to go home.*

The sounds of voices and breaking twigs snapping off in the distance caught my attention. Bob Monroe couldn't tell the rescuers where to find me, so the six-man team headed intrepidly into the woods like a pack of bloodhounds. However, they were going the wrong way! They went south instead of west, and it seemed they crisscrossed everywhere but where I was. At one point, through the brush, I caught a glimpse of them heading away from me and watched them move slowly out of sight. Their image grew smaller and smaller and there was nothing I could do! I couldn't yell and I couldn't move. I just stared at the forest floor—long and hard, this time thinking or dreaming of nothing. Nothing at all. Time was nonexistent. I faded out again.

Suddenly, I was startled awake. Somehow, Sergeant Moony of the Foster PD was standing over me, surrounded by a blue aura with a black outline that traced his tall and lean body. I tried to adjust my blurry eyes to respond to his presence but couldn't.

Is this another dream? I thought, while focusing on his reflective badge that floated with his surreal movements. I continued to adjust my pupils by squinting narrow, then wide, kind of like zooming in my binoculars before a clearer picture comes into view.

It can't be a dream; I have never felt such brutal pain in a dream!

"Where is your weapon, sir?" he asked. His synthetic uniform and patent leather shoes gave him an artificial appearance that contrasted sharply with the natural surroundings.

He doesn't belong here, I thought, still squinting hard through my puffy eyes.

"Weapon? What weapon?" Dazed and confused, I answered him slowly with barely a voice as he paused to speak into his radio.

"I don't know," I said. "I'm not hunting, I was moving my tree stand." It even hurt to think, so I decided to keep my answers short and brief. "I may have hit my head because I keep passing out and coming to. I'm not sure."

"Have you been holding your back off the ground like that the entire time?" he asked. My arm was quivering involuntarily and he wouldn't stop staring at it while he spoke.

"I think so," I sighed before answering again. "It's broken. My back is broken, and I need to keep it off the ground. I won't lie on it. I need something strong for the pain because it hurts like hell. Please tell them that for me, okay?"

He nodded at my request. "How long have you been out here, sir?" Then, looking beyond his left shoulder, I could see a response team making its way to me.

"I don't know," I said, just above a whisper. "I got out here about ten or eleven I think."

"Well, you've been out here for quite some time now, sir."

"How long?"

"Hours," he replied.

Hours? I thought. *Really? I wonder how long it takes to bleed internally...to death?*

He pulled a small notepad from his wrinkle-free, baby blue shirt pocket.

"What's your name, sir?" he asked, with some authority.

He knew me only by sight because we both attended the father-daughter dances at Paine Elementary School. I thought of Lauren again. *I will never walk her down the aisle.*

"Robert DePalo," I answered.

"Please spell it, sir."

I did. "I can't move my legs," I announced, and wanted to take it back as soon as I said it. He tried to disguise his concern, but I saw it in his face. I thought it was bad, and he just confirmed it.

I reluctantly answered his annoying questions, including my address and telephone number.

"Is there anyone you'd like us to notify?" he asked. That question sounded so weird to me.

Notify? I thought. *Like in, notify my next of kin?*

Then the volunteer rescue team encircled me and went right to work. When questioned, I told them I did not hit my head. I don't know why I said that.

"Why is your ear bleeding then?" one of them asked. I shrugged my eyebrows instead of my shoulders.

"Do you prefer, 'Robert' or 'Bob'?" he asked.

"How old are you?" another one asked.

"It's Bobby," I growled. The barrage of questioning annoyed me enough to stop answering when it broke my concentration and allowed the pain to come through. I begged again for something to ease the agony.

"Okay!" the leader said. "I am starting you on morphine right now." The sight of so many people hovering over me triggered the start of another anxiety attack.

"I can't breathe guys!" I blurted out. "Please back off!"

"Get an oxygen mask on him right away!" someone in the background shouted.

"No, that's not what I mean, you guys are crowding me and making me feel anxious! I feel like I'm being buried alive—kind of."

I had just realized how silly that sounded but didn't know how else to explain it. I felt like a wimp the minute those words left my mouth.

"Can you feel this?" the leader asked. He was down by my feet, that's all I knew.

"What are you touching?" I bargained.

"You tell me," he said.

I wouldn't say without knowing what he was poking. I couldn't bear to be wrong. He quit asking so I assume he got the answer he was looking for.

"Please give me more morphine, it's not working!" I announced, with a raspy voice but was ignored. "You guys don't understand, please listen to me. I can take a lot of pain, but this is different, and now that you guys are poking at me, I really need more!"

"You can have more morphine when Life-Flight gets here, sir."

"Life-Flight?" I responded.

"We have a helicopter coming out of Connecticut," he said.

"A helicopter? Connecticut? Why?"

"It will be faster getting you to the E R that way," he answered, while hooking me up to things I didn't understand.

Shit, I thought. *It is bad. I knew it!* "Where are you taking me again?"

"Norwich City Hospital I believe, in Connecticut," the team leader said.

"I need to go to Rhode Island Hospital! Please get them to take me there!" Not only would I get the best care at Rhode Island, but I also needed to be close to my family in order to look after them.

"I will request it, sir."

"Thank you," I whispered.

The stocky one bent down on one knee and held my head straight.

"What's in your mouth, Bobby?"

"A stick to bite down on, for the pain," I said.

"John, look at this, he's got a stick in his mouth and says it's for the pain!"

"It's gotta come out!" John answered back. With that, anxiety reared its ugly head again and alerted me to a defensive posture.

"No, don't! I need it!" I hollered back.

"It has to come out Dan, just take it out," John ordered, as Dan reached for the stick and pried it from my teeth. I held it tight and it hurt as it scraped my gums coming out. As he threw it over his shoulder, I watched it tumble through the air and felt sadness in the way we parted so unexpectedly.

Another guy strapped a brace on my neck and almost sent me into orbit.

"You're killing me!" I screamed. "Stop, don't move me!" I pleaded. "Please give me something stronger. I can't take it!"

"We can't just yet, Bobby!" John said. "I know it hurts but the hospital has ordered me to keep you alert and conscious, and that's what I've got to do. I'm sorry."

They tied me down to the stretcher way too tight. I held my breath for long periods and exhaled quietly in the bear-like growl again. I wondered if they thought I was a bear too.

Facing into the sun, four or five of them began to clear a trail for our long trek to the road. It was wrong, so I spoke up.

"Not that way guys! Take me over the stone wall and through the cow pasture, it's easier. Just head northwest and you'll find it. It's out there! Northwest is that way. Take a hard right at the sun and go over the stone wall!"

"How do you take a right at the sun?" one guy muttered, as they spun me in the right direction, twisting, bumping and banging my stretcher off their hips as they turned.

14

MY HANDS AND arms were strapped down, so I pointed with my eyes each time they weren't sure of the way. They agreed to try it. After all, I don't think they knew their way out of the woods on their own.

The volunteers, my heroes, struggled with my stretcher as they walked sporadically through the underbrush. Every few yards, they got tangled in the razor-sharp bull briers and complained out loud with each tear to their clothes and skin.

"Sorry guys, I'm so sorry to put you all through this," I shouted up towards the treetops in a raspy and pitchy voice.

"That's what we're here for," an unfamiliar voice sounded off. I was getting dizzier and even nauseous by now and sensed some blood in my stomach by the iron-metallic taste I had on my tongue and gums.

We made it to the stone wall, and half of the team hopped over it in order to receive my stretcher from the other side. On our way over, they tried so hard to keep me level, but I tilted at a steep angle anyway and they toppled like dominos, landing on shins and knees on the stones, then unsure footed on the other side. They didn't totally drop me but the jarring hurt like heck. I couldn't blame them for any of it though. It was all my fault. The skinned knees, the torn clothes, all of it. It was all my fault.

I thought of the bulls after we cleared the wall. For a second, I thought I smelled them. With the neck brace, I couldn't see anywhere but up, so I envisioned people standing on each side of the stretcher, three on each side, like pallbearers, paying their last respects to me.

I remembered the white mare too. I envisioned her dancing sideways, trying to get me to hop up on her.

The stretcher bearers were quiet, just struggling to keep me level. I listened to the grass parting as their boots and shoes pushed through the cow field. Swoosh, swoosh, swoosh.

We must have come upon a downhill grade because with my head higher than my feet, I could see just the tops of vehicles, parked willy-nilly across the beautiful field where the bulls once roamed. They seemed to be encroached on land made just for animals. Because of me. Another feeling of guilt filled my belly.

I closed my eyes and wished it all to disappear. When I peeked, I saw the bright red, square-shaped rescue truck waiting for me at the edge of the field, and as they prepared to load me in, I cringed. None of it would disappear. Whatever dose of pain meds they gave me started to work on my psyche but did nothing for the pain. I was high for sure but the pain still came through.

Once strapped down inside the rescue truck, we sped to the helicopter landing spot with the siren blaring and hit every bump on the way. Engine 2 Ladder Truck raced ahead of us so they could tape a large X-marker on the ground for the helicopter to see from the sky. We slowed to a stop.

The helicopter had circled and landed. This, I knew by the sound of the idled prop and the smell of the cut grass particles slipping past the ventilation filters and into the back of the rescue. They had me unloaded and carried to the sound of the massive engine idle in no time.

Even at idle, it was loud and windy. They began loading me into the helicopter feet first but stopped me half way in. I began feeling quite high from the morphine and lost some perception at this point.

I watched myself surrealistically, far above, looking down at them loading me into the helicopter, and maybe it was the morphine that slowed time down again, I am not sure. I just know I didn't like it.

I shook my head from side to side to shake it off and widened my eyes to the spinning propeller blades above me. The massive prop parted the air with a constant 'woof' and seemed to be slowing down, rather than speeding up.

Someone hollered, "Bobby, your wife is here!" and my heart sank.

How did she get here? I wondered, embarrassed, slapping the sides of my lifeless thighs through the stretcher straps. *How did she know?*

Amongst the faces, hers appeared above me and our eyes locked sadly in an eternal millisecond. There was no reason to speak; there was nothing to say. She just stared down into my eyes and shook her head. I mouthed the words, "I'm so sorry," as she was quickly pulled away.

I was moved into the whirlybird on some type of conveyer, I think. I wasn't sure; I couldn't see it but I was in.

Leaning over me appeared a military-looking figure in a large helmet with futuristic headgear, communication devices, I presumed. Dark sunglasses and a wide chin guard covered the alien-like face, along with a helmet that appeared too big for the body. I couldn't tell if it was a male or female, and it didn't seem to speak.

Looking up and out the opened door, I watched the spinning prop blades again, still slowly emitting its muffled "woof—woof—woof." It was blowing my mind. The morphine was blowing my mind! *I'm so high!*

This is so familiar, I thought. *I know where I am! This is Vietnam! I knew it! I knew I would have to go someday! But why am I wounded already? I don't remember fighting! Did I fight?* I think my imagination took real thoughts and rushed them into real dreams.

I can't believe what I'm seeing! The whirling propeller, the medivac unit! Am I there? Am I in Vietnam? I was afraid of Vietnam.

As a boy, I watched the nightly news with my family and saw the images from Vietnam of the wounded and dead getting loaded into Army helicopters, as the Vietcong fired upon them from the rice paddies. Some soldiers returned home on stretchers and some in body bags, and I felt that it would eventually be my turn to grow up and come home in a body bag too.

The propeller blades blurrily spinned above me, and the morphine threw me into a dazed stupor.

I envisioned my Grandma Dena crying like a baby. She was sitting at her kitchen table with a broken heart and her head hung low. My Uncle Joe kissed his mother goodbye and promised her she didn't have to worry about his deployment to Vietnam. I was sitting in the den pretending I couldn't hear.

He didn't quite go when he was supposed to though. I was there when the Military Police showed up at the house after he pulled a switch with Cousin Sonny in order to get more furlough days before having to ship off. Sonny was drafted also and was scheduled to ship off two weeks later. The close cousins swapped I.D. cards and one went in the other one's place. You see, Auntie Jean was pregnant with Cousin Gina and my uncle was not about to miss the birth of his first child. I always thought that Sonny was so cool for going in his place two weeks before his scheduled time.

Every weekend, our family got together to assemble care packages of homemade wine, cookies, tomato sauce and pasta which left each week for the two boys overseas. We mailed the packages on a Monday morning and watched the war news Monday night. Body bags and all.

I was just ten years old when I heard Grandma cry, and it bothered me deeply. I calculated the amount of time I had left before I turned eighteen, and then I too would be drafted and receive *my* care packages.

In 1975, Saigon fell to the North Vietnamese and the U.S. pulled out. That was a year and a half before my eighteenth birthday and draft eligibility age.

15

T HEY LOADED ME farther into the helicopter and the engine
noise changed its pitch and mimicked the rapid fire of an
AK-47, with its bullets bouncing off the helicopter's fuselage! I fran-
ticly tugged on the restraints that tied down my arms.

*They'd better load me in fast and take cover before we get hit!
Where's my rifle!* I screamed silently; *I need my rifle!* I jerked on the
straps that crisscrossed my arms.

Yelling above the noise, the alien-looking thing finally spoke to me.

"Robert, sit still! I need to secure this IV, so just relax!" By the
sound of the voice, I knew it was a woman.

"Okay," I thought. *At least we're inside now and taking cover."* Another
crewmember appeared out of nowhere and yelled out to me too.

"How are you doing there?"

"I need more morphine!" I said, through clenched teeth.

"Not until we get there!" he said.

"But they promised me some more when I got in the helicopter!"

"I'll ask the attending in Providence when we open communica-
tions after liftoff," he said.

"Providence?" I said. "We are not in Vietnam?"

"You're not where?" he asked.

"Viet...," I caught myself in midstream as the notion sounded
strange to me too. I didn't answer him. I felt like an idiot. *Ugh, these
drugs are really doing a number on my mind but nothing for my body!*

As I felt the ground leave us, I must have tightened up a bit because the pain spiked. The flight nurse's face appeared above me once again and spoke with confidence.

"Our ETA to Rhode Island Hospital is eight minutes, and the attending ER resident has just authorized an increase in morphine for you!"

I thanked her and closed my eyes with some relief. I thought about my family. I thought about what I said to God. I thought about a lot of things.

"You're going to feel a little bump when we touch down shortly," the male one shouted. The little bump felt more like a crash landing.

"A transport ambulance is waiting at the landing pad for you, Robert." With that information, I felt I could relax now because my job was done. I stayed alive so far, and I knew there was a lot more ahead of me. More of the unknown. Needing my strength for what lie ahead, I let my heavy eyelids fall and turned myself off.

16

"ROBERT! ROBERT! ROBERT!" Someone was shouting at me from far away. "Open your eyes, Robert!"

With my vision still blurred, it took me a few seconds to focus in on a bald man, about thirty, dressed in light blue scrubs and slowly coming into a hazy view. He had a stethoscope hanging from his ears and a coal miner's light on his forehead. The light was blinding.

I know this guy from somewhere! I thought. *Who is he?*

I blinked intensely, searching for a clue, and then it hit me.

Holy shit! It's Dr. Green, the character on ER! It's him! The television show ER was a big hit back then and Doctor Green was one of the stars. *This is good,* I thought. *This is good! This guy will fix me!*

"Robert, I'm doctor so and so.

No, you're not, you're Doctor Green! I thought, confused. "Do you know where you are?" he asked.

I knew the answer but forgot the words. Thinking for a moment, I answered, "I'm in the emergency room, you're Dr. Green, and I can't feel my legs. I need to walk my daughter down the aisle someday."

"Did you hit your head, Robert?"

"No, I don't think so."

"Did you lose consciousness, Robert?"

"Um, twice at least, I think."

"Then how do you know you didn't hit your head?"

I didn't answer.

Suddenly, I screamed in agony! "My legs are burning! What are you doing to my legs? Please stop!"

"We are not touching your legs," someone answered.

"They are burning like they are on fire!" I screamed, again. "Stop!"

"The nerves may be dying," another one whispered.

That comment cut right to the bone and has stuck with me all these years.

"We are giving you something now to ease the pain," the doctor said. "You will feel better in a minute. Try to answer my questions. Do you know who the president is, Robert?"

I thought about it. "Yes, it's Clinton, unfortunately."

He chuckled.

"Okay, Robert, what year are we in?"

That answer I blew. I was off only by a year though.

"Was I right?" I asked.

"It's okay, close enough," he said.

I must have had a half dozen people hovering over me by now. They were cutting my clothes off, effortlessly it seemed, with super sharp and bent-looking scissors, while scurrying like worker ants to hook me up and plug me into a web of boisterous monitors. Bright lights beamed down on me from all angles and made me feel like a specimen in some weird science experiment. A high-pitched voice came out of nowhere, a nurse I presumed.

"Robert, you brought the whole forest in here with you! You've got pinecones and pine needles stuck to your pants and socks, and leaves under your tee shirt. You even had an inchworm hitch a ride in here!"

"I can't feel my legs!" I announced. No one seemed to care.

"I can't feel my legs," I said again, softly and sleepily to myself...

––––––––––

I WAS SUDDENLY IN A different scenario than before. Same room, I think, but now lying on my side and nowhere to look but downward.

I noticed the tips of two pairs of shoes planted motionless on the floor next to my gurney. I stretched my eyeballs as high up as I could. Filling those shoes stood both my father and my wife, Debbie. I couldn't see their faces.

"We are here, Bobby," my father said, with sadness in his voice.

Busy bees worked around me in unison, prodding and prepping as they went. A clear plastic tube filled with white, milky liquid was inserted into my mouth and fed forcefully down my throat. I sensed my stomach filling with the putrid slime and gagged in disgust.

"I'm gonna puke!" I announced, while lifting my head some.

"Just a little more, honey," a gentle voice said. "It's only dye; we need to get it all in."

"I can't hold it down anymore!"

And with that, I turned my head and shot a stream of the milky goop across the room and onto my father's shoes. He jumped back and did a little jig, avoiding some of it while a nurse sprang into action, clearing the floor area of roll-a-ways and drip bag trees.

"I'm so sorry," I sighed.

"Don't worry, it happens all the time," she said.

Not to me, I thought.

Things intertwined with things and I was on automatic pilot now. My mind was being navigated by my emotions. Whatever I felt, I thought. Whatever I thought, I felt, and the morphine eventually produced a hallucinogenic effect that soon plunged me deeper into a world of unconscious fantasies and dreams...

17

NO MATTER HOW many times I killed it, it still kept coming! It just wouldn't stay dead!

The never-ending dream played out repeatedly, as I plunged the knife again deep into its face, causing massive blood loss and yielding thin strips of torn flesh. Each massive blow dropped it to the ground in a certain ending, yet it rose up from the dead to chase me again, clutching at me like a mental patient in a prison gauntlet.

My skin crawled as its long, pointy fingernails brushed the backs of my leg calves. I was terrified and couldn't make a sound while trying desperately to end the replay!

This time I thrust the blade violently into its eye socket, twisting and turning until it reached the cerebellum. Brain matter splashed into my face and stuck to the corners of my mouth.

One last push sent the steel blade deep inside until it protruded through the back of its scull, leaving the wooden handle imbedded in its wet, gooey eye socket. Down it went and took its last putrid breath.

I held firmly to the knife handle and pulled it from its head, dragging with it strands of colorful meat that oozed with mucus and puss. Its eyeball remained stuck to the blade while a lengthy tail of tendons followed. Brain matter speckled the floor, like splashes of spaghetti sauce on a clean white shirt.

My chest was rising as I stepped closer for a better look—but as I leaned over to view the hairless body, both of its bony hands reached out and grabbed my bare ankles!

Running away once more and dragging the heavy load behind me, I prayed to God that I'd shaken it free.

My legs were like rubber and moved with so much resistance. Everything was thick, thick like peanut butter. I tried to move my legs to get free, but as the thickness consumed me, panic emerged and disabled me further.

Unable to shake its grip, I reached around and plunged my knife deep into its mangled face again, praying that it let me go...

———

TREMBLING FROM THE NIGHTMARE, I awakened in an unfamiliar room. My chest was rising and falling and my breath was fast. Awake, that thing still had me terrified.

"Bobby, you are in the Intensive Care Unit. Can you hear me? Do you understand me?"

Slowly, I nodded my head. It was my mom standing over me. Then Debbie spoke from a point out of view.

"Do you remember what happened to you?" Debbie asked.

My heart began to hurt as I started to remember. I didn't answer. The pain was numbed and I was higher than a kite.

"You're fine,—and everything is going to be okay," Mom said. She was talking too loudly and I didn't understand why.

"This is Dr. Lucas. He is a surgeon here that specializes in spinal injuries!" She pointed her hand in his direction as she spoke. My mother navigated the conversation, as Debbie was known to be more reserved.

"We're very lucky to have him here!" Mom said. "He is one of the best surgeons in his field, and he's going to talk to you about repairing your spine, okay?"

With a small build and a preppy haircut, the handsome doctor looked a bit like a middle-aged, flannel shirt model from an L.L. Bean catalogue.

I liked his warm bedside manner in the way he moved in close to speak to me. Besides, I sensed that Mom and Debbie liked him too. That was a plus.

Just then, someone or something caught the corner of my right eye, and I blinked hard to focus in on what looked like a person standing to my right. The abstract figure then slowly faded away, so I stared at the spot for a brief moment, then back to Dr. Lucas, all the while keeping one eye out for the anomaly.

Great, I thought. *Now I'm seeing things that aren't there. Anything else?* I thought. *Is there anything else you want to throw at me? I don't need this crap. Just drop me right down into hell and then reel me back up for more. Go ahead, just keep it coming because I'm gonna fight you all the way!*

I wasn't seeing God's face this time. This time I was thinking of Satan.

Was it Satan who I swore at like that after I fell? Would I have really spoken to God like that? I couldn't have. It must have been the Devil. Who else would have let me fall out of that tree? Who else would paralyze me and let me suffer like this? It was him. It had to be. It was the Devil for sure.

I immediately liked blaming him. Fighting God made me feel ashamed, fighting Satan I could do.

Mom broke my train of thought again.

"We're very lucky, Bobby, Dr. Lucas just happened to be available when they brought you in!" She sounded too upbeat, too delighted. I knew what she was doing.

I struggled to keep my mind clear while looking down. I became aware of a bunched-up hospital johnnie that was opened at my chest and saw lots of sticky tape holding needles and things to my hands and arms.

Sensing other patients in the vast room, my curiosity was piqued but just for a brief moment. With my head forced flat on the bed, I couldn't see much unless it was practically over me.

Beeps and buzzers sounded all around me, aggravating things. I couldn't concentrate, but more importantly, I still couldn't feel my legs. My stomach did flip-flops and I knew why. I just remembered that I was paralyzed.

I can't believe this, I thought. *I can't believe I'm paralyzed. Me, a paralyzed person. A paraplegic. How nauseating.*

I despised my conscious state because at least sleep allowed me to forget. I was imprisoned in a body that reeked of despair, and I felt that I couldn't take the heartache for another minute.

I've gotta get out of this body. I replayed those words in my head over and over as the surgeon spoke.

I gotta get out of this body, now!

Although he seemed nice, I hoped that the good doctor would finish up with his spiel so I could concentrate on fighting off this affliction, and knowing that I was drugged, I tried to act sharp enough to understand what he was telling me but caught myself saying yes even before he finished his sentence. I didn't understand what he was proposing but the tone of it sounded good enough to me, so I nodded my head on intuitive cues.

He held up a plastic model of a spine or something, I don't know, and explained that the operation would attempt a repair to my shattered vertebrae, using titanium rods and screwing them into my spine as a bridge or brace. This much I understood.

That's great! I thought. *He can fix me and I should be able to walk again! I should, shouldn't I?*

I wanted to ask that question so badly but didn't want to hear the wrong answer. I didn't need any more disappointments for a while, so I never asked the number one, burning question. *Will I ever walk again?*

Dr. Lucas asked if I could wait until morning for the procedure because his surgical team would be fresh and rested by then. Apparently, his team had just spent eight hours operating on another patient. Who was I to say, no?

As he spoke, I imagined him making his long incision down the length of my back and pinning my skin flaps opened widely, exposing the raw and multicolored meat that surrounded my backbone to the infinite number of airborne bacteria and dirty germs in the air. My thoughts grossed me out, so I tried to concentrate on what he was saying but instead drifted away again.

In my mind's eye, I could see him slicing through my flesh and muscle, like a butcher cutting up a prime Hereford for baby back ribs. I used to butcher my own wild game, so I'd gotten to learn the anatomy fairly well. Probably not a good thing though, maybe it would have been better not knowing the details.

Dr. Lucas then closed his sales pitch by stating that if he could not repair it completely by going in through my back, he could turn me over and get to my spine through my belly. By removing my innards and placing them on the table alongside me, he could gain access to my back from the front.

I visualized the scenario with repulsion while he placed a clipboard on my chest and pointed out the disclaimer.

"You do understand that death may occur during the procedure?" he asked.

"Yup," I answered him back without hesitation. "I understand, let's go for it."

The pen fell lazily over after I scribbled an unreadable signature, and with that, I felt another task was complete, so I thanked him, smiled at everyone as they spoke with lowered voices while walking to the door. Then, gave in to the sleep I wanted so badly and lapsed into unconsciousness. For how long? I don't know.

18

I JUMPED UP FROM my sleep and threw my hands out, grasping for the imaginary tree branch to latch onto. I had been falling again— and my heart was still pounding hard.

There was a nagging hurt deep inside my back, so I started a small stretch to relieve some of the stiffness but was stopped short due to the immense pain. An involuntary deep breath was also quickly squelched for the same reason.

Frustration, Anger, Sadness and Fear - all of these emotions swelled as I got my waking wits about me. I waited and prayed for death, then life, and then death again.

I wish I didn't have two kids to think about. Why couldn't I be alone with no one to miss me? Why couldn't I have children that could under-stand my suffering and just let me die? It would be easier contemplating suicide without the thought of my kids being hurt and preventing me from doing it!

A loud, irritating buzzer was sounding on and off at about fifteen second, uneven intervals—and I suspected was pushed manually.

It was dark all around me so I knew it was nighttime but wasn't sure of the day. The last thing I remembered was signing the opera-tion death disclaimer for the next day. *I must have fallen asleep.* After taking it all in, I let it all out with a long-lasting, audible sigh.

My mother sprang up from out of the darkness and grabbed my arm.

"I'm here, Bobby. I'm right here," Mom said, as she reached for my needle-punctured and medical taped-up hand. I was surprised to see her and it showed.

"Did I have the operation?" I whispered. My voice was hoarse with soreness and sounded like someone else's.

"No Bobby, it's scheduled for the morning, it's still nighttime."

"What time is it, then?"

"It's 3:30 a.m.," she whispered.

"Why are you here? Is Debbie here, too?"

"No, I've been here all night with you while Debbie went home to be with the kids," she said, sympathetically, and in the tone of a question rather than a statement.

"I'm sorry I put you through this, Mom, I'm sorry I put everyone through this."

"Bobby, you keep saying that, why are you sorry? It was an accident, so don't be sorry!"

"I can't help it. I've ruined everyone's lives, now. I know I did."

She leaned in closer.

"Don't be silly, you've ruined nothing, and we're going to get through this no matter what it takes." Her voice got softer but sterner.

"It's only temporary. Remember that, alright? It's only temporary. Please just have hope."

"Okay, I'll try, but the pain is wearing me down now and I can't get any relief." Just then, a nurse approached out of nowhere. "That's why I'm here," she said, busily moving about with a chart in one hand and a needle in the other. "See this button on the bedrail?" she asked. I nodded yes without looking for it, I don't know why. I was more curious as to who she was and what that needle was for. By her seasoned look, I figured she must be the head nurse. Her name tag read, Donna. *A young name for such a distinguished woman,* I thought.

"Just push it in when you need more pain medication, okay? You can push it all you want because it will only give you what it is programmed to give you."

"What's in it, morphine?" I asked.

"Yes, well there is morphine in it," she said.

Reaching for that button was like torture. It hung by its cord, attached to the right bedrail and I had to push it with my left hand because I was leaning a bit on my right side, and it took all I had to attempt the reach.

Raising my arm, I saw the plastic tubes and wires crisscrossing over my chest like a circuit board. My ribs ached as I took deeper breaths to hit the button. Donna knelt to view something down on the side of my bed. She lifted it from the dark and into the light. It was a clear plastic bag, attached to a tube that led to my right side and was hidden under the bed sheet. The bag and hose were filled with thick, reddish-purple stuff that stained the lining of the bag.

"Is that stuff coming from me?" I asked.

"It's a fluid drain. It drains the blood and the other bag is for urine."

"Where is the other bag?" I asked.

"Oh, it's right down here."

I couldn't imagine all those hoses being plugged into me and yet not being able to feel any of it.

I wondered where the bloody bag was draining from but was afraid to ask. Still higher than a kite, I rambled on a bit about nonsense, although I caught myself doing it and corrected my words on the fly.

My voice revealed my discomfort by rising and lowering at an uneven keel, and my mind was still on that blood-filled bag as I watched Donna leave the room. I needed to know how and where the tube entered my body, so I reached down under the sheets with my left hand and automatically went for my groin. What seemed like a thin cable, snaked out from between my legs and pulled things outwards, out towards the side of the bed.

This thing is yanking on me way too hard, I thought. *Things on me could tear off and I wouldn't even know it.*

Next, I felt for my thighs. They weren't burning anymore. I found both legs and traced their outline down to my knees. That was as far as I could reach, but it didn't matter because I felt nothing down there. Then I tried to move my hips. Nothing. Then my legs and feet, and still there was nothing.

I noticed that I held my breath each time I tried to push to move a body part. That made me lightheaded and searching for air.

My mom was filling a water pitcher with ice when she spoke.

"Are you okay, Bobby?"

"I think I've been getting panic attacks or something, Mom, and I think I'm getting one now."

She looked a little worried but kept filling the pitcher.

"Just try to relax; I'm right here with you," she said.

Trying to sound nonchalant, I asked her a question. "Mom, you know when I can't feel my legs, or I try to move them? Well, I get anxious, I think. Is there anything they can give me for that?"

"What exactly do you feel, Bobby?"

"I don't know exactly how to say it, but when it happens, I feel like I'm being smothered. Like being buried alive." I took a short breath. "I imagine that I'm in a coffin, being buried alive."

She reached for the call button and summoned the nurse. An unknown voice responded and listened to my mother's request for anxiety medication. The nurse explained that she'd have to page the attending doctor and the request may take a while. Hearing that only escalated even more anxious thoughts. So, I fought them as best I could by pushing them to the back of my mind and pushing down on the pain medication button again. Twice.

I spent the next few minutes watching my mom speak to me but I never heard a word she said.

Donna appeared with another needle in hand, and that sporadic and irritating buzzing was still coming from the bed across the room. It sounded off every minute or so, each for about ten or fifteen seconds. Some of the buzzes were accompanied by phlegm filled, high-pitched moans, that ran goose bumps down my arms. I cringed and then stretched my neck out in an attempt to get a peek at the culprit.

Donna sensed my concern and began to explain.

"When she feels as though she can't breathe, she hits the call button."

"She?" I asked. "Since when do they mix men and women together in the same room?"

Donna shrugged, then continued.

"She thinks she is suffocating, but actually we don't know if what she feels is real or not because she can't speak. She has been in the intensive care unit for almost a year now, and the nurses still must respond quickly to each and every call. It's a hospital rule. Therefore, we walk back and forth, back and forth to her, never knowing if the calls are for real or not. Is she really suffocating? We never know."

"Why is she still here?" I asked.

"Because she has no insurance and no family, and no one else will take her. It's very sad. And to answer your question, this is the I C U; there is no separation between the sexes here."

That's just what I didn't need to hear. I began imagining how that woman felt. Suffocating, smothering, being buried alive! All of it!

The thought of it got my heart rate to rise, and again I tried secretly to fight off another panic attack. Watching my mom and Donna converse, I was suffering inside, and I kept up the façade until once again and thanks to the medication that snuck up on me, I nodded off and fell asleep.

19

I FOUND MYSELF DICTATING my final wishes as my mom jotted it all down on bits of scrap paper. I don't remember waking up or asking her to do it, I just found myself right in the middle of it. It was morning, that much I knew but I didn't remember waking up. I also knew that the operation was scheduled soon, my pain level was up, I couldn't move my legs and my life was over. But everything else was pretty much unknown.

"It's important, Mom, just please keep writing. If something happens to me after the operation, you need to know these things in order to protect Debbie and the kids from my ex-business partner. He'll move in like a vulture to steal back what he feels he has lost."

"What do you mean?" she asked.

"After learning how my company was thriving, he made a comment that he was going to sue me over the buyout deal because he now felt as though he got the short end of the stick. This was typical of him, so I had saved every document that would incriminate him in his nefarious endeavors. Boasting to others was always his downfall, and he's his own worst enemy."

"Hard work and getting rid of *his* dead weight are what got my company back on the right track," I told her. I think the sun was beginning to rise so I picked up the pace before they came to get me for the operation.

"You should have seen how fast he wanted out when our gas station failed its annual test, leaving me to deal with the cleanup. He ran like rats fleeing a sinking ship. Now that things are going well and the business has grown so much, he wants back in, threatening to sue, claiming he went into a bad buyout deal. It's not going to happen. I am going to arm you with enough ammunition, that if he messes with my family, he will have to think about it from a jail cell. Give this info to my lawyer and have him release it in the event of the following conditions."

I must have spoken for an hour, and when I was done, I felt a huge sense of relief.

———

THE SUN CAME IN THROUGH the slits in the window blinds, and the first shift nurses trickled in—bringing in raucous and laughter that carried throughout the corridors.

My head was pounding from all that thinking, and it lowered my resistance to the pain. I wanted to sit up and get off my back in the worst way, but my stomach muscles didn't work anymore, and I couldn't lean forward. That kept a lot of my own body weight on the injury.

I reached for the morphine injector and hit the button eight more times. That was the maximum injections allowed in an hour's time. Mom then kissed me goodbye and acted as if it were no big deal to leave. I knew she was trying to keep it light.

"I'll see you in the recovery room after the operation, Bobby, and this will all be behind us by then. Remember, it's all just temporary. Just keep having hope."

With that, she tidied up the room and put all essentials within my reach. She covered me with an extra blanket and kissed me again. I waved with a smile and tried to look brave. I hated myself for what I had done to her.

Listening to the sound of my own breathing, I stared at the ceiling and wondered what was to become of me. I didn't want to live like this.

My back, ribs, and heart were all broken, and depression was keeping me from thinking hopeful thoughts, like trying to look on the bright side. There was no bright side.

The cheap, soapy smell on my pillow caught my attention and reminded me again of where I was and why I was there. An emergency announcement came over the intercom. It called for a surgeon, any surgeon, to report to the O.R., stat!

An announcement like that may be for me soon, I thought.

I remained very still and reflected on parts of my life, and able to dream with my eyes still open, I went back to my early teens. Back to when I was invincible...

FLOWING PAST MY HALF-CLOSED EYES, were fifty-yard dashes, karate tournaments, Little League and hockey games, all played with meat and muscles on my leg bones. Those were my glory days.

My calf and thigh muscles remained hard and muscular right through to my kickboxing days and well into my thirties. And, I could still throw a decent round kick. Well, not anymore.

I can't live like this, I thought, as I lifted the blanket for a peak at my legs. I despised them.

If I could chew off my own legs to get away, I would do it in a heartbeat. Animals do it. I was reminded of the Indian in the trap. Forgetting to blink, I stared up at the ceiling again, this time with heavier eyelids.

I would chew them both off to get away from the dead parts. I'm like the Indian in the trap. I didn't want to think about that Indian but I knew I would. I began to think of last month's Wyoming elk hunt which was still fresh in my mind...along with the Indian in the trap.

20

WITH MY EYELIDS getting even heavier and my mind yearning for any remembrance of the *before*, I began to leave the present and lift the heartache that filled my entire being.

I found myself leaving camp just before the sun came up on that really cold October morning in Kemmerer, Wyoming. Tucked cozily into the mountainside, our white canvas wall tent sat almost two miles above sea level and glowed warmly from the gold flickering lanterns inside. It was just five weeks before my accident.

I was in the Jim Bridger National Forest, some fifty-five miles from the nearest town and so thankful for another invitation from my friends from out west.

Bridger was a mountain man from the eighteen hundreds and one of the best explorers, trail guides and fur trappers that had ever lived. He was also the young scout that left Hugh Glass to die from that grizzly attack and was later tracked down but forgiven by the vengeful survivor.

The closest I ever came to meeting a real frontiersman was with a gentleman by the name of Bill Bean, a trapper who guided for the legendary outdoorsman and archer, Fred Bear.

Bean was a heck of a storyteller and kindled the imaginations of the guys in my hunting group as we sat by his log cabin's fireplace back in the late eighties.

As a younger man, Bean made his living as an Alaskan fur trapper during the fifties and sixties, when fur trading was still part of the American culture. He lived in a hand-sewn tent, flushed and tanned his animal skin blankets, and trapped, hunted and fished for his own food.

When the animals hibernated, Bean moonlighted as a bush pilot in a second hand and dilapidated seaplane. He made chartered runs to South America by dropping religious volunteers into sometimes hostile, native country, in an attempt to fix people who didn't want to be fixed.

On his last run, Bean said he urged a group of missionaries not to disembark the plane and return to Alaska with him. He said he didn't like the look of the inhabitants that day and just had an overall bad feeling. But the volunteers left the airplane anyway.

Well, Bean was right because moments after takeoff, and as he circled the drop zone, he looked downward to witness the entire landing party being viciously slaughtered by the inhospitable natives.

Bean's stories were still fresh in my mind as I continued down the steep Wyoming mountainside and around the soft-wooded blowdowns, (fallen pine trees) from storms past. Laid out like "pickup sticks" and trying to slow me down with their pointy dead branches, they reached skyward like witches' fingers, concocting spells and praising the dark side.

It was a thrill like no other. And, with my loaded Remington rifle slung proudly over my right shoulder, I found a comfort zone that I couldn't find anywhere else but on that mountainside.

My 7-millimeter magnum, I jokingly called Old Betsy, which I named after Davey Crocket's trusted Hawken rifle, had been with me on many unforgettable treks. Her worn-out, rawhide sling fraily bore an embroidered bald eagle, and her checkered, walnut stock was full of shallow dents and crooked scratch marks.

When my friends teased me about all the nicks and scratches that she wore, I simply told them that each one was a memory, and I could never just sand them away.

The fresh smell of pine needles made me sigh with exhilaration as I rummaged through my belt pack full of Hershey Bars and Sun Maid Raisins.

After taking a bearing with my compass, I made a mental note of my heading for the eventual return home. That was important.

I loved this part. The part I waited for all year long: to locate a fresh elk track and follow it wherever it may lead me. And never knowing what was over the next rise just thrilled me to no end.

In the pursuit of game, for me anyway, the thrill of the hunt far outweighed the thrill of the kill.

On my slow descent from the campsite down the mountainside, I kept thinking of Bill Bean and the stories he told us. I could still hear him boast of the time he stitched up his own leg with corn whiskey and a used fishing line, after almost cutting it in two with a dull hatchet blade.

The story that moved me the most was this one.

Bean ran a fur trapline that strung out for more than 150 miles through the Alaskan wilderness and was accessible only by foot or horseback. Beaver and fox pelts brought earnest profits to the trappers, but the life was lonesome and the work was strenuous.

One snowy day while checking baited beaver traps on foot, Bean found an Indian in one of his old bear leg traps. He said it just like that, too!

"One day, I found an Indian in my trap."

Bean told us that the Inuit man's leg was bleeding profusely, and each time he fought to set himself free, the steel jaws clenched tighter and dug deeper into his leg, cutting through flesh and muscle with its razor-sharp teeth.

"And it didn't matter that he had a boot on neither!" Bean said with surprise, as he puffed his corncob pipe and blew rings of smoke into the air.

"Those rusty teeth bit straight through the shoe leather and clear to his mangled leg bone, aiming to bite all the way through if it could! If it were a fox and he survived the bloodletting, he'd a chewed his own leg off to get away. I found just a chewed off muskrat leg in a trap once. The critter got away with just three legs and probably lived a good life afterwards. They're resilient creatures, they are."

Bean explained that there was a heavy chain welded to the bear trap that bit into his leg. The other end of the chain was secured to a large fallen pine tree. A padlock protected it, but Bean's lock keys were long since gone. The market for bear furs had vanished years before and so did Bean's bear trapping business and equipment.

Bill thought that he had rounded up every last bear trap years ago, but he must have missed that one hidden beneath the leaves on the bank of a cool-water trout stream.

"I even sold off the C-clamps along with the bear traps," Bean said. "I should have kept a few."

C-clamps were used to spread apart the bigger trap jaws because of the tension on them. You could never pull them apart with your bare hands.

The Indian conveyed to Bean that he had stepped in the trap two days before and had lost a lot of blood. And with the eight-foot chain running out of links just feet shy of the stream, he had no water to drink during his captivity. "He was so close to the stream he could of spit in it, but he couldn't draw a drop to drink. Poor soul."

Bean gave the Indian what little food he had and filled his hat with water from the creek. The nearest trading post was in a small mining town a day and a half away, one way, so he set out immediately for the three-day journey.

He had to wear his snowshoes for most of the way because a blizzard hit just 10 miles into the trip. He endured the arduous trip, but upon arrival to the town, he was disheartened to learn that the storekeeper had no C-clamps, nor did he have a carbide saw blade to cut through the hardened-steel chain.

The trading post carried a chisel and anvil, and a four-pound hammer; all which would prove quite heavy to carry back through the deep snow. Bean explained just how their conversation unfolded next.

"After explaining my dilemma, the storekeep pondered on it a bit, reached down under the counter, and threw down a box of 30-caliber rifle cartridges." Bean paused before continuing, as he relit his cherry, tobacco-filled, corncob pipe.

"You got your 30-30 rifle with you, ain't ya?" said the storekeep.

"Yeah, I do," said Bean. "She's in my back pack."

"Well, why don't you just shoot him?" the proprietor asked. "You said he was an Indian didn't ya? Then why go through all that trouble? Just shoot him out there, I won't say nothin'."

As his story wound down, I think we all guessed the ending.

Bill Bean was a good man, so he set out with chisel and anvil, and the four-pound hammer, back through the deep snow and back to where he left the bleeding man. And, much to Bean's surprise, the Indian in the trap was still alive.

Bean spent the next two days chipping away at the unbreakable chain until it broke, then carried the weakened man over the snowdrifts and into the mining town where he left those rifle cartridges behind. Amazingly, the Indian survived and so did his leg.

After the evening tales ended, we all wondered if his stories were exaggerated, but we soon became believers when he pointed to a scrapbook under the handcrafted coffee table, which I fished out and opened for the rest of the guys.

There, in that old scrapbook was a news article along with two photos taken by a local news station in Anchorage. The photos depicted two, one-thousand-pound grizzlies, lying dead with nine 30-caliber bullet holes in both of their thick hides.

The article described Bill Bean traveling alone along his trap line, when the big bruin man-eaters stalked and attacked him from behind.

After opening him up with a gash that would later take 165 stitches to close, the grizzlies forced Bean to unload on them, reload and then unload again, in one of the fiercest bear encounters on record today. We then knew for sure that this guy and his stories were for real.

I continued down the mountainside still thinking of Bean and the Indian in the trap. I wondered if I'd be able to find my way back up the steep climb and back to camp in the dark, so I already decided that I would end my elk hunt well before dusk that day.

Down below, either an elk or a mule deer had kicked up some brush, leaving a trail of upturned pine needle patches behind. I must have jumped him up when I noisily snapped my way through the blowdowns and witches' fingers.

As I got closer, the tracks revealed the elk's bedding area by exposing impressions of its body's outline in the leaves and needles. Elk and mule deer bed down during the day and feed at night.

I walked down to the tracks below to see how fresh they were, but either way, I'd found their beds and I knew that they'd come back this way every morning around sunrise. I figured I'd have to get back there to stake it out before dark the next morning...

21

MY CONCENTRATION WAS broken when a food orderly rapped on the door with two quick knocks before entering my room with a tray of food. Daydreaming of the Wyoming elk hunt and the Indian in the trap made me forget my troubles but not for long.

"Morning! Breakfast!" he said, without looking up at me. I was angered that my daydream was cut short and my nose was rubbed in my shitty reality.

"Morning," I responded, then looked to the generic clock up on the wall. I noticed how institutional looking the clock was and was amazed at how much time had passed since my mom had left.

When I glanced back to the orderly, he was gone. In his place was a breakfast tray haphazardly tossed atop my roll table and parked about four feet from my bed. I could smell the pancakes and see the eggs through the clear plastic plate cover.

First of all, I wasn't even hungry. Secondly, I wasn't allowed to eat anything before the operation. Third, even if I wanted it, I couldn't reach it! That was my first experience of the able-bodied being clueless to the needs of the disabled.

So, I just lay there feeling bad for myself, smelling and viewing my breakfast just out of my reach.

Where is my rifle now? I thought. *I need it now more than ever.* I pictured myself holding its cold, blued barrel to my warm aching chest, while reaching out for the trigger with my right thumb. At the moment of the blast, it would all be okay again.

A lasting sleep, I thought. *A body without pain and a clear head without thoughts.* I wanted it so bad, and I fantasized about it over and over - the act of suicide by gunshot. I fantasized about my death, as I enjoyed the smell of my pancakes, four feet away.

Where could I do it? I wondered. *How could I do it? The rifle is too long though, a handgun would be better. I've gotta get my Beretta here instead. There's gotta be a way.*

I pondered the possibilities. Then it hit me. *Debbie said that Cuckoo called her for an update on my condition. Maybe he'll come. Maybe he'll fly out to see me and I'll ask him then. I'll tell him what to do. He'll understand. He'll do it for me. I know he will.* Cuckoo was the one person I could count on for sure. I knew I could count on Eddie too, and for everything else, but not for that.

Eddie would do anything for me; we were as close as brothers were, but this was different. Eddie's one of the toughest guys I ever knew, but he also has the softest heart. He could kill at the drop of a hat if someone hurt his family, but he couldn't help me die and that I knew. Cuckoo could put down a wounded animal and that's what I needed him to do now. He would finish off a suffering animal if need be, and I was truly that.

Retiring to Wyoming had been a dream of Cuckoo's ever since we first hunted there years ago. He was so impressed with the Wild West and its old-fashioned way of life, it was able to lure him back to settle out there for good with his wife, Debbie, just after he retired from the Woonsocket fire department.

My first experience with the ways of the west was not so impressive though...

22

THE YEAR WAS 1991. Cuckoo and Moses drove out to Wyoming from Rhode Island in just under 36 hours, in a 1986 Ford F-150 4x4, with a trailer in tow and an old chest freezer strapped down to its truck bed. We couldn't afford the meat processing fees or the shipping costs, so we rigged up our own mobile butcher shop for the ten-day hunt. We planned to feed our families with meat for 2 years if we were lucky.

I flew into Casper from Denver on the single-engine prop plane we called, "The Vomit Comet." I couldn't take the extra time needed to ride out with the guys because of my business, so I had to fly out while they drove.

By writing ahead to a rancher, we arranged for a stay on his twenty-thousand-acre ranch, which was eight thousand feet above sea level and bordered the Medicine Bow National Forest.

The town of Medicine Bow had a population of 223 and was where the television show 'The Virginian' was filmed, back in the sixties.

The town has wooden sidewalks lining its dirt streets and an authentic saloon, equipped with poker tables, brass spittoons, and a hand-carved cowboy bar.

The Virginian Hotel still preserves two-dollar-a-night rooms outfitted with old, springy beds, porcelain pitchers and washbasins that sit atop solid oak dressers with lion-clawed legs.

Across the muddy street, stood an old cowboy eatery that proudly bares its bullet holes in the flower-papered walls, leftover from gun-fights and shootouts of long ago.

Our pen pal rancher lived 75 miles outside of town, just off the old schoolhouse road. His sweet wife invited us in through the farmer's porch and introduced us to the man of the house.

He was a tall, lean cowboy in his early eighties, yes eighties–but with the physique of a nineteen-year-old. He sported a worn out, tight fitting pair of Levi's, held up squarely by a black leather belt with a great big silver-scrolled belt buckle.

A brownish-paisley, button-down shirt had ironing creases in it, and a red-checkered handkerchief hung loosely around his wrinkled neck. The handkerchief made him look like a bank robber, I thought, and I kept imagining him pulling it up over his nose and pointing a pair of six-guns at a bank clerk with hands held high.

My first hunt in Wyoming.

And, like most cowboys, his back pants pocket bulged in the form of a circle, which was about the size of a half dollar. He reached back into his dungarees pocket and pulled out a can of Indian Head Chewing Tobacco, and with two fingers, he packed a wad into the side of his checkered and leathery cheek, then spat a hunk of the tarry clam into an empty coffee can on one corner of the dining room table from which we sat. The coffee can sat right next to his mug of black coffee. I got a kick out of that.

I was told that when cowboys were done with their old blue jeans, they could drop them off at a thrift shop in Cheyenne. There, they could get six bucks a pair for them, no matter what their condition.

From there, they were exported to Japan, where they were sold to and worn by the Japanese chic, for as much as three hundred dollars a pair for an American Cowboy original. And if a pair of jeans were lucky enough to bear the tobacco can wear mark around the back pocket, they could fetch upwards of one thousand dollars!

A pair of cracked and dry-rotted boots fit the old cowpoke's feet as if he were born with them on, and I wondered just how comfortable they could possibly be.

And, of course, at the top of his meticulously short haircut, was a worn out, tan colored Stetson cowboy hat, faded and marred by the wind and sun. His name was Jigger Jones.

Jigger drew us a map to the log cabin we were staying in but cautioned us not to leave for it in the dark of night.

"You fellers are welcome to sleep in the bunkhouse tonight if it pleases ya," Jigger told us. But we didn't intend to waste another minute of our trip, so we set out anyway under the countless stars with that tiny map as our only guide.

I remember asking Jigger a question as he drew a small pencil line on the map he had drafted for us. It was on the back of an old electric bill envelope. The whole map that he drew was only about the size of a matchbook.

"That little line, is that a dirt road Jigger?" I asked respectfully.

"Hell no, that's a two-tracker!" he said. "Ain't no roads out there but more like cow paths zigzagging through the prairie sagebrush. Careful or you'll miss one!"

"So, tell me, Jigger, just how far would that little line be there on your map?" I asked, pointing to the one that was less than an inch long.

"Oh, son, I'd say that one's about seventy miles or so." I just looked at Cuckoo and Moses through crossed eyes and a mischievous smirk.

After driving all night in pitch-black darkness, we miraculously found the base of the cabin's mountain. The steep, rocky trail was too treacherous to navigate at night, especially with the sixteen-foot open trailer that we towed behind us.

The trailer was weighted down with a Polaris 4-wheeler that I borrowed from a friend, some wooden boxes filled with cooking and eating supplies, army cots, a gas grill which we shouldn't have brought, hunting gear, way too much clothing, and enough ammunition to defeat the Mexican army. Oh, and, of course, our coveted hunting rifles.

Exhausted by the campfire.

Usually, the cabin was only reached by horseback and used as an outpost by cowhands to camp out in after a long day of checking barbed wire fence lines. Thinking the climb might be rough, we decided to disconnect the trailer, leave it at the bottom and come back for it in the morning light.

We took our rifles and ammo with us, along with just the supplies we had in the back of the pickup and started up the steep incline. The climb took our four-wheel drive pickup over an hour and a half to reach the top that night. It was so rocky, we could only do about 5 mph most of the way. I don't think anyone minded that we would need to make that trek twice a day, as the camping was at the top of the mountain, yet the hunting was along the bottom. We never cared about things like that.

We found the one-room log cabin in good condition when we lit the glass-globed lantern sitting on the handmade cottonwood table. The cast iron wood stove was the center of attraction with its fancy scrolls that lined the outer edges of the firebox.

The four bunk beds held our curiosity while we examined their bedding. There was none.

Tossed loosely across each bunk, laid the rusty coil springs, naked of any mattress or cloth material.

"Where are all the mattresses?" I said.

"I don't know," said Moses, as he opened the only cupboard in the only room. "Oops, here they are!" he announced. "They're all shredded up and stuffed into this small cupboard! I think we have a mouse."

"Ya think?" I said, through squinting yet smiling eyes.

Thank God, we had our sleeping bags in the back of the pickup.

———————

THE THREE OF US GOT up early the next morning and raced down the mountain to fetch our gear, only to find that our trailer was gone! We glassed the area with the binoculars we had in the truck's cab and backtracked for a while, thinking that we left it somewhere else in the dark but just couldn't find it.

Unbeknownst to us, we had left our trailer on a small strip of land that crossed over Jigger's property, and unfortunately for us, a wealthy rancher named Saib Dakhil, owner of the Broken Arrow Cattle Ranch, owned that strip.

Dakhil was rumored to be an unneighborly and bold landowner. His ranch boss had been in a small fight with Jigger's eldest son, Paul, over some barfly at the Beacon Bar and Dance Hall in Casper. It created bad blood between the two cattle ranches and its hired ranch hands, too.

The ranch boss and hired hands didn't have a trailer hitch on their pickup, so when they swiped it, they just dragged our trailer by its tongue, right on the ground across the open prairie, snapping off brake signals and marker lights as they went.

We found broken pieces of red and amber lenses ground into the dirt along the drag marks left behind. We tracked it for a mile but lost the trail when they tied the tongue to their bumper. Good thing we took our rifles with us up that mountain the night before.

The next two days were spent searching for our gear and tracking down the thieves. We got a lucky break from an old friend of ours, Maurine, a Rhode Island native now living in Casper and working for a Wyoming State agency.

Maurine made several calls on our behalf and got a lead from an anonymous source. She then telephoned the owner of the Broken Arrow Ranch and inquired as to the whereabouts of our trailer without directly accusing him of the theft.

Dakhil informed Maurine that he and his ranch hands were indeed in possession of our property but were not inclined to return it. He stated it was now his and his to do with what he pleased. He then recited his rendition of Wyoming laws on trespassing and ownership and scoffed at her request to return the trailer to us.

"Besides," he said, "It's up to my ranch foreman because it's his

4-wheeler and trailer now, not mine." He ended the conversation with the phrase, "it's the Wyoming way."

We didn't have cell phones back then, so Cuckoo guarded the cabin while Moses and I made the long journey to Medicine Bow for supplies and to call the Sheriff Department which had its closest office located in Laramie, about eighty miles south of our location.

We made it back up to camp just before nightfall and saw the lights of the deputy's Blazer, making its long climb up the mountain and to our supply-starved camp. Cuckoo had a campfire going for us.

That lawman drove about two hours just to get to the base of the mountain, then another hour to get to the top, all just for us to fill out a police report! I thought that was so weird but was glad to see him just the same.

Black coffee was offered to the veteran lawman, (every man out west drinks his coffee black) with an invitation to join us out by the campfire to warm his cold hands and feet. We apologized for the lack of firewood as our chainsaw was stolen along with the trailer.

As we sipped our coffee together by the hot embers, the deputy's star-shaped badge reflected the firelight, which danced on it like a moth to a flame.

The deputy questioned our hunting plans, then changed his demeanor and seriously warned us of a rogue mountain lion that was terrorizing farmers in and around the national forest.

He described how just that week, he took a complaint from a local rancher who found his mare standing alone and in shock, with two long claw marks imbedded deeply in her haunches. Her three-month-old colt was nowhere to be found.

Other residents called in similar reports complaining of big cat encounters, too. Yet, the deputy warned us not to shoot the rogue cat, as it was protected under federal law, and shooting the animal carried strict federal penalties.

Cuckoo told the officer not to worry because if the lion encountered one of us, there would be no report filed. The officer thanked us; I don't think he got what Cuckoo meant.

Later that week, Cuckoo did come upon the mountain lion as he stalked a mule deer across the rolling prairie at the base of the mountain.

He would find the big cat perched in the only tree in sight, stretched out along a forked limb. The massive cat flagged his curled tail and watched Cuckoo make his way toward the tree.

Cuckoo would stop dead in his tracks as the cat slithered down the trunk of the tree and slinked into the windy grass facing him. Then the big cat squatted into a long sneaky posture before closing in on its prey—Cuckoo.

The lion crouched lower and took slow, deliberate steps, never taking his eyes off Cuckoo. The hunter had become the hunted.

The ghostly image came and went, melting into the background as he steadily crept closer to the ever still deer hunter. But I'm confident that the stealthy lion didn't know he only had two more steps to go before Cuckoo would unload his 300 Winchester Magnum, which was loaded with 195 grain Nossler Partition, big game, big ass, bullets.

Cuckoo makes his own bullets. And Cuckoo doesn't miss.

The lucky cat would veer off just in time and live to terrorize another day.

Before the sheriff's deputy left, he took our complaint and much to our surprise, informed us of his conversation with Mr. Dakhil earlier that day. We were surprised to know that they had spoken.

"The rancher was arrogant with me also," the deputy said. "I went out there to the Broken Arrow Ranch and spoke to Mr. Dakhil on my way up here. He told me I had no right to trespass on his land, either, and to tell those easterners up there that they had better learn that this isn't New York City, and things are done differently out here."

"We are not from New York," I interrupted but was ignored.

The deputy sipped his coffee and continued with Dakhil's words. "Out here, men have to pay to trespass, and my land is just that, mine. They need to understand, to claim personal property left by a trespasser is my right, but more than that, it's the 'Wyoming way.'"

The deputy paused for a moment with another thought. "Even on my way out to his ranch, and as I was going through the front gate, I stopped to read the warning poster tacked to the gatepost. It read, 'No Trespassing! *Survivors* will be prosecuted!'"

With one last slurp, the deputy drank down the coffee grounds at the bottom of his cup and suggested that we take Mr. Dakhil to civil court in the spring, to try to recover our possessions.

As the deputy left us, we thanked him for his advice but assured him that we wouldn't wait months to get our property back but thanked him just the same. That part I know he understood.

We sat in the dark late into the night and watched the falling stars with great disappointment.

"I'd expect this treatment from foreigners," I said. "But not from fellow Americans. I'm disappointed."

"I don't think Dakhil is an American," Cuckoo said.

I impatiently quipped back. "His ranch hands are!"

Just then, I noticed a light in the dark about half way down the mountain, which seemed to be driving away from us.

"The ranch hands are riding our four-wheeler!" I shouted. "Who else would be driving something way out here at night?"

"Those lights look close out here but could actually be as far as 20 miles away!" said Cuckoo.

I reached for my rifle, which was lying right beside me and ran to the pickup, shouting for someone to stay and watch the camp. Moses jumped through the passenger door and held onto my rifle as we raced from the camp like a bat out of hell.

"Moses, load my rifle up for me, it's only got three rounds in it, there's a box of shells under the seat, hurry up!" As he rammed each round into the gun, Moses screamed at me over the wind noise from the open vent windows.

"Just shoot them below the knees, okay, Bobby? Don't kill them!

It will be hell to pay if you kill them, so don't. Below the knees, okay? Bobby are you listening to me?"

"Okay, okay, below the knees! I will, I promise! I'm not going to kill anybody!"

We hit every rock on the way down and drove way too fast. And it was all in vain, too. They must have seen our headlights racing toward them in the dark and doused theirs, making it impossible to see them in the blackness!

We limped back up the mountain, unsuccessful, discouraged and exhausted. It killed us to give up.

The next morning, we got up early and went to town to use the only pay phone. I asked Cuckoo to get Maurine on the phone for me, never letting him know what I was about to say. My end of the conversation sounded like this:

"Hi Maurine, how are you? I'm okay, thanks, but could be better as you know. Hey Maurine, I want to thank you for all you've done for us and want you to know how much we appreciate it. I know you are. It's okay, I know you did, I know, the Wyoming way, I know, thank you. Maurine, please do me one last favor. Will you get a pen and paper please? I'll wait, thanks."

"Ready? I need you to call Saib Dakhil and give him a message for me, please. And I need you to tell him that you are just the messenger, and I want him to know that I asked you to write it down, word for word. I know. Please, just do this for me, okay? Thanks, ready?"

"Mr. Dakhil, my name is Robert DePalo. I am one of the hunters who crossed your property by only thirty feet, I am told. And I am the one whose trailer and property you and your employees stole from. And you should listen to what I am about to say to you if you are as smart as you think you are.

"I am giving you until four o'clock today, to call your ranch boss and instruct him to return our trailer with all its contents and deliver it to the spot from where he stole it."

"If you do not, Mr. Dakhil, I will come to your home tonight, drag you out by your hair in front of your wife and children, and beat the living shit out of you on your own front lawn. There will be no discussion."

"Oh, and Mr. Dakhil? That's the 'Rhode Island Way.'"

We got word through the sheriff's office that same day with instructions on where we could find our trailer. We never did know if Maurine delivered the message.

Surprisingly, it was only six miles from our cabin and hidden in the hills at one of the Broken Arrow's bunkhouses where they rope and brand their cattle. That's why we saw their headlights that night. We never knew that outpost was there!

As Cuckoo and I rode up on the bunkhouse, we were outraged at the condition of our trailer and gear. All the wooden lockers had their padlocks sawed off and were tipped over, spilling their contents on the dusty ground throughout the area. The 4-wheeler sat with a flat front tire, broken lights, bent bumpers, out of gas, and an ignition key switch that was hacked open with a screwdriver or something.

Every tail lamp, parking light, marker lens, and turn signal light was smashed on the trailer. Entangled in one of the trailer wheels was its entire wiring harness, which had been ripped out from the undercarriage during the drag.

The worst of it all was the trailer tongue and coupling. That's the long, neck-like piece that you hook onto the trailer hitch ball when towing. It was twisted and mangled when it was dragged across the rocky prairie, and we were certain it would never fit on our truck's trailer hitch ball again.

After a careful look around, I stepped out of the truck with my rifle in hand and leaned it over the truck's hood, while staring down the barrel at the darkened windows of the wrangler's bunkhouse. I was only looking through the scope, but it looked intimidating just the same.

The rest of the trip was amazing—wild horses roamed the prairie.

Cuckoo wrapped up the wiring harness and picked up the tossed gear that was spewed about everywhere. I never saw any movement in their camp but was sure they were watching us from inside.

After he chained the trailer tongue to the rear bumper, we slowly made our way out the open gate and away from the Broken Arrow's outpost.

Out of sight and earshot, we stopped beside a Black Angus bull who was grazing on some sparse grass on the edge of the two tracker we traveled on. The massive bull was blacker than night and must have weighed 1000 pounds. The brand on its rump depicted Dakhil's ugly burn mark, and I immediately knew what Cuckoo was thinking.

"How much money do you think that bull stands him?" he asked.

"A lot," I said loudly, eyeing the massive horns that weighed heavily on its gigantic head.

With that, Cuckoo locked up the brakes, jumped from the truck, and pulled his rifle from its gun case behind the seat.

"I'm gonna shoot his fuckin' bull. Don't say a fuckin' thing, Bobby! Fuck him, I'm gonna do it! I'm gonna put a fuckin' bullet right between its fuckin' eyes!"

He raised his rifle at point blank range and....

23

I DRIFTED OUT OF that memory and found myself back in my hell. Daydreaming was my escape but coming back to reality hurt each time I did.

Motionless in my hospital bed, I wished I was back in the prairies and foothills of Wyoming again but knew it could never be.

I zoomed in on the cracks and crevices on the ceiling panels above. A rabbit's head appeared out of some squiggly lines, and different shades of light and dark made up the rest of its body.

When the kids were small, we played this very game, I thought, as I tried to make out more figures.

I thought of Sunday mornings and the fun-filled times we had as the kids waited for me to wake up. I could hear them in the kitchen, whispering things like, "when is he going to get up?" Or, "I think I heard him move a little!"

When I was still half asleep, I would whistle twice, duck under the covers, and brace myself for the impact, as the kids raced like nuts to be the first to dive on the bed and jump up and down on my quilt-covered head.

Uncontrollable laughter prevented me from telling them to stop. Debbie always had to step in by breaking it up and saying things like, "What's wrong with you, Bobby? Are you five? Someone's going to get hurt!"

After they calmed down, they hopped under the covers, and we all looked up at the ceiling to find animal shapes up above.

Our log home interior was full of cracks and crevices, as the dry tongue and grooved pine had split over the years. There were lots of pine knots that gave the house character, but more importantly, they made great animal eyes. It was amazing how many figures could be seen in one area. When one of us found an image, the other two would have to find it and try to make it out as well.

My kids, as most kids, had vivid imaginations. It hurt me to think what they were imagining now. I stared at the rabbit's head on the ceiling until the tears blurred my vision and forced me to look away. Then the orderlies came to get me for the operation.

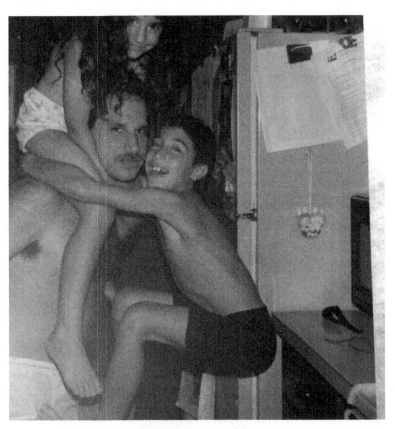

Lauren, Derek, and me.

24

THE RECOVERY ROOM nurse held her freckled face at about six inches from mine and yelled way too loud! Her words were barely audible but I knew what she wanted. "Time to wake up, Robert! Wake up!"

Moving my eyes downward, I saw what looked like tie straps holding my arms down. *Why do they keep doing this to me?!*

An ice-cold oxygen mask, sealed tightly to my face, left me feeling smothered again! I couldn't stand any of it!

I tried to sit up but was forced back down, and feeling the restraints across my arms, well, I began to pant like a dog through the fogged-up mask. For a moment or so, I was back at the beach and under the heaviness of the cool, wet sand! I tried to move my legs but felt nothing at all, that made things even worse so I squirmed the top part of my body before being stifled by the restraints. Again, I thought of the Indian in the trap.

Please kill me, I prayed. *Please God, let me die!* I turned my head in both directions, looking for a way out and searching for something sharp to drive through my skull.

I wish I had my pistol with me. I wish Cuckoo were here. Please God. Please help me to end it now and go into a peaceful and lasting sleep. Panic took hold of me like a boa constrictor, squeezing, squeezing...

I'm suffocating again! I screamed in my mind. *I'm suffocating!*

"Get these restraints off me!" I screamed aloud and through the oxygen mask that was now sideways on my face!

Just hearing myself scream frightened me further, so I struggled to get free and worked myself up into a short-breathed frenzy!

Freckle face leaned back into view, and I latched desperately onto her presence as kind of an anchor. Without speaking, she quickly pulled the blanket off me and unbuckled the restraints. I didn't take my eyes off her until I was able to calm myself down, still wondering just how much more of this I could take.

I pulled the mask down from my face and onto my chin, inhaling the world's air as if for the first time. "This is driving me insane," I said aloud to myself, trying to fight off the grog by shaking things from my head like a wet dog that just got out of the heavy rain.

"Stop tying me down! Everyone! Everywhere! I can't move my legs and it creeps and freaks me the fuck out!"

My head fell back on the pillow. I wondered just who heard my *big* speech and was immediately sorry that I cursed. It seemed I was doing that a lot lately.

What did they give me, opium, or something strong like that? I can't shake off the grog! I closed my eyelids and rolled my eyeballs back to think.

I'm just glad that this is happening to me and not to someone else. As long as it has me, it'll leave my family alone. I was chosen for this misery because no one else could handle it. Who could? I know that now. I know... that...now...

I don't remember falling asleep in that recovery room; but I did. Time passed—but I don't know how much.

Clutching at air while falling fast, I threw my arms out and jolted myself awake again! I kept waking up like that. It was the same nightmare of me falling fast towards the earth, over and over, and it was frightening!

My heart pounded hard and I still couldn't shake off the grog. I think I was in a different room now. Maybe not.

Movement caught my eye off to the side of my bed when Mom and Debbie slowly came into view. They were whispering something to each other, and I immediately became embarrassed, knowing that they saw my flailing arms as I awoke. Mom stood to speak.

"Are you okay, Bobby? Did you have another bad dream?"

"I'm okay. I'm just so sleepy and I can't wake up."

"It's fine, Bobby. We have great news! The operation was a success, a complete success!"

"What?" I said, dazedly.

"You had the operation, and Dr. Lucas said it was a success!"

"Really, a success? The operation was a success? So, I'm going to be okay?"

A huge sense of relief came over me. *I'm going to walk again!*

"It was a major operation that took over seven hours. All day in fact. But it's over now and you're going to be alright! Are you happy, Bobby?"

"I'm happy," I answered, barely, with the most slurred, drunk-ard-like and soft, raspy voice. "That's good," I said, and fell back to sleep, back into the abyss.

25

MY COMATOSE-LIKE HAVEN was taken from me when fear suddenly erupted with a ghastly explosion and threw me into a terrifying panic!

Falling fast, I told myself to wake up and grab onto reality. As I reached out to grab something, the slick branches of the neighboring tree slipped through my desperate fingers. I screamed terrifyingly in my mind! *Wake up!* I told myself again. *Wake up!*

With a pounding chest, my eyes opened wide, scanning the room and searching for something solid! Something real!

Where is everyone? I wondered, breathing heavily through my cotton- mouth. *My back is killing me!*

Beyond the half-closed door, the dimly lit nightlight illuminated the corridor and created an ambiance of horror. Moreover, the inability to detect direction left me feeling uneasy and out of control.

Which way am I facing? Which way is north? Where is my world?

Alone and vulnerable, I felt utterly exposed to the nighttime predators. So, in a defensive posture, I raised my shields and prepared for the worst.

I had been fantasizing snippets of horror scenes in my head. My classic horror scenario involved myself reaching for the call button, only to find it missing or just out of my reach. Then, forced to lay there, alone, insane, and rotting from the inside out.

I played out the fantasy in my mind as I reached out through the dark and felt for the call button's plastic cord. For a nanosecond, part of me didn't want it to be there, my usual addiction to flirt with danger, I guess. However, the insulated wire found my grip and I held on tight.

Something in the dark spooked me, something in the corner of the room. I kept one eye on that spot and one eye on the corridor through the small opening in the door.

Where is everybody? And why weren't they watching me? I've been abandoned, abandoned to suffer all alone in this terrifying place.

They must know what I'm feeling right now! Where are they? I listened. *This must be part of the conspiracy,* I thought, as my drugged mind worked obsessively to create all sorts of plots. I listened some more. I badly needed someone to latch onto. Someone to bring me back to reality.

I needed to reposition my legs to reach easier for the nurse's call button, so I pushed. I pushed my legs. Nothing. I pushed again. This time the anxiety rose to a higher level! *Why won't my legs work yet? I thought the operation was a complete success?*

I pushed on the call button long and hard; the clock in my head started the countdown. I knew that if the nurse had not responded soon, starting now, I would lose it—really lose it. While praying to God that I wouldn't have to wait, a terrifying notion entered my mind! *I didn't see the light go on when I pushed the call button! Oh my God!* I cried in silence. *Please no! Please God, no!*

I dreaded having to try again but knew that I had to. I pushed on it again and held it down hard. Pausing briefly to reflect on the situation, I found myself not really surprised at my predicament, but I prayed to God that I was wrong.

I released the button, and the moment my finger sprang back up, I could not believe my eyes! The light did not come on! The light did *not* come on!

It's broken! God, please, come on, no more! I pleaded to Him, thinking that if I both begged and commanded in the same sentence, one of them might get through.

With my throat closing shut, I began spiraling downward, out of control and into unadulterated fright. I was more afraid right then than I had ever been in my entire life! And Debbie was wrong about me! I wasn't brave, I was afraid.

This fear was different because I couldn't end it! If you are afraid of the dark, you put the light on. If you're afraid of speed, you slow down. In the back of your mind, you always have that out. But there was no out for me now. This kind of fear was the worst of all fears because there was nothing I could do to end it! It would go on and on and on, until I went insane.

My outcry for the nurse suddenly broke through the nighttime's quiet, terrifying me even more! And it both surprised and startled me, because I hadn't expected it from myself!

Silence fell again and all I could hear was a loud ringing in my ears! The ringing sound of panic! Again, I yelled out in the dark, "Nurse!" Silence. Just silence. My hands trembled. Once more, I hollered out into the dark. "Nurse!"

She must have been walking by my door because the outburst hadn't completely left my lips when she landed with both feet into my room.

"What's wrong?" she screeched, as she held her rising chest and panned the room for the answer.

"My call button is broken!" I yelled back through the dim light. "It doesn't work and I'm having a panic attack! Please, it's really bad!" Unable to move I squirmed in place, bouncing up and down with just my upper half. "I can't move my lower half! Can you give me something for this feeling? Anything, I need something, please!"

Her nametag was missing, so I asked her name. I had to know it! "It's Tammy," she said.

"Please Tammy, it's really bad! I know you don't know me but I'm not a complainer, I'm not. It's really bad!" A look of pity suddenly leaked from her eyes.

"I'll page the doctor, okay?" she replied, still holding her hand to her chest.

"No, please, I can't wait! I'm losing it Tammy, is it day or night?"

My palms were soaking wet. I tried to sit up and get out of my body and away from it all, but in trying to pull myself up, my hands slipped off the guardrails and I fell back into my hell.

"It's nighttime. Can I call someone for you?" Tammy yelled. All nurses yell, they all yell as if all patients are deaf.

"Maybe if someone comes and sits with you, you might feel better. Can your wife come in? Does she live close by?" The caring nurse was obviously concerned and trying to help. I fixed and locked my eyes on her and would not take them off.

"No, she is an hour away. We have children!"

"How about your mom? I met her last night; she seemed so nice. Want me to get her on the phone for you?"

Embarrassed, yet desperate, I said yes.

"Okay, but I feel like a baby, Tammy. I'm really sorry about all of this."

"What's the number?" she asked, as she dialed the phone that was in my view but out of my reach. I hadn't heard her make the connection; I was too busy fighting off the demons and nighttime predators.

"Hold on please, Terry, here's Bobby. Here she is, honey." Not knowing what to say, I timidly accepted the telephone with sweat soaked hands.

"Hi Mom, I'm so sorry, I know it's late. I feel like such a baby!"

"Bobby," she said firmly, "I'm leaving right now; I'll be there in 15 minutes!"

"No, Mom, you don't have to, I'm okay now; I feel better already. I don't know what's wrong with me but I'm okay now. I think just talking to someone has helped. I'll be okay now."

"Bobby, I'm coming right now. Hang up the phone and try to relax, and I'll be there before you know it. Jim is taking me now!"

"I feel like such a jerk Mom, okay, all right and thank you. You don't have to rush." I handed the phone back to Tammy while regretting the call and embarrassed about the sweat.

"Thank you," I told Tammy, "I'm fine," I kept saying. "I'm fine."

I was too embarrassed to say, but I didn't want her to leave me. I needed to keep her in my sight and even made some bogus small talk in order to stall her for a few extra moments.

I sensed someone in the other bed across the room but couldn't raise my head up enough to see. Whoever it was, was much quieter than the last one, and I was sure he or she was awake by now. I was embarrassed about that too.

Mom made the thirty-minute trip in less than fifteen and stormed in with a worried but determined look on her face. I latched onto her glossy eyes and slowly began to pull myself back from the abyss.

"Ma, I'm sorry I made you come," I said, while wiping my forehead with my forearm. "I just... I was falling again...I couldn't grab onto the branches and...and I woke up alone. I'm sorry.

—————

SHE BENT OVER ME AND softly said, "Close your eyes and get some sleep now, I'll sit right here in case you wake up again. I'm not leaving you alone tonight."

Resting my head back down on my pillow, I took a long deep breath, closed one eye and then the other. My breathing slowed, my heart rate dropped, and a calmness slowly overcame me. I was okay.

I think that God created moms to help defeat the nighttime predators.

26

HOURS PASSED. I kept waking up and fighting the overwhelming urge to sleep. Each time I nodded off, I jumped up to stop the falling process, clutching at air as if to grab the passing branches that slipped through my fingers as I fell out of that tree. Since the accident, I must have fallen from that tree over twenty more times. It was exhausting.

"I'm still right here, Bobby, it's okay to sleep. I won't leave you; I promise." I had forgotten she was there.

"Mom, I can't..., don't let me sleep. It's horrible! I keep falling! And the drugs are helping to create these things!" I then pushed on the morphine pump like a junky needing a fix. Pain wasn't the only motivator that time. The drug was now becoming a means to escape and from that point on, I relied on the drugs to do just that, escape.

I remained quiet until I calmed down a bit.

"Mom," I said, without looking up.

"Yes, Bobby?"

"What did they say..., about when the feeling in my legs would return?"

She paused a second to choose her words very carefully. "They just don't know, Bobby."

What? Did she mean they didn't know "when" it would return or "if" it would return? What has changed? She told me the operation was a complete success! I was afraid to nail her down.

"I thought you told me that Dr. Lucas said the operation was a complete success? Did I dream that? Didn't you tell me that?"

Her expression changed and I didn't like it. "Dr. Lucas is a very good doctor." My heart sank. "All there is, is hope," she said. "That's all we have, and I'll never let go of that." My heart sank further and butterflies filled my stomach. *Wait, I was told I would walk,* I thought. *What is going on?* I couldn't tell her what I was thinking or feeling so I kept it to myself and suffered in silence.

She paused in thought before she spoke again. "I need to tell you; your brother Ricky is having a hard time with this."

"He was here yesterday, Mom. He was okay."

"No, Bobby, he is not dealing with this very well at all."

It's funny, I thought. *Even at a time like this, the two of us are looking out for him. It's what we've always done.*

"Okay, Mom, I'll keep that in mind when talking to him. I'll be more upbeat."

She must have left before daybreak. I really don't know. I just knew that something was wrong. They told me that the operation was a success, and now they seemed to be backpedaling. I didn't want to think about it and pretended there was no problem. I couldn't face it. I just couldn't. So, I didn't.

27

THE NEXT MORNING, the words "just a pinch" got me to open my eyes just in time. A needle, or should I say, a javelin was plunging sideways into my belly, just under the naval, by a pair of ice-cold fingers and hands.

"Yow! What's that for, and why there?" I asked.

"It's to prevent blood clots," 'Nurse Ratchet' said. That really wasn't her name.

"Now don't move. I'm not doing it twice!" she said, and a little too fresh, I thought.

"Well, it really hurts!" I complained.

"Oh, come on, don't be such a baby," she said, as she peered over her church-lady style, eyeglasses.

This one is a bitch! I thought.

Her lips pursed and remained pressed tightly together, and her undyed hair was strictly pulled back in a regimental fashion, which reminded me of a prison guard in an all-women's state prison or a Russian gulag. She ran her unit like a boot camp.

"Only two visitors at a time and family members only! No exceptions!" She ordered.

I caught wind of a scuffle between her and my family, but everyone did their best to conceal it from me. I asked my family if there were a problem. And if so, would they please not make any waves, for fear that I might suffer from neglect late at night. I was completely at her mercy and was petrified of being ignored in my darkest hour in case anxiety arose. Later on, I told my other nurses about her and they weren't surprised. One of them jokingly told me that some nurses are brutal, in fact, "they are known to eat their own young." I really missed Tammy.

A team of orderlies appeared and took direction from my 'Nurse Ratchet'. She barked out orders and had them slide me onto an empty stretcher in order to install an air mattress on my bed. For the first time, I was able to see what my bed looked like from another angle. It had a body impression so deep into the mattress, it looked like a huge dinosaur fossil.

They plugged in the mattress air pump with a clicking noise that I knew would just wear my already thin nerves down to nothing. I didn't gripe though, maybe I'd get some back pain relief. They also installed a chain above me with a triangle shaped thing at the end, in hopes that I could reach it and pull myself up. No way. I was too weak, too sore and my arm muscles were already experiencing atrophy. I liked having it dangle there just the same.

After they transferred me back over to my bed, I reached for the morphine button again and pressed it eight more times.

Nurse Ratchet's job was done, so she efficiently and neatly wrote in the chart on the clipboard that hung at the foot of my bed. I so desperately wanted to know the contents of that chart because I was convinced that it contained the answers that were being kept from me.

That log, just out of my reach, holds the answer to my question. Will I ever walk again?

A foreign speaking woman came in to give me a mini-sponge bath. She was round in stature and exceptionally jolly, from Yugoslavia or one of the Baltic States, I think. She had that Russian-sounding accent, and I liked the way she floated around my bed as she hummed an unfamiliar tune.

I focused on her walk, wondering if she appreciated what she could do.

"I am Olga," she said in broken English. "How did you get this?" She didn't give me time to answer and asked me a bunch of more things all at once.

This one will not keep things from me, I thought. That was apparent by the personal questions she asked and by the comments she made.

A little too insensitive, I thought. *How dare she bring up the events of my accident and speak freely of my tragedy. No one else did! She is supposed to pretend that my current condition doesn't exist!* I liked her immediately. I liked her a lot.

Her humming paused as she looked up to speak. "*Eet* is very sad, but an *odder* hunting man fell also last *veek* and *vas* not able to *leeve* long. He die. He *vas* in *theese* very bed as you, and he die last *veek*. Very sad," she said, and continued humming.

That's encouraging, I thought. "How did he die?" I asked.

"He had inside bleeding from *hees* fall. *Eets* very sad."

As she washed my legs and feet, I replayed the detailed events of my accident. I pictured myself climbing the oak tree again when she commented that my "feets" were hot.

"Are they really? They're hot? That's good, right?"

I had ignored my legs up to that point. I couldn't bear to look down at them, only to check to see if my hips were in line with the rest of me. Just the idea of my legs lying crooked gave me the feeling that they might snap off and that caused anxiety.

"*Eet* is good," she answered.

"Are my legs warm too?"

"Ya, is hot."

Finishing her chores, Olga left as quickly as she came, while humming a polka-sounding melody all the way out.

The unfounded worries compounded by the hour. I'd look at the water pitcher and worry that if no one was standing by to pour it for me, I might panic and suffer all alone with no one to hear my cry. And most of the time, I wasn't even thirsty.

My nerves were on overload and everything bothered me now. I believed the meds had a hallucinogenic effect on me too, which added to the problem.

How will I go to the bathroom? I asked myself. *Would I need to live in a state hospital to be cared for? Would I need to wear a bag?* I had no clue what a bag does, or even where it plugged into. I just knew I didn't want one.

I think it was the unknown that scared me the most. I had no one to talk to or answer any of my concerns. Everyone just wanted me to heal from the injury and keep up my will to live, but little did they know that pretending that my paralysis didn't exist only made things worse.

More and more, I was seeing strange figures standing off to the side, and more and more, it took longer for them to fade away. I sometimes blinked profusely, so sure that I wasn't just seeing things. I was determined to catch them in the act so I could prove to myself that they did indeed exist.

28

PEOPLE BEGAN TO treat me differently now. It was as though everyone was keeping a secret from me, except I knew what the secret was, and it was so obvious at times, it became sickening. They told me I would walk again and now it seems taboo to talk about it.

It was midmorning when a team of medical students wearing long white coats arrived from Brown University, without warning, and to gawk at my condition like a specimen on exhibit.

I pretended to be upbeat and attentive as the students stared impolitely, untied my call button and lowered my bedrail, all the while speaking in front of me as though I couldn't hear them. They just took over, closed the curtain that surrounded my bed, with me inside of course!

I didn't like that they removed my call button, my lifeline; they could have lowered the rails without doing that.

Clueless, I thought. *Oblivious to my feelings too.*

The team leader chatted to the rest as if I weren't even there. It was humiliating. Before I knew it, they walked away, immersing themselves into a deep medical discussion that made them seem oblivious to their surroundings.

Because of my prior episodes with anxiety and broken call buttons, everyone knew to make sure that the call button was always in my reach and tied securely to the bedrail. But, without warning, the graduate students just left without saying a word, and guess what? They left without reattaching the call button. Yup, it was out of my reach! It was dangling from the bedrail just inches from the floor and definitely out of my reach! To make matters worse, they left without fully reopening the curtain that surrounded my bed! I could not be closed in!

The second I noticed it, I broke out in a cold sweat. I couldn't find the words to call them back before they were out of speaking distance. I was afraid that hollering would freak me out even further. I was doomed!

I laid back on my pillow, shut my eyes and tried to clear my head and breathe! Thoughts kept creeping in though. I began to imagine myself in a coffin, six feet below the earth's surface with tons of dirt piled on top. My chest felt heavy. I saw myself inhaling deeply, keeping my lungs inflated so the weight of it all wouldn't crush me.

I could imagine the coffin's ceiling only inches from my face, with my hot breath bouncing right back and telling me just how close it was to my nose. The inside of the casket had no padding, just wood that rang hollow when my knuckles knocked the insides by accident. The inner walls were so close that I couldn't get my elbows out from beneath my sides, only my wrists and hands were somewhat movable but only to flex them. With my arms stuck between my thighs and the casket, there was no way I could bring them to my face!

I visualized lifting my head a few inches and banging the casket ceiling with my forehead straight away. That whole scenario played out in my mind in just a millisecond.

That call button is so important to me. How could they just leave and forget to put it back? Maybe they'll come back! Stop imagining the coffin! I screamed silently to myself, as I rubbed both eyes, hoping it all go away.

The closed curtain felt so close to me. Almost as close as the casket's ceiling did. *Stop thinking about that!* The closed curtain was closing in on me. *I can't breathe!*

Gasping for air, feeling nauseous and before thinking, I yelled out to the new patient in the bed across the room. I'd learned he'd been in a car accident that left him with a crushed and shattered leg bone. The scuttlebutt was that he was from Venezuela with no family here, and without medical insurance, the hospital had no choice but to keep him in the I.C.U.

Although he spoke no English, we had a common bond that needed no common language. Neither one of us wanted to be there.

I had helped him in the middle of the night when he summoned the nurse, only to be denied his needs because of the language barrier. He kept saying the words "Resfriado, Resfriado" while the nurses threw their hands in the air, shouting back that they couldn't understand a word he said.

Knowing that Spanish and Italian were both romance languages and can be similar at times, and knowing very little Italian myself, I yelled out a guess from the dark and suggested that he was cold? The Italian word for cold is *freddo,* so I figured it must be close. And, I was right; he got his extra blanket that night.

Then, in the morning, he was trying to ask for a cup of coffee from the young food attendant.

Now that was an easy one, I thought, but the attendant still couldn't get it.

"Café? Café?" he mumbled, in the middle of a bunch of fast-talking gibberish that ran right over those two words. But I had an ear for broken English and I think that helped.

I helped again by announcing that he wanted a cup of coffee. And when my liquid breakfast came, which I was unable to eat anyway, I had my nurse bring my coffee over to him. He raised it up to me and said something I didn't understand. Then ended it all with the word, "Gracias!"

I answered back with the Italian response, "Prego," welcome— and think he got the drift.

But now I needed him. I thought that my breath might bounce off the curtain so I tried to yell through it.

"Amigo!" I screamed, moving my elbows and wrists just to see if

I could. I waited and listened. No response! *This curtain seems even closer to me!* I thought.

With a louder yet shakier voice, I hollered through the curtain again. "Amigo!" No response.

"Come on!" I said desperately through tightly clenched teeth. "This could drive me mad!"

"Si?" he finally answered, meekly.

Okay, I thought. *I have his attention.* Just having contact with him made me feel a little better.

"Call the nurse!" I yelled, guessing that he didn't understand a word I said. He didn't answer.

Please don't make me yell through the curtain again! Please understand me! "Amigo!" I yelled out again, breathing through my mouth as I watched the inside of the curtain closing in on me further!

"Si?" he answered, once more.

"Call the nurse!" This time I sounded like I was about to cry. I hated that.

I thought I heard him fumbling with his call button but wasn't sure. Wishful thinking maybe.

Can it be that he doesn't know how to call the nurse? I thought.

"Amigo!" I screamed louder and more desperate.

"Awkay..., awkay," he answered with his heavy accent. I could hear him fumbling around with something—it seemed like an eternity! I didn't know if the nurses were just busy, or he hadn't understood me. Everything was closing in on me, fast!

I flexed my hands and wrists again!

"Shit!" I said aloud. "This is like friggin' Chinese water torture! Just friggin' like it!" Then I sat in silence with my eyes closed, trying to push it all away. Yet, I couldn't. *Chinese Water Torture!* I thought, and kept thinking it! *Here we go! Now you're going to start thinking about this!*

The Chinese used the technique to extract military intelligence from an unwilling prisoner. And I read that it was highly effective too.

The prisoner was strapped down tightly on his back to a hard table, with his head locked in a stationary position, preventing him from moving it up and down or from side to side.

Suspended high above him, hung a large wooden barrel containing water. The torturer opened a small spigot, which released small droplets of water that landed squarely on the subject's forehead. The droplets were timed to release one droplet at a time at five-second intervals. It would be like, Drip...Drip...Drip...

The water droplets mimicked the echo of a leaky faucet, except with the most intense and nerve racking, amplified splash. After many days of this, the maddening effect would eventually drive the subject over the edge and quite insane.

I can't wait another second, I'm losing it! I was in a full-blown panic!

"Aprirei, por favor?" I yelled out, and the loudest yet!

I thought I knew how to say the word *open* in Italian and *please* in Spanish, so I mixed the two, together.

"Open please...! Aprirei, por favor!" I hollered and listened.

"Che?" he responded.

"Aprirei!" I repeated with my still raspy voice!

Because of their Latin derivatives, I was hoping that both words for *open* sounded the same. It paid off. The Spanish word for *open* was *abrir,* which wasn't far off from the Italian word *aprirei.*

"Awkay! Awkay! He called back. Either blowing me off or agreeing to help, I wasn't sure!

I took a deep breath and rested my head back on my pillow. Although I couldn't see him, I listened and envisioned his every move as he slowly made his way out of his bed and over to mine.

His crutches propped him up all right, but he struck and bounced off every obstacle on the way. I could hear him scuffling toward me with little grunts and groans but he kept coming! Leaning more so on one crutch, he reached out with the other and hooked a small part of my curtain. Then, with just one swipe, the rings screeched across the metal curtain rod and rushed in a breeze of welcomed air. We both looked stunned to suddenly see one another!

"Open wide," I said, as I gestured with my hands to do it. He struggled by hopping on just one foot, clearly tiring himself out. However, he kept trying for me.

He bunny hopped over to the other side of my bed and with his lengthy and top-heavy crutch, slid more curtain rings along the noisy curtain rod. I was exhausted from the trauma and drenched in sweat.

I could tell my amigo was definitely pooped as he looked up at me with a concerned face to seek my approval.

"Thank you, buddy, gracias, gracias," I said.

He nodded and then made his long journey back to his bed. I watched as he hopped up on his bed and settled in with a long and drawn out sigh. I called out to him one more time.

"Amigo!"

He looked up.

"Gracias," I said.

He just nodded.

29

NIGHTFALL CAME AND brought with it my dad and my step-mom Irene. They sat by me and after a while they ran out of things to say. So, I asked it. I asked it without inhibitions. I surprised myself as soon as it came flying out of my mouth.

"Did they say when I'd walk again?" "Did you know I still can't feel my legs?" Each time I asked a question, my father looked to Irene to answer it. *Is he afraid to goof up and say the wrong thing?* I wondered. *He knows she's better at hiding the truth than he is.*

I scrutinized her every word, looking for a slipup that I could catch her on. I even matched her expressions with her words, hoping for a clue as to my true medical condition.

"I need to sit up a little to relieve my back pain," I said, as I grabbed the bed rails and attempted to rise up, this time making it up a little higher, before collapsing back down again.

While grabbing for my sore ribs, my elbow brushed against a puffy clump around my numb, lower waist. I lifted the sheet just enough to expose a diaper that was fitted loosely to my bottom.

"When did I get this?" I sighed. "I didn't see them put this thing on me. I must have been out of it when they did." Irene sprang up to touch me.

"It's been on you for a while. We were waiting for you to notice it."

"No, it wasn't! I would have known it! There was just a johnny on me before—with a pull ups type underwear underneath, not a baby diaper!"

"Don't get depressed, Bobby, don't, okay? It's going to be fine. Just think, you still have your children, and they love you and miss you very much! Try for them, okay? Do you think you're ready to see them?" she asked, with tears in her eyes.

"I can't, not like this," I said.

She stared down at the floor and asked again.

"Do you think you can see them soon?" she squinted, while looking up at me waiting for my answer.

"I can't," I said.

I raised the sheet again to take another look at the baby diaper. The sight of it produced a deep breath and a lethargic exhale.

"I knew something was on me, but I don't remember wearing this big thing."

I lifted the sheet higher. My eyes continued downward to discover a pair of white nylon stockings donning my legs. Starting at the knee, they covered my calves and ran down to the tips of my toes.

They look extremely tight, I thought.

"What are the stockings for?" I asked.

"I don't know," they both answered, simultaneously. "To squeeze the fluids back up to your heart maybe? I thought I heard someone say that," Irene said, timidly. "I think they call them Teds or Teddies or something like that," she said.

Old ladies' stockings, I thought.

"Will I need to wear them forever?" I asked.

"We don't know, maybe you could ask your doctor that question," Irene replied.

"Yeah, ask your doctor," Dad agreed, with eyes cast downward.

I couldn't help feeling that things were being kept from me, but I played along with the charade.

Irene must have sensed something, as mothers usually do, because she leaned over me to whisper in my ear.

"Please don't give up, I love you," she said, in a shaky voice. "I wish I could make it all go away, but I can't. If I could, I would trade places with you in a heartbeat."

"I know," I said. "I love you too."

"Please don't give up. Ask God for help. He loves you too, you know!"

I turned to her, smiled, and said, "God loves me? Yeah, right, He's the one who pushed me out of that tree. And if He didn't push me, He sure didn't catch me when I fell, that's for damn sure!"

"Don't say that, you son of a bitch!" Her face reddened and her eyebrows came together in a fake anger. "How could you still fool around at a time like this? You'll never change!"

I chuckled without smiling.

The click-e-t-y clack sound of a broken caster wheel interrupted us, as two orderlies out of nowhere entered the room with a noisy transport gurney.

"Robert? It looks like you're wanted in operating room twenty-two, otherwise known as OR 22." I looked at Irene with a somewhat concerned expression. "Wasn't that the name of a horror movie?" I asked, to no one in particular.

"We wanted to prepare you sooner," she said, "But didn't want to wake you. They want to implant a filter of some kind into your chest, so the blood will flow freely to your heart and prevent any blood clots from forming."

I took a deep breath. "Another operation and at night?" I asked.

"No, no Bobby, it's not a big procedure at all. They can go in through your groin and feed the line up to your heart from there." She looked as though her dog just died. "I know you're going through so much." I immediately felt bad for her and realized that it was I, who had caused her pain.

"Oh, okay," I said. "That's good, at least I won't have to worry about a blood clot. It's okay, I can handle it." The false, upbeat facade expended more energy than I had, but I had to keep it up so my family wouldn't worry as much about me.

So, I went to OR 22, waving goodbye with wide eyes and a forced smile.

———

I WAS WIDE-AWAKE AS THEY fished the filter line up through my groin and towards my heart. A young physician joked with the nurses all throughout the procedure, as though I were not even there. This made me feel nervous and wishing for death again. I had control of nothing and again found myself in a helpless and humiliating situation.

Listening to him flirting with the pretty, young nurses while working on my body brought me down yet another notch.

"How are you doing, Robert?" the anesthesiologist asked.

"Fine," I said.

However, I wasn't fine; I was far from fine. I was dying inside.

My mind must have sensed my despair, because I pushed my surroundings and the insensitive people far away from me. So far away, that I left OR 22 and found myself in the viewing room at Woman and Infants Hospital, in the year 1986...

———

MY NOSE PRESSED HARD AGAINST the glass window, in view of the lineup of newborns on the maternity ward.

Lauren's little face melted my heart as I prayed that her birth defect would reverse itself and leave her alone.

How could this happen to her? I thought. *What can I do to stop it?*

That morning, I walked in early and caught Debbie eating breakfast from her hospital bed by the fourth-floor window, overlooking the Providence River. She was weary from the cesarean section she'd gotten the day before and looked up at me with a tired, yet odd look on her face. I knew something was wrong the moment she started to speak.

"Morning, Bobby, uh, the pediatrician examined Lauren this morning."

"Yeah? ..., and?"

"He discovered a hip disorder that is common in a small percentage of girls."

My heart sank.

"What do you mean?" I said anxiously.

"He explained it, but I was too nervous to grasp it all. He said she might end up with a limp and possibly one leg looking shorter than the other one. It's some kind of a hip deformity, I think. She may need leg braces too."

"Can't anything be done for it?" I asked.

"Well, the doctor is going to put a plaster cast over her bottom, it's in the shape of a diaper. Sometimes they can correct it, but there is no way of knowing."

Debbie explained that a full examination was scheduled later in the day, and a consultation with a specialist from Orthopedics was to follow.

Gazing through the viewing window's noseprints, smudges, and upon my little girl's rose-colored cheeks, I prayed. I begged and pleaded, and prayed as if I had never prayed before. I couldn't bear the thought of her growing up different or having to deal with teasing or ridicule from the other children. I knew how cruel kids could be, and it broke my heart to imagine her future with such a handicap. That was the only other time I had pleaded with God, and I found it odd that in both cases, I was praying against a disability.

I leaned against that window most of the afternoon and until the first set of grandparents arrived to soak up their new granddaughter through the glass. They weren't aware of my troubles or the tears that were evident just moments before.

I left the hospital that night with a huge weight on my shoulders and continued to pray most of the night. I told God that I had always tried to be a good person and that I would continue to do so if He answered my prayer.

After a sleepless night, I returned to the hospital to find Debbie smiling from ear to ear.

"Guess what!" she said, "Lauren's hip went back into place all by itself! It is as if it never happened! The pediatrician can't explain it either!"

"What? Wow! No cast?" I asked.

"Nope, no braces, nothing!"

Recalling how happy I was that day, reality stepped back in and brought me back to Operating Room 22 and the sound of the flirting doctor.

Maybe that's why I thought I could change God's mind after I fell out of that tree, I wondered. *He did it for my daughter.*

Looking up at the bright examination lights, I imagined them snaking something carelessly through my body, ripping and tearing things as they went, while joking and giggling about what they did the night before.

God, I have never forgotten the promise I made to you, or the prayer that you answered for me all those years ago. Have you forgotten me?

30

THE NEXT MORNING, I opened my eyes to the morning light, while my mind raced frantically with emotions, and as usual, the one of fear emerged the victor. For some reason as I viewed the upright bedrails, I noticed a feeling of security being forged within the confines of my bed. I hunkered down to keep out the rest of the world. I was beginning to like my fortification.

Thoughts of suicide became mixed together with strategies for survival. I was getting good at reaching for the medication button now and could find it just by feeling for it.

I summoned for the nurse and asked her to come in and lift me onto my left side, as I'd fallen asleep on my right.

Shifting position was the first order of the day and checking for any leg movement or sensation was the second. I couldn't try too hard to move things though; anxiety was always looming in the dark and just around the corner.

Debbie walked in with my mom behind her.

"I wanted to leave you this magazine and let you know I was here," Mom said, as she rolled the table over to me within arm's reach. "I'm going to give you both some time alone. I'll see you later, okay, Bobby?"

"Yup, thank you, bye Mom."

I squinted at the tops of my hands and saw that they were puffy and dark yellow in color. With streaks of blue running through the tops, they looked like someone else's hands, someone I didn't like.

Debbie sat by me and released the lock on the bedrail to get in closer. It fell heavily, with a cold and hollow clunk, like the barren and sterile sounds heard in a state-run institution.

"Deb, I am so sorry," I whispered.

"Bobby, I can get through this, but only if you can. You are my strength. I can't imagine what you are going through. You are still the bravest person I have ever known, and I just want to take you home so that I can take care of you. I don't care if you ever get better, I just want you and just the way you are."

"I'm okay..., I really am," I said, with lowered and saddened eyes.

"Well then please, please see Derek and Lauren. It has been too many days now, and they can't understand why they can't see you. Your son is very hurt that you won't see him. You know how he is."

"Didn't you explain why I don't want them to see me like this?"

"Yes, I did."

"Then please don't ask me to, not yet, okay? I don't want to cry in front of them, and I know I will."

My eyes filled up by just the thought of them seeing me that way. And I couldn't stop it.

Because my head was back and flat on the pillow, the tears pooled up in the outer corners of my eyes and streamed down into my ears. I still couldn't raise my hands high enough, so Debbie had to stand over me with a damp cloth, blotting my eyes with the four corners of it.

My eyes had leaked for so long that the salt from the tears burned my skin and left me with raccoon-like eye marks off the outer corners. Everyone commented on my raccoon eyes.

The following day I agreed to see my children.

I'm still not able to recall the first time I saw my kids–and don't know if I can ever talk about it. I purposely left it out of this book.

———

THREE OR FOUR MORE DAYS passed with more of the same. The Foley catheter was removed from my bladder and intermittent insertion was repeated every four hours to prevent bladder extension. Because of the intermittent catheterizing, I had to be awakened to pee at two a.m. and then again at six, leaving me perpetually tired and groggy. Each nurse told me that functions down there could return and it was too early to tell. I hung onto that hope.

My lips had become dry and blistered due to dehydration, as I avoided drinking and eating as much as possible.

What goes in must come out, I thought, and I didn't want anything coming out.

Because I hadn't moved my bowels in almost a week and was petrified of having an accident, I asked the shift nurse to check my brief about every hour, each time with just as much embarrassment.

Tones of frustration and irritability became common. I couldn't stand myself. My hands ached from being clenched tightly all the time, and I had to try to remember to open and relax them whenever possible. My jaw also hurt from being clenched tight, to fight the constant pain. I had to remember lots of things.

Other family members came and went, leaving me all sorts of foods and Italian delicacies.

My windowsill was lined with trays of almond biscotti and baskets of cellophane covered Wandies, while has-been flowers overpowered the room with the morbid look of an old-timer's wake.

Dozing in and out one afternoon, I sensed that someone was in the room. I opened one eye and was surprised to see my friend Vinnie standing against the wall with his hands hidden in his pockets.

His face said it all. He just stared at the floor, deep in thought and unaware that I was awake. I felt so bad for him at that moment and wondered how long he had been standing there.

I knew what he was thinking too. We were close and I felt bad that he had to worry about me. It was my fault that he felt the way he did, and that bothered me.

"Hey," I said.

He looked up slowly and shook his head from side to side.

"I'm okay," I said flatly.

A sad smile crossed his face, and again he just shook his head. I felt awful. We hardly talked at all. We didn't have to, besides there was nothing to say.

Someone warned that Debbie's Uncle Reginald was waiting to see me. That's how it was. Each visitor had to wait to see me, as if it were their last chance to pay their respects. Vinnie stepped out for a moment to let Reginald in.

Reginald was an ex-Catholic, born-again Christian, who spent most of his time preaching the reasons to convert to his newfound faith.

He was a good-hearted man, although most of the family felt that his particular church took advantage of his generosity, as he seemed naive and gullible.

He entered the room with his eyes sparkling with tears and couldn't look directly at me. After some small talk, he got right to it.

"Bobby, I want to pray over you and bring Jesus into your heart. I am going to ask him to save you and let you walk again."

Oh boy, I thought. *This ought to be good.*

He placed his hands on both of my legs and bowed his head. With his eyes shut, he prayed aloud for a minute or so, but then abruptly stopped.

"Bobby, I need a commitment from you. If Jesus heals you, will you accept Him and serve Him and always worship Him?"

There it is! I thought. *Always a condition. Jesus wasn't a deal maker, so why was his love always conditional with these people?*

I remembered why I was turned off by Reginald's faith and how his church demanded that he give at least ten percent of his earnings each month to support the parish while keeping people from other religions "at arm's length."

His pastor played a huge role in the lives of his flock, so I was especially curious to finally meet the infamous man at a family wake one night.

The guy had a meticulous hairdo, with not a single slicked-back strand out of place on his jet-black, dyed hair.

The shiny, gaudy, rocks on each ring finger stood out like a sore thumb and portrayed a carnival-boss-like image, at least to me anyway.

Sometime thereafter, I heard that the good preacher ran off with one of his parishioner's wives. I wasn't surprised.

Any other time I would have scoffed at Reginald's offer, but I wanted this to work more than anything. And even though I doubted the outcome, I looked down at my legs with him and began to ask Jesus to help me.

But soon after, I looked up at Reginald and felt unsure of it all, and although I appreciated the gesture, I started to become distracted, distracted by thoughts of phony healers and fraudulent con games that ripped off the weak at heart.

I couldn't concentrate on his prayers anymore and the more I tried, the more impatient I got. Over his shoulder, I could see Debbie in the background, rolling her eyes as he mumbled on with such conviction. And although I tried to remain receptive, I kept one eye on the door and couldn't help think how ridiculous we must look to a passerby.

As Reginald summoned Jesus to command me to walk, I tried to open my heart and keenly waited for a sign. Without anyone knowing, I pushed my leg muscles with all my might, but got no feedback at all. It was even hard to know if I were actually pushing. The intensity of the push was unknown, and that bothered me, yet it fascinated me at the same time.

Some small part of me was still amazed at the whole ordeal, and I needed to learn more about it all.

As I pushed, together with Reginald and Jesus, the anxiety demon briefly reared its ugly head again, only to retreat at the sound of Reginald's sudden rhythmic chant.

The chant-like thing reminded me of what I didn't like about his religion. Kind of cultic, I thought.

Years ago, I was watching an investigative report on one of the networks. The show aired an undercover documentary which exposed the myths and truths of self-proclaimed healers of God.

A Southern healer was mesmerizing his flock by randomly picking out a woman from the first row and seemingly reading her mind.

Among gasps of astonishment, he identified the sufferer as a dying and disease-ridden cancer victim and even guessed the right afflicted organ too.

As he pressed on the forehead of the pain-stricken woman, he zapped her with energy from the power of God. The inflicted follower then fell, knee-buckled, back into the awaiting arms of a couple of muscle bound no-necks, wearing secret service style earpieces.

The suited gorillas portrayed a bit of overkill, as they stood over the fragile, ninety-pound woman. They then lifted the healed woman to her dancing feet and demonstrated the miracle of God to wide-eyed believers.

She danced around the stage and sung with delight, praising the all-powerful healer and the Almighty God.

The miracle man validated his divine ability by asking the woman if they had ever spoken or met before that moment and then stressed the fact that he could not have known her affliction if it weren't for the Almighty Himself, who was whispering in his ear.

Evidentially, it was revealed that God wasn't the only one whispering in his ear. Undercover investigators were successful in intercepting a signal, which was being transmitted into a listening device hidden in the ear of the healer, exposing him as a fraud and a charlatan.

When the preacher chose a subject from the audience, a backstage accomplice identified the chosen one and transmitted useful background information to the all-knowing healer.

Even after the con game was exposed, many followers still refused to doubt the psychic and continued to believe in his God-given ability to perform miracles.

The healer went on to swindle many more trusting souls out of their life's meager savings before meeting his match from a young and diligent state prosecutor, which finally sent him to prison for ten years.

"Bobby, open your heart to Jesus," Reginald commanded. "I have opened the door and now it is up to you to let him in." He paused with thought and wanted to say more, but started to break down, and with his voice and lower lip beginning to quiver, he stood up and left quite abruptly, waving a goodbye as he walked to the door.

"Thank you, Reginald," I said. But he never turned around. He just waved his hand as he left the room.

I don't remember seeing Vinnie leave. It was a bad day.

31

Hours had passed as I drifted in and out and in again. I took inventory of my body and noticed that I had no urge to blink. I stared off into space—numb to things that used to matter.

With my mind's eye, I started at the top of my body and worked my way down. My jaw and neck hurt when I focused on just those specific parts. The corners of my mouth stung like my eyes did, and my lips were cracked with blisters. I couldn't drink lying down and lifting my head to reach for the ginger ale straw hurt my chest, so I fought off temptations to drink. I badly needed a shave, and I was dying to brush my teeth.

The six broken ribs on both sides of my chest still hurt and were not getting better. I was afraid to cough and petrified to sneeze, and that yellow thing I had to blow in six to eight times a day may have strengthened my lungs but sent me into orbit with rib bone pain. It looked like I was just blowing into those DUI testers.

I then traveled farther down and zoned in on my back. The outer skin tingled with nerve pain and felt like I was getting electrical shocks everywhere.

With my mind, I journeyed deeper within my back and sensed a nagging agony way down deep. I'd been incised from my shoulder blades, down to the top of my tailbone. No wonder I was so sore.

I remembered that Dr. Lucas told me one of my vertebrae had exploded and burst into hundreds of pieces, shooting bone chips into my spinal cord. Another vertebra split cleanly in two. He said he gently picked broken bone chips from my bruised spinal cord in an attempt to prevent nerve damage.

I grabbed the left bedrail with my right hand and pulled my torso over an inch or so, trying to lean on my left side. Those tender ribs sent shooting pain signals around to the front of my breastplate, so I released my grip and settled back to where I started.

My hands and fingers really ached from being closed so tightly. Even in my sleep, I think I clenched my fists.

Again, I journeyed lower with my mind and landed at my midsection. Bladder spasms erupted every so often with a burning-type pain, causing a perfectly timed flinch. If I thought about the spasms, they would increase their frequency, so I thought that at some point in the future, I might develop some control over them.

My bladder area was also quite sore. The nurses came in every four hours to insert a catheter in me, trying to void pockets of trapped urine. They pressed down hard on my abdomen and tried to push out all the remaining fluid left behind. That really hurt. Then they probed my belly with a sonogram-type machine. They wheeled that thing in every time I peed, searching for every last drop.

Some nurses left a little in there while others left none at all. It took so much time out of the day and night, and so much energy out of me, that eventually they decided it wasn't as important as they had once thought and just stopped using the machine altogether.

With my eyes closed, I journeyed further down.

At my waistline, where the sensation met no sensation, I experienced what they called hyper- or hyposensation. I never did get it right. That area drove me the craziest. I couldn't stand even the slightest touch to my skin there. It felt like I was sticking my finger in an electrical outlet. Even just the thought of being touched there set it off!

Now to my bum. It felt like someone was ramming a telephone pole up my butt all the time, and when the neuropathic pain started, it looked like I was going into convulsions as I jerked and doubled over in a fetal position, rocking back and forth like a mental patient in a horror movie.

I was like a pregnant woman, enduring contractions, I think, and I soon realized that if I breathed in a relaxing rhythm, I could decrease its intensity and calm it down.

I reached down with one hand and discovered butt cheeks that were opening and closing from involuntary nerve signals. Dealing with all this, my morale dropped yet another notch.

I then reached around and felt for my thighs but wasn't sure which leg was which. I thought about how each night I instinctively awoke from a deep sleep to feel for my legs because I was petrified of bleeding to death without knowing it. I also needed to know just where the two limbs were at all times.

When I thought down to my legs and feet, I sensed a far away, pins-and-needles type feeling, mostly in my left leg. My right foot was pretty much dead, but the small toe on my left foot was really hurting and felt as though it were in a vise, being pinched and squeezed so tight, I thought it would pop.

How could it hurt? I thought. *I can't feel my toe, but it really hurts? Is this phantom pain?* I had heard of people who lost a limb and still experienced pain from the extremity that was lost.

After taking more inventories, I became aware again that I still hadn't blinked in a while. I tested my overall health and imagined that my organs felt sick. I didn't know it then, but later discovered that my fingernails had stopped growing. This became evident by the horizontal depressions that later showed up on each nail. I was told that this was not uncommon, due to the deficiencies and overall trauma to the body.

Still not blinking, I listened to the swishing sound of the air mattress pump, as it breathed in and out like a sleeping dragon. Before I knew it, my breathing matched its rhythm, and my body and the dragon became one, one in a perfect, shitty harmony.

More time passed as faces came and went. A third shift nurse caught me wide-awake and staring off into space. She asked if I was okay, reached for my arm, and spoke to me in a soft, comforting tone.

"It'll be okay," she whispered.

"What is your name?" I asked.

"Akiki," she said. Her accent told me she was South African. She had the smoothest, coffee-colored skin I had ever seen.

Akiki told me stories of her homeland, and we talked about our children. For a short time, she took my mind off things. I couldn't get enough of her, and as she spoke, I listened to the call buttons buzzing in the distance, hoping that they weren't calling for her to go away. I wanted her to stay with me indefinitely because I drew strength from her. Akiki was the first on my new list of inspirational people.

It was late, yet, a young resident doctor came in and asked to speak to me alone. He closed the curtain behind him.

"Robert, you've been here at Rhode Island hospital for eight days. Tomorrow we're transferring you to Kent Hospital. There, you will receive intensive medical care as well as rehabilitation therapy."

I looked at him very seriously and tried to clear my head in order to grasp what he was saying.

"I'd like to speak to you, Robert, on a personal level if it's all right with you."

"Sure," I said.

"Well, Robert, no one here knows this, but when I was in med school back in St. Louis, I was involved in a severe motorcycle accident that left me with a broken neck. I wore a halo for eight months and received therapy for over a year. It was the hardest thing I have ever been through, and I'd like to give you a piece of advice if I may."

I nodded for him to continue.

"What lies ahead of you will be extremely hard. Rehab can be your worst enemy but can also be your best friend. I can't stress that enough. Remember what I'm telling you. 'Your worst enemy, yet your best friend.'"

He repeated the statement one more time as he shook my hand and wished me luck. His advice made me somewhat nervous because it represented yet another unknown. I thanked him and said that I'd remember what he said. I did, and I have, and I always will.

———————

DR. LUCAS STOPPED BY TO authorize the transfer and sign my release form. He held up his fist before him and, with a stiff upper lip, he told me to fight hard at rehab.

"Dr. Lucas," I said. "Are you going to have the people at Kent give me something for the panic attacks?"

"Yes, I will." He then rambled on about all the other medications he was prescribing, but I didn't care about them in the least, just the anxiety meds.

As he shook my hand to wish me luck, I thanked him and said, "Please don't forget to write a prescription for the anxiety?" He said he wouldn't.

As a team of nurses and orderlies loaded me into an awaiting rescue, I asked Nurse Donna to check my diaper one last time because that always weighed on my mind. I still hadn't gone. It was still empty.

Debbie got approval to ride along with me in the rescue, because I was convinced that the closed-in ride would produce yet another anxiety attack. I was right. Being tied down on that stretcher fostered a full-blown panic attack that stayed with me throughout the entire trip...

32

"WELCOME TO KENT Hospital and Rehab!" The chipper sounding voice said, as we rolled past a busy nurses' station. "My name is Elsa!"

Thank God, I thought. *"I can finally get some help here. I am going to be rehabilitated. I'll work hard and get back on my feet again in no time.* I wasn't sure I fully believed it but thought it anyway.

Still feeling extremely dizzy and nauseated from the ride, the nurses gingerly transferred me to my new bed and hooked me up to the new needles and tubes all over again.

I was introduced to the gentleman in the bed across the room even though I couldn't lift my head to see him.

The new environment felt lonely and cold because all the kind cards and fresh flowers had been left behind. I couldn't help feeling uneasy. I glanced over and noticed that I had a window—and by the angle of the clouds, I guessed that I was about four to five stories up.

Hmm, I thought. *I'm high up and I have a window.*

I checked out the window and its latches but was unable to make out how it opened from where I was. I spent most of my time fine-tuning my vision and honing in on every inch of that window from across the room. How to get over to it was a puzzle too but not one for that moment. I was determined to figure out how that window opened. *Four stories up,* I thought. *It's there if I need it.*

A woman in a long flowery dress blew in and introduced herself as Dr. Toms, the physiatrist on the unit. I had no clue what a physiatrist was and didn't really care. She was the boss.

"On a scale of one to ten, how would you rate your pain level?" she asked.

"Eleven," I replied, with a serious smirk.

"Alright, well, we're going to address that immediately by adjusting your medication. On that marker board hanging on the wall beside you, there is a list of meds that I'm starting you on. You're in good hands, so if you need anything, just ask, okay? I'll see you on Monday because I'm heading to California to attend a pain management clinic."

"Thank you, Doctor Toms," I said. "Have a nice trip."

A quick look up at the message board revealed a list of narcotics that could have choked a horse. I wondered which one of them was for the panic attacks. Before my accident, I didn't even like taking aspirin, so I didn't recognize any of them

A bald, stocky man appeared at the foot of my bed.

"Robert? I'm Dr. Capella. I'm a urologist here at Kent Hospital. I just want to let you know that you need not worry about sex. When you are ready to talk to me about it, just have the nurses' station get ahold of me. I have many things that can benefit you. Don't let that issue worry you in the least, okay? When you are ready, I will make you happy. I just wanted to tell you that. You take care now."

"Thank you," I said. Then he was gone. *That was weird.*

———————

SUNDOWN SUMMONED THE BRIGHT FLUORESCENT lights, whose ballasts vibrated a low drone overhead. The window darkened to a one-way mirror, emanating emptiness beyond the glass, and with the disappearance of the sun, my thoughts darkened too. I studied the workings of the latch.

Here it comes, I thought. *Here it comes again!* The fear of anxiety brought on more anxiety. My hands became clammy, my mouth dry and butterflies filled my stomach. I couldn't breathe!

I jerked my head in a robotic motion toward the call button, and unlike the one in my previous bed, this call button wasn't plugged into the bedrail. Instead, it was mounted on the wall, about three feet above me and a foot behind the headboard.

It had a long, unwound gauze bandage tied to its short pull chain. The other end of the bandage was tied to my side rail for me to reach and yank on from my end when I needed the nurse. That was okay, but I wanted the ceiling light over my bed turned on. That light control was mounted and out of reach on the wall too, and had an eight-inch chain hanging from it also. I couldn't reach that chain either, but someone had tied an unrolled gauze bandage to the chain. Unfortunately, the other end wasn't tied to anything and just hung against the wall a foot above the floor, way out of my reach!

How was *any* patient supposed to reach it if they needed light?

"Goddamn it!" I said aloud.

Calm down, I told myself, as I leaned my head back to think. *I've got to stop cursing*, I thought. *Especially in God's name. Calm down and fight it. Fight it and beat it. It feels like the end of the world but it's not! Just fight it!*

I noticed a brown shopping bag on the floor under the rollaway table, about three feet from my bed and out of my reach. It was filled with socks, clean underwear, and some button-down shirts on wire clothes hangers. Debbie packed the hangers just in case the room closet had none.

It hurt to do, but I pulled the rollaway table over to me by grabbing the corner of it, barely catching the underside's sharp edge with just my fingertips.

As I pulled the table closer, the two front wheels snagged the opened bag on the floor, dragging it sideways across the worn, tiled floor until it got close.

Looking in the opposite direction, I stretched out my right hand and felt around for the paper bag on the floor. Two fingers caught the bag's edge, and I began to lift it up to my bedside. I couldn't believe how weak and hurt I was.

The lopsided lift tore the bag in two, so I flipped the little piece of bag I had as high as I could go and just enough to grab hold of a few tangled shirt hangers in midair.

The clothing spilled on the germ-ridden floor, which I didn't like at all, but I held onto my catch and gripped those hangers, like a hungry barn cat clutching a live sparrow. I had to rest a few seconds before untangling then untwisting the wire hangers, which showed just how weak I really was.

By switching them back and forth between sore fingers and hands, I straightened two of them out into a long and straight wire. Then I joined the two by intertwining them together to create one long and wiry, homemade fishing pole.

Next, I bent the wire and formed a small hook on one end and shaped a hoop on the other end to serve as a handle.

Because the gauze was dangling against the wall behind me, I knew I wouldn't be able to see what I was grasping for, so I studied the location of the dangling bandage very carefully before fishing for it.

The distraction lowered my pain level, so I slightly raised my left arm over and behind my head, then slowly brought the hanger back until I heard it hit the metal plate on the paint-chipped wall.

Moving it from left to right, a small resistance told me that I had found the hanging bandage and my mark, so I rotated the hook by twirling my end of the wire by its handle. I caught it! Then, I slowly reeled in my catch, grabbed hold of the gauze and tied it to the bedrail, in a double knot! Tight!

Out of breath, I leaned back and held my sore ribs. I felt a small sense of accomplishment and almost enjoyed the challenge. And after all that, I forgot to pull the chain and turn the light on!

This was a pattern of stubborn "MacGyver" behavior that would follow me from that day forth—often with slightly humorous results. That was also the first time I noticed that "distraction" helped lower my pain level, significantly.

33

I DOZED IN AND out, keeping the anxiety at a distance but never very far away. Mom and Debbie arrived with a forced smile and a cell phone that was set up for emergencies only. (Back then, before calling plans, you paid by the minute and it was expensive to use.) I put it under my pillow.

"How do you feel?" they both asked.

"Okay, um, when do I get my anxiety meds?" I asked. "It's getting dark." Just then, a stocky male nurse walked in and introduced himself as Joe, the unit's charge nurse.

"Can I get something for anxiety please? I need it now," I told him.

Joe looked puzzled. "I don't know anything about that, and I certainly can't administer anything without a doctor's order," he said.

"Dr. Lucas from Rhode Island Hospital said that I could get them here when I needed them! He wrote the order!"

"You will have to talk to the doctor tomorrow about that." He left some extra blankets for me on one of the chairs, as if I could really reach them, and said he'd be back later.

I turned to Deb and Mom and said, "I knew it! I knew this was going to happen!"

I felt the walls closing in on me like never before! It all came down on me heavy and hard, like the older sibling sitting on your chest during horseplay, with nothing you can do except pray to God you won't suffocate!

I grabbed the bedrails and tried to get up to fight for myself but just squirmed in place with nowhere to go. Yelling aloud, I desperately tried to convince my family of Dr. Lucas's promise to me. They just stared at me in disbelief, as if I were crazy or something! This made me angrier and more frustrated. And, much more anxious!

"He promised he would arrange anxiety meds when I got here! Especially for when the sun went down! I knew it wouldn't happen! I knew it!" I was out of control now and didn't care.

"The one thing that terrified me, the one thing that I really needed! I knew it! Why are you two just looking at me like that! Can't someone fight for me! I can't live through the night like this, and I'll either die or go insane!"

With a tremendous holler, I yelled at the top of my lungs. "Why are you two just looking at me?"

They both just stood there, staring at me with confused expressions.

Mom abruptly left the room and Debbie stayed behind, still just looking at me. I couldn't look at her. I just gazed off to the side, to the window mechanisms.

Mom returned moments later with the charge nurse. She motioned for Joe to speak, and with a slight smirk, he began to do so.

"I didn't say that you couldn't get anything for your anxiety. I meant that I couldn't give you anything whenever you wanted it. I checked your chart. Your meds are ordered and are to be given to you at 10:00 p.m. and, yes, I just read your chart, there is an order for Xanax there."

I whipped my head around to the clock. It was only eight-thirty. "Xanax, that's for panic attacks, right?" I asked.

"Yes, he said, it's for anxiety, nervousness and unrest."

"Listen Joe, please understand, I'm getting these attacks daily, and the nighttime really brings them on. I don't want to sound like a wimp, but they're really strong, and it's getting harder to deal with them. I can't just get up and just walk them off!"

He smiled and said, "Don't worry; you will get what you need." His smile made me feel worse, as if he were humoring me. I felt more alone than ever and was sure that there was no person on earth that understood or even cared to the extent that I needed them to. I was shrinking in my world and nobody cared.

Shirley, a second shift veteran nurse heard all the commotion and stood listening at the door. I had briefly met her when I arrived and liked her down-to-earth demeanor when I did. Earlier, she asked me some questions while Denise changed my ever-clean diaper.

As Joe walked past her, he whispered something that changed the expression on her face. She then stepped forward and asked if she could have a word with me, alone.

"We're leaving now, anyway," Debbie said. They kissed me good-bye, did a thorough check around the room and assured me that they'd be back in the morning. Mom leaned over the bedrails and quietly handed me a religious card.

"This is a picture of Saint Jude; he's the patron saint for healing the sick. I have always liked his face. Whenever I needed hope, I looked at his nice face and I prayed to him. Keep it with you and if you feel that you need hope, pull it out and look at his face. Here, I'll tuck it under your pillow."

"Thanks, Mom."

Shirley closed the curtain behind her and sat on the edge of my bed by my right knee.

"Could you leave it open, just a little? And remember to open it when you leave?

"Of course. Now, I'm going to tell you something that I have never told anyone in my capacity as a registered nurse. I never get personally involved, but I'm going to do it this time. Okay?"

"Okay," I answered.

"You are Italian, right?" I knew what she meant. Americans of Italian descent, refer to themselves as Italians rather than Americans when speaking about family.

As I nodded, she fired back. "Well, so am I! That's why I know that you have the ability to overcome this thing that has happened to you!"

Then Shirley leaned over me and got right in my face. Her expression became sterner, while her voice louder and more powerful.

"I know that you have the means to reach deep down inside and pull up that strength that you carry within you. And the reason I know you have it is because I have it! It's a passion and strength that we Italians all have!"

She looked into my eyes, grabbed both my hands, and squeezed them tightly.

"Now, call upon that strength, give it your all, and overcome this! Because, you can and you must! Your family needs you to do this!"

I was surprised but appreciated her candor and immediately felt close to her. She helped me to relax that night until my meds came, which helped me to fall into a deep and much needed sleep.

———————

I AWOKE ABRUPTLY IN A strange room and was bothered by the raised volume on my roommate's television. Something was wrong, very wrong.

I was itchy. I was itchy everywhere! When I scratched one itch, I immediately became itchy somewhere else. It drove me crazy! I began to scratch faster and faster in a race with the itch until my nerves wore thin. *What is this, the drugs? It has to be the drugs!*

Some time passed, and I dozed in and out, unable to stay asleep because my skin was crawling! It was as though thousands of ants were scurrying around inside my body, trying crazily to find an exit. Even my scalp tingled!

I couldn't cover the entire surface no matter how fast I scratched, so I switched to half scratches and quickly jumped to the next one, never really satisfying the one before it.

I shook my head from side to side just to see if I could snap out of it, but I couldn't. I just scratched myself raw.

"What the heck is this?" I said aloud. The audio on the TV stopped dead, only to be replaced by an ear-piercing static, like the sound a local station makes after its nightly sign off. I could imagine the still picture of the Indian chief in his colorful headdress, letting you know that there is nothing left. The volume of the static was really, really, loud!

Where am I? I wondered. *Am I in a different room? Am I alone? I am itchy. I am so damn itchy!* I don't remember much after that.

34

SUNRISE CAME AND found me exhausted. The itching was gone, but my skin was still tender. Another unnecessary diaper change and teeth brushing was followed by a series of shots, including the daily and painful javelin to the belly.

During my morning routine, I thought about the room I found myself in the night before. It made no sense to me, but not much did lately. Maybe it never happened.

Midmorning arrived with a pleasant looking woman appearing out of nowhere and standing by my bed.

"Hi Bobby, I'm Bess, and I'm a therapist here on the unit. They sent me in to try to get you some pain relief."

"Hi Bess," I said. "How are you going to do that?"

"I use a technique called Cranial Sacrum therapy. I work on the fascia, deep tissue and other layers surrounding the muscles. It's kind of like peeling an onion. I peel back one layer at a time, and then I apply pressure and heat to the area."

"How do you apply heat?"

"Just with my hands, you'll see," she said confidently. "Can you sit up, Bobby?"

"Not without your help and only a little I think."

I tried but I was wrong. I couldn't sit up at all, so she left me on my back and slid one hand under it and placed her other hand over my chest.

"Let me know if any of this becomes too painful to take. Wow, Bobby, are you tight! You're all knotted up too. Alright, just relax the best you can for me, okay?"

"Okay," I replied.

She put her head down on my shoulder and closed her eyes.

"I can feel the heat, Bess! This is unreal. Wow! It's hot! How are you doing that?"

"If it gets too hot, think of the color blue," she said.

"Blue? Okay. Hey Bess, is this like, witch doctor stuff?" I asked with a chuckle.

"Anyone can do it," Bess said. "You just have to know how to. It's not a gift, and no, it's not magic. Am I hurting you, Bobby?"

"Yeah, but it's a good hurt," I said. "I can take it."

"Okay then, I'm going a little deeper now and turning up the heat, too."

"Jeez, Bess, can I see your hand?"

I grabbed the one she had on my chest, turned it over and felt her palm.

"It's so hot!" I said. "Amazing. And how are you directing heat to that area in my back?"

"It's all done with the energy that's flowing between my two hands. Our bodies are full of this energy."

"Well, Bess, it is amazing. I never would have believed it. How come I never heard of this?"

"This type of treatment is not endorsed by the whole medical community. Some still don't believe in it. They want to believe it works, but need to see evidence of it in writing," she explained.

I put her hand gently back on my chest.

"Maybe they can't read the proof, Bess, but they sure should be able to feel this heat."

Before she left, Bess dug her fingers deeper into my back away from the incision, shot in some more heated energy, and I don't care what anyone says, I felt the energy from her fingers, and it felt great. I was and still am a believer.

The sound of heels clicking against the tile floor snapped me from my thoughts, and I knew it had to be a woman coming through the door.

It was Irene with my stepsister Teri. Teri hadn't seen me this way yet, so it was awkward to make eye contact with her right away. I didn't want her to detect any sadness. I was glad she came.

Irene came right to me with her usual two or three kisses on my face and always whispered that she loved me after the last kiss.

Teri carried a red-flowered plant that caught my eye right away. It was a poinsettia. A poinsettia!

Finally! I thought. *Finally, a way out!*

Poinsettias are poisonous if eaten. I knew that's why cats and dogs steered clear of them. Deer could be starving to death and still have the instinct not to eat them.

"Where would you like this plant, Bobby?" Teri asked.

Just in reach, I thought.

"Um, could you put it over here by this window so they get the sun?" I replied.

"Sure," Teri said.

I felt relieved at the possibility. As they spoke to me, I was far away—far away plotting and planning my way out of this hell.

I glanced over at my water pitcher. It was made of nontransparent plastic and had a hinged lid that covered the top, hiding its contents.

Placing a handful of poinsettia leaves under the water line and closing the cover could create just enough heat, I thought. *And, that would activate the fermenting process. It would be like making wine, only with one hell of a deadly kick.*

Teri spoke on, telling me a story about the family, while my eyes shifted between the plant and the water pitcher.

This is it, I kept thinking. *This is my way out. It's better than the window, too. Now I just have to figure out how to get that plant over here. Soon,* I thought. *Soon.*

———————

ELSA GOT ME READY FOR my first day of physical therapy by giving me a sponge bath, which left me shivering from the lukewarm water. I couldn't help her and just had to watch as she lifted my legs as if they were dead logs.

I felt bad for her, watching her struggle as she washed my feet. I felt ashamed. Washing someone's feet is such a humble act, and I didn't deserve it from that woman. I didn't deserve it from anyone. Yes, she was a saint for doing it and I was ashamed.

35

I TOLD ELSA THAT I wasn't up to my first day of therapy because my pain level was high and my energy level was low, really low. I hadn't sat up in a couple of weeks, and they said it was important that I get vertical a little bit at a time. But I had no desire to try and decided to stay in bed.

Their plan was to slide me over onto what they called a tilt table. By strapping me down to it tightly, a remote control device would tilt the table up until I was completely vertical. Because of blood pressure dangers, my body would be brought to a standing position very slowly. Paralyzed patients lack the nerves to fire muscles needed to squeeze and pump blood up to the heart and brain and have to be careful of that.

I didn't relish the idea of relying on another button-controlled device, and I was petrified of falling over, face first onto the rock-hard floor while having my arms strapped down by my side to a heavy table behind me. All the anticipation, along with rushing to prepare for therapy left me tired with a pounding headache. I closed my eyes as Elsa worked around me.

A knock at the door startled the both of us. Elsa and I quickly looked at each other before noticing a middle-aged Roman Catholic priest standing in the doorway. His white collar stood out like a beacon of light.

"Oh boy," I said under my breath, but was sure that Elsa heard me.

"Robert? I am Father Riccio, how's it going today?"

"Fine," I said slowly and cautiously, while a thousand different things ran through my mind.

"That's great," he said.

"Um, do you know something I don't, father? Am I going somewhere?"

"Ha, ha, ha!" he laughed. "No, not that I know of, Robert. Not today anyway. But we all have to go sometime!"

"Good, because I haven't packed my bags yet." I reached up a few inches to shake his hand. "How are you, Father, and please call me Bobby?"

"I'm okay, but how about those Red Sox though?" he asked, as I grabbed my side to chuckle a little bit before answering.

"Well, I really can't comment on them lately, I've been a little out of touch for a while." *I like this guy,* I thought. *I wonder if he was a ball player in his Catholic school or somewhere in a church league. He looks like he could have been a shortstop. No, a second baseman.*

"I can't talk about it without getting emotional. We came close but there's always next year," he said. "So, what happened to you, Robert? I mean, Bobby?"

"I fell out of a tree."

"Hmm, well, as they say on the outside, Bobby. That's the shits."

"Yeah, I know," I answered, pretending that his curse was no big deal, but in reality, I was cracking up inside.

"Would you like to receive Holy Communion on Sunday, Bobby?"

"I would, Father, but I haven't been to confession in..." I was about to lie a little, but I figured I'd be barking up the wrong tree. "It's been... it's been too long, Father. And after some of the things I said to God when I got hurt, I need more than just confession."

"Not a problem, how about I give you absolution, Bobby?" he asked, while leaning on and tapping all his fingers on the top rung of my bedrail.

"You can do that?" I asked.

"Sure, I can." He pulled an instruction or praying card or something from his shirt pocket.

I wonder how they keep those white collars on. I thought of the Saint Jude religious card I had under my pillow and imagined what face *his* card depicted.

"Absolution?" I asked. "Does that mean my slate will be wiped clean, Father?"

"Yes."

Smirking, "So, it's kind of like, one step away from sainthood, right, father?" I couldn't resist.

"Don't push it," he said, and continued by leaning in closer and over me, peering upward to the ceiling while clutching the card to his chest. This time with remnants of a small smirk on his face.

"Heavenly Father...," he recited, while most of it I can't remember. I do remember him asking God, among other things, to forgive me.

With his head raised high and his eyes shut closed, he prayed.

"Heavenly Father," he said again, softly, "Bobby is sorry for his sins and asks...wait, you *are* sorry for your sins right, Bobby?" he said, while looking down at me with just one eye open.

"Oh yes," I answered matter-of-fact like.

He closed his eye again, raised his head and continued without missing a beat.

"Bobby is sorry for his sins and asks for absolution," he said.

This priest is so cool, I thought. *How refreshing he is. Nothing like some of the stuffy ones I'm used to.*

We talked more about the Red Sox and when he'd be able to come back again to shoot the breeze. I truly looked forward to it. After he left, Elsa reappeared.

"How's your headache, Bobby?"

"It's still there. I'm exhausted, Elsa."

The sound of shuffling feet and low murmurs brought my attention to the doorway again, this time with five physical therapists standing ready, each wearing sweatpants and matching V-neck polo shirts.

"Are you ready, Bobby?" Michelle shouted, with lots of energy. I had met her the day before in a brief meeting that explained the upcoming exercise as well as her P.T. credentials.

I looked up and smiled before answering her. "Oh, I pass today thank you," I replied.

"Excuse me?" Michelle fired back, with her neck stretched out and her eyebrows raised high.

"I pass today. Sorry, but I'm not feeling up to it, not today...but thank you." The others quickly looked over at Michelle to catch her response, and I knew it was coming. As she showed me her five fingers and the palm of her hand, Michelle shouted at me even louder than the first time.

"I'm giving you five minutes to have Elsa get you ready, and then I'm coming back to get you! You pass, huh! I haven't heard that one before! Are you kidding me? You can't pass! Elsa, can you get him dressed in five minutes?"

Elsa smiled at her and then spoke. "It's up to him," she replied while changing a fresh pillowcase on my pillow.

With that, Michelle turned and left with her little army and their matching V-necks. Before she hit the door, she yelled out the words, "five minutes!" and then she was gone.

I looked over at Elsa, held my ribs and began to laugh very slightly. It just struck me funny. I think it was the first time I attempted to laugh in weeks.

We had forced grins on both of our faces as we struggled to put brand new gym shorts on my nonresponsive legs. I still couldn't get over the response from Michelle.

The team returned to get me exactly five minutes later, and this time I didn't put up a fight.

"Before we do this, I want to check something," Michelle said. "Put your head back and close your eyes, Bobby. This will only take a minute."

"What are you going to check?" I asked. Michelle worked down at my feet but I couldn't see.

"I want to check your proprioception," Michelle answered. "I'm going to lift your right leg, and I want you to tell me where it is in space. Keep your eyes closed." It was quiet for a few seconds, and I tried to detect her movements. "I am either going to lift it straight up, or up and to the right, or up and to the left. Think about it and tell me where it is now."

I concentrated on my right leg and felt good about my guess. "It is up and to the right, I'm sure of it. Am I right?"

"I'll let you know when we're finished. Where is your right leg now?" she asked.

"You are holding it up and to the left, I am sure of that."

"Where am I holding your right leg now?" she asked.

"Straight up and in the middle," I answered quickly and confidently. It was a good feeling to make that connection to my leg and foot, especially after disowning everything from my waist down.

"So, Michelle, how did I do? Did I get them all right?" A few more seconds passed.

"Okay, Bobby, you can open your eyes now."

I lifted my head and raised my eyelids. I was shocked! I was shocked to see Michelle standing down at my feet, holding up not my right leg, but my left one! She held my left leg by my left ankle and was holding it up to the left.

I immediately felt strong vibrations in my legs that irritated the heck out of me. I threw my head back and closed my eyes again. "I can't believe it," I said quietly to myself.

"You have no proprioception. Do you understand what that is?"

"No."

"Proprioception is a sense of where your limbs are oriented in space. Sorry I tricked you. Are you ready for the tilt table?"

"Yeah, I guess."

My arm muscles had shrunk in size and were like rubber, so I was no help in sliding myself over to the tilt table. It took three of them to do it.

After I landed on the table, the first strap was cinched across my chest—a little too tight for my liking and the feeling of being tied down got my mind racing again. *Don't think about it,* I said to myself. *Just do it.*

Then, the second strap landed across my hips, and I didn't like that either. I put my fingers under the nylon webbing in an effort to create some space between it and me. That seemed to help.

The third strap was thrown over my lower half, but I don't know where it landed. Across my knees, I presumed.

A blood pressure monitor was hooked up to my right arm, and then I was handed the remote control. When I got the go-ahead, I slowly raised the table but got dizzy at first, so I was told to stop and wait.

When I resumed, the sight of becoming almost eye level with everyone else was exhilarating. I rushed to bring myself all the way up and again became dizzy. I didn't care about that though; I just wanted to simulate standing.

I thought I felt taller than before. *Could the rods in my back have made my spine longer?* I couldn't feel the floor under my feet and pondered on that a bit before Mike and Bethany came in to watch. Mike was a newbie and Bethany was a veteran. I liked them both.

They lowered me back to a horizontal position and rolled the table and me to the P.T. gym for my first physical therapy session. It hurt to do but I lifted my head to see along the way. The hallway wasn't anything like I expected. Each room had a triangular light above their doorway that lit up each time a patient hit their call button. Most were lit.

Nurses scurried from room to room like hectic soldier ants busy at work. As we rolled into the gym, all eyes were on the contraption I rode in on.

Paula C, another PT therapist, met us as we arrived, while onlookers stared at us with uncouth curiosity.

The gym was small and neat with a spotless kitchen off to the side. Two large bed-like mats filled most of the main room, each one with a patient receiving leg therapy on them.

As we rolled past, lethargic patients in wheelchairs paused from their therapy to check out the new guy and try to figure out his affliction. Mike and Paula parked me in the corner and proceeded to raise the tilt table, but I stopped them right away.

"Can I do it, please? I must be in control or else I'll get anxious."

Paula handed me the remote control and took my blood pressure as I held the button down. A nauseous feeling quickly came over me so I released the button. I needed some air.

"Not too fast!" Paula warned. "We need to make certain that enough blood is being pumped up to your heart and brain. So not too fast."

I was a little nauseated and bothered with hot flashes, but the feeling of being upright blew away any desire to quit.

I pressed firmly on the up button and felt like I was at the top of the world! The straps dug deep into my chest and stomach, and must have done the same to my lower half, but I couldn't tell.

I felt much taller. And it made sense now. My spinal column had been rebuilt with bridging supports, quite possibly lengthening my spine. I always wanted to be taller and finally got my wish. How ironic.

The gym was filled with mostly elderly women in wheelchairs, and by now all eyes were on me. Being a little self-conscious was a huge understatement.

Don't stare at me! I yelled in silence and tried to become invisible by wishing for it.

Bethany and Liz were just a few feet away, tending to their helpless patients while looking my way.

Through the dizziness and nausea, I still worried about my appearance. I hadn't showered in weeks and tried to remember if Elsa had combed my hair that morning. I hoped I had put enough deodorant on too and prayed that Paula would detect only a nice, clean, fragrance, as she got closer to me.

When she leaned in for another blood pressure reading, I held my breath, remembering that I wasn't able to brush my teeth after drinking my orange juice that morning.

Hurry up, Paula, I thought. *I can't hold my breath forever.* I exhaled my juice-breath slowly, while she deflated the tightly secured armband. I hated being unclean.

Then, while inhaling deeply to recover all that I had let out, I paused for a second. I suddenly detected an odor. The first thing that crossed my mind was coffee beans.

Do I smell coffee beans? I wondered. Then it grew increasingly stronger and a little more unpleasant, so the coffee bean theory was out.

Man! I thought. *Some elderly person must have had a wicked accident!* I was somewhat familiar with the odors on the unit, namely bedpans and soiled Johnnies from across the hall. This was very strong though, so I immediately felt compassion for the culprit.

How humiliating for them. I'll pretend I can't smell it, as not to embarrass them.

Glancing over at Liz, I noticed her still staring at me. I smiled back, as if to say, "It's okay, I don't mind the smell. I just feel sorry for the elderly person who did it." However, she never turned away. She just kept staring at me. And, as her eyes saddened while locked on mine, and as the stench grew to a disturbing level, the blood began to drain from my face.

It was like being hit by a ton of bricks! I was mortified! Liz's saddened eyes told me it was *me!* The disgusting odor was coming from me! And as I stood tied helplessly to the tilt table, there was nothing I could do about it. Nothing!

BETHANY GAZED DOWN AT MY lower half while Paula ran to summon the nurses' station by using the outdated phone hanging on the wall.

Are you kidding me? I asked God, in a shocked tone, still not able to see anything down below. But I visualized it. I visualized dark lava, flowing endlessly from my rectum for the whole friggin' world to see. I don't know why I imagined lava. I just did. I hadn't gone in almost two weeks. Remember, that diaper was always empty.

The unwanted stink began to fill the gym when Mike walked back into the room. Our eyes met immediately.

"Mike!" I yelled at him in a strong whisper. "Get me out of here, please!"

I feebly pressed on the down button without asking. Liz's face flashed before me again, and as the tilt table began to level out where I could see my lower half, I saw the unthinkable. It was surreal. So damn, surreal.

"Please get me back to my room, Mike! Please, hurry up! Don't let the girls do it, okay, Mike? You do it! Get me back there, hurry up man, please."

He must have heard the desperation in my voice because he moved about in a nervous panic, wheeling me past the other patients and heading out of the gym. I looked everywhere else but in their eyes. I wanted to die right there.

From then on, when things went wrong, it seemed that death was the first thing that popped into my mind. Death was first, and a way out was second.

As countless ceiling tiles flowed by, I thought, *Things have really changed, since that climb up that oak tree,* I thought. *I used to fight for things at every turn. Now I pray for the easy way out.*

Mike rolled me past the small crowd of occupied wheelchairs and into the never-ending trip down that never-ending corridor.

In my room, nurses Jean and Denise were waiting for us with their arms full of clean towels and generic soap supplies with label-less spray bottles. The whiteness of the towels stood way out, and it bugged me that they'd soon be ruined to no end.

Sliding me from the table and back onto my bed created a catastrophe, and the sight of it was beyond embarrassment.

Why, God, why are you torturing me like this? I asked him the same question repeatedly in my head, while sinking lower and lower into a deep depression. Mike left the room and I didn't blame him. Then the call monitor cut through the silence, and Denise was called away to another room, leaving Jean to deal with things all alone.

"I'm so sorry, Jean. I can't believe I did this. I am so, so sorry."

"Bobby, shush, it's fine," Jean whispered. "Just shush. I'll take care of everything."

I watched her moving in and out of sight, with flowing and angelic-like movements. I listened to my own breath—just lying there and trapped in my own body.

Jean gently placed one hand on my shoulder, while working vigorously with the other from behind me. Then...a tranquil humming graced my ears...and slowly began to soothe my wounded soul.

She's humming to me? I asked myself. *And all while immersed in this horrible mess? What a beautiful person she is and what a comforting sound. Where did she learn to do that? I know where. She is a mom.*

As I listened, she hummed her beautiful melody, which drew a long sigh of calm and contentment from me, and as I melted into my mattress, I wondered if her technique was a learned response or an instinctive, nurturing one, which only a mother could possess. Either way, she soothed me.

Lying naked and vulnerable on my side, I was left to reflect on my existence, and for the first time since my accident, as sweet Jean hummed in my ear, I finally began to cry...

36

First shift nurse Gary woke me up to a neckache, coupled with upper body stiffness, and a memory of my misery. I must have slept on the same side all night. Usually, the nurses would wake me and turn me over to avoid getting bedsores, but last night, it seemed that everyone had left me alone.

Gary moved methodically through his morning chores as if he'd done it all before. As he wrote his name on the box of latex gloves, the smell of magic marker reminded me of the other world, the one I left behind. The one with my kids in it.

By placing his own glove box by each room entrance, he could be assured that they'd be readily available when he needed them. I think he spent more time preparing for the task, than he did performing it, and I admired him for that.

Even the bathing supplies were laid out beforehand, as not to waste precious seconds that might turn warm water to cold.

A new bottle of body lotion was peeking out of Gary's smock, and soon the pink goop found its way to my muscleless calves.

"What's that for?" I questioned.

"I like to massage the legs," Gary said. "The massaging helps with circulation."

"Do I need help with circulation, Gary?"

"Why, hasn't anyone done this for you, Bobby?"

"Nope, you are the first. Do the other nurses do this for their patients?"

"They should," he quipped.

I was surprised at the lack of standardization between the staff. But they couldn't do anything wrong in my book.

"I don't know about other nurses," Gary said. "But I like to do it." He rubbed a glob of lotion deep into my skin and massaged it up and down the length of my legs with his thumbs.

"Do you feel any of this, Bobby?"

I hated that question. I hated to have to answer it and all the other questions like it. But I did it with a smile and as if it didn't bother me in the least.

"Hmm," I paused. "Let's see, nope, I don't think so?" Like, I really had to think about it. I was always playing the game and faking answers as not to hurt feelings. Gary wanted the best for me, though, and I knew that, so I went along with it and answered him with a smile.

"So, I'm sure you've heard what happened to me yesterday?"

"No, I didn't. What do you mean Bobby?"

I knew that he knew. I just changed the subject.

"Gary, I have a question. I have deep horizontal grooves in each of my fingernails. What is that? Do you know?" He pursed his eyebrows together and spoke in an honest tone.

"Well, the nails could stop and then start growing again if the body experiences things like, a vitamin deficiency, or an infection, or even stress or trauma."

"Oh, okay," I said, as if I didn't care much.

"I hear Sherry Brown from Mass. General is coming to speak to you in a few days," Gary blurted out, never looking up. He was really working the legs.

"Yeah, what can she do for me? Did she ever help anyone to walk again? Do you think she can get my bowel functions back?"

Gary described Sherry as knowing a lot about spinal cord injuries and seemed to build up the upcoming visit to excite me. However, nothing excited me. I was intrigued though, mainly about her experiences with other SCI patients, but was disappointed with her prior postponements.

"So, Gary, what will this woman show me? Level with me, huh? Did she get that guy you told me about walking again?" Gary still never looked up from oiling up my legs. I know he didn't want to give me false hope and I felt bad for putting him on the spot.

"I'm not sure what she does, Bobby, but I do know that she is very good in her field. She used to work in this hospital. She was a good nurse."

"She was just a nurse here? I thought she was a specialist in spinal cord injuries!"

I knew it was too good to be true. I said to myself.

"There really are no specialists in this field yet are there, Gary?" He still didn't answer. "How can there be 250,000 people in the U. S. suffering from spinal cord injuries, and yet there are hardly any doctors that specialize in the field?" I paused to reflect on that for a moment.

"Sorry, Gary. I don't mean to complain to you, but whenever I ask a question to anyone here, I get more I don't knows, than anything else. It's unreal," I mumbled more under my breath than aloud.

Gary still never looked up.

37

PAUL CAME TO get me for physical therapy. Two nurses tried to transfer me from the bed onto a seat-belted wheelchair but couldn't, and I couldn't help because my torso muscles had atrophied and I was like a jelly fish with no spine. Pam, one of my favorite nurses pushed everyone away and grabbed me under my arms with my face touching hers. With her bad back and all, she picked me up like a lifeless ragdoll and gently placed me in the wheelchair. She left the room holding her sore back without one complaint. Then they wheeled me to the gym for 'armchair therapy', *whatever that is*, I wondered.

I was excited about it yet still a little mortified over the accident the day before, but Jean's angelic humming and loving care inspired me to jump back up on the horse again and get over it.

As I waited, buckled in and parked in one of the smaller gym rooms, I wondered just what they would have me do to fix my legs.

I can't imagine the equipment they must have here to rejuvenate my spinal cord and me. Maybe they'll put me on some kind of advanced electrical stimulus machine or something like it.

I watched patients trickle in, one by one, all in wheelchairs and all over the age of seventy. Six in all—and all were woman.

One had an amputated leg. Diabetes maybe? Another had been in a car accident and had broken her tibia and fibula above and below the knee, I think. Three had hip replacements, and the last one had had a stroke, a paralyzed face and couldn't remember how to do things. She couldn't speak and needed to learn how to all over again. I felt so bad for her, because I knew she was afraid. I could just feel it. I wanted to put my hand in hers and hold onto it for comfort, but I knew it would frighten her. I decided to stay close to her in case she needed anything.

Paul had us roll forward in our wheelchairs, make a semicircle and face him in his folding chair, as he sat, blowing up a big red balloon from a helium tank. Yes, he was blowing up a balloon.

What's going on here? I wondered. *Where are the therapists? Where are the other paraplegics? And where's the high-tech apparatus that's going to rehabilitate and get me walking again?*

I couldn't understand why those elderly women needed the same advanced therapy as me.

When the big red balloon was inflated to the size of a beach ball, Paul sent it slowly floating through the air, over to the amputee and where she reached for it, tapped it and sent it floating even slower to one of the hip recipients next to her.

The eager patient cautiously leaned out of her wheelchair, stretching her seatbelt to the limit and just missing the balloon by a few inches. It bounced off the floor once before slowly drifting over to the accident victim on the end, where she whacked it and leaned back in a victorious posture.

The balloon floated sluggishly over to Paul, as if it were a ball in flight between two astronauts playing catch on the moon.

And yes, Paul sent it directly over to me, in a high arched path, which gave me plenty of time to contemplate my situation.

Now I know what armchair therapy is, I thought to myself. I felt like I had been had.

The balloon took forever to glide over to me. I contemplated spiking it off the head of one of the nice ladies, but instead, I gently tapped it over to the stroke victim, where she tried to hit it but couldn't, allowing it to bounce tenderly off her chest and onto her lap.

She tried to push it off but couldn't remember how. It was so hard to watch her struggle to remember her motor skills.

As I had no choice but to watch, I began to feel ashamed for the way I had just thought and felt. The frightened woman made me realize how fortunate I really was. At least I could hit the big red balloon...

———

AS DAYS WENT BY, SOME strength and balance began to return, unnoticed. Michelle teased me about my karate background and challenged me to a push-ups contest on the gym mat. Michelle was six months pregnant so the challenge drew a small crowd. I took the bait, hook, line and sinker.

I was trained to do push-ups on my knuckles, so my fists partially sunk into the soft mattress, making it tough to do without resistance. Michelle had no problems at all, and even with the huge belly bump, she was amazing.

And after forty-five tough ones, I'm still not sure if the tie was legitimate or she planned it that way. All I know is my spirits were lifted, thanks to Michelle.

38

THE MOMENT OF Sherry's arrival from Mass. General finally came and I couldn't wait another second for the S.C.I. specialist.

Debbie and I sat in wait as the nurses scurried throughout my room, rearranging chairs and medicine bag stands in preparation for her visit.

Gary entered the room and announced her arrival as if he were introducing the Queen of England. I quickly sized her up and began analyzing her mannerisms right away.

She was nothing of what I pictured, with her matronly hairstyle and business power suit. She looked like a CEO. I don't know what I expected. Just not her.

She seemed nice, very nice, and as she told us about her prior S.C.I patients, I tried to appreciate her coming to see me, but I couldn't. I couldn't get past her pretentious chitchat. I was already tired, so tired of all the letdowns and disappointments.

I felt that she was giving me a pep talk rather than real solutions, and within the first three minutes, I decided that she wasn't going to get me walking again and dismissed her as just another person that couldn't possibly know what I was going through. I kind of resented her for pretending to do so.

I straddled between listening and daydreaming, because for me, daydreaming was a tool that allowed me to escape.

She spoke of anatomy and spinal cord function, but about nothing that would let me walk again. She covered all the things I couldn't do and nothing of what I could.

Is this it? Is this the last bit of hope I've been waiting for?

From time to time, I instinctively nodded when her tone called for it, although I wasn't listening consciously.

"Do you have any questions for me?" she asked.

Finally, she's done, I thought. I was afraid to muster up a question for fear she might start again. Over her left shoulder, I could see the wall clock. One hour had already passed. One long and tedious hour.

"I do have one question, Sherry. Could you briefly tell me how I'm going to be able to go to the bathroom? Move my bowels, I mean."

"That's easy?" she said. "Sometimes the function comes back on its own. Yours may return just fine; you never know."

"You mean those functions could come back? When?" I eagerly asked.

"You never know what functions will return. But in the meantime, I have a device that will enable you to go, unassisted!"

"Unassisted? On my own?"

"Yes sir," she said proudly.

Now I was interested and wanted to hear more. The doctors told me that some people with my level of injury may regain bowel control, and I was determined to be one of those people. She bent down to pick up a plastic bag that was stored under her chair. I had forgotten that she brought it in with her when she came in.

"Do you know what digital stim is?" she asked.

I shook my head no.

"Well, these are your digits," she said, as she wiggled her fingers in the air. "And stim stands for stimulation, digital stimulation.

If you take a finger, gloved of course, and gently touch the opening of the rectum, you can stimulate a bowel movement."

I didn't know how to take that. I was somewhat dumbfounded.

Part of me felt grateful for an option, but another part felt hopeless again, and again reminded of my hell.

"How will I do something like that while sitting on the toilet? I can't even hold myself up yet without holding onto a grab rail with both hands," I said.

"Well, Bobby, here is where this contraption comes in." She pulled out a white plastic, stick-looking thing, about the diameter of a pencil.

"This is a great device for quads," she said.

"I'm not a quadriplegic, Sherry, my arms work just fine," I snapped, as I waived them about.

"I know, that's okay, this will still be a great benefit to you too," she said, confidently.

Holding up the funky device made her look like a street vendor, peddling her wares.

Her contraption was about two feet long and hinged in two different places, allowing it to fold over twice and swivel at different angles. It kind of looked like a foldout carpenter's ruler, only not as long.

"You hold one end from up here," she said. "And send the other end down there, to your rectum. Once you find the rectum opening, you simply stimulate it by making small circles, until it finds the urge to move the bowels."

Simply? I thought. *Okay, I've seen enough.*

Feeling depressed, I slowly blinked my eyes and politely thanked her for coming. She said that would be fifteen-dollars for the stick thing, and at my request, she left it in the bathroom for later use.

Yeah, I can't wait to try it. I thought, sarcastically.

I blew off my armchair therapy that day and lay in bed the rest of the afternoon, thinking. *I can't believe there are so many questions and so little answers,* I thought. *I should write a book.*

39

I OPENED MY EYES to see my friends, Little Charlie and Moses standing over me with goodies from the bakery and a partially folded copy of the *American Hunter* tucked under Moses' long-sleeved, red-plaid shirt arm.

The back page of the magazine peaked out at me and just enough to reveal an ad depicting a father and son, sitting in a duck blind, sharing a cup of steaming hot soup atop a box of Winchester shot-gun shells. Immediately, I thought of my son Derek. I missed him. I missed both my kids. My heart hurt each time I thought of them.

Moses placed the magazine down on my tray table while I forced a smile with just my eyes, as I was aching from lying on my back for so long.

"How are you doing, Kid?" Moses asked.

Moses sometimes called me Kid because I was the youngest one of the hunting pack, and I used to be saddled with the chores around camp that the older guys couldn't do. When strenuous tasks were needed, they'd say things like, "Get the Kid, let him do it, he's just a puppy." I didn't mind though; they were my friends.

I looked up at the two of them as if nothing were wrong.

"I'm alright guys. I know...I did a stupid thing. I should have worn my safety strap, I know."

"Well, it's water under the bridge now," Moses said. "So, you just need to get better now, and get your health back so we can get your ass out there hunting with us again."

"I don't think that's ever going to happen. I think my hunting days are over forever."

"Don't say never," Moses said. "You never know what's down the road, right?"

"Yup, I know. Have you guys talked to Cuckoo?"

"Yeah," Little Charlie nodded. "Why don't you give him a call? He's really broken up over this. We were going to wait and visit you this weekend, and then he called me this morning and asked us to check on you today instead. He wants to know how you're doing. He's worried about you."

It hurt me to think that he was worried about me like that.

"Yeah, I will," I said, meekly.

"You'll get through this, you're tough, kid," Moses said.

"Moses, I may not want to," I stated, in a matter-of-fact-like tone.

"Don't talk like that, will ya?"

"I'm serious!" I said, and then pulled the waistband on my pajama bottoms out and downward, exposing my diaper for both of them to see.

"You see this? I won't live like this. I'll give it a month, one month at the most, and if I still have to wear this thing, if my bowel function doesn't return, forget it. I'm not living like this, and you guys will have to help me do it."

By sliding the waistband across my stomach, I triggered a nerve spasm that doubled me over in a semifetal position. I quickly grabbed for my side and pinched off its pathway. While talking through the hurt, I switched gears and assured the guys that I was fine for now and tried to explain the spasms away like this:

"I have kind of a hypersensitive zone, where feeling meets no feeling. The nerve endings are broken and shooting out wacky signals all over my body, and most times, it's in the form of pain. Right now, it feels as though my intestines are being pulled out through my rear end if you can imagine that. But other than that, I'm fine."

I realized how stupid I sounded, in one minute declaring suicide, and another trying to convince them of how well I was doing.

Neither one of them said a word. There was nothing to say. Maybe they thought I was losing my marbles.

Before they left, I asked them to tell Cuckoo that I was doing great. They said they would and wished me well.

"Remember guys," I called out, as they slowly walked away, "One month, and then you'll help me!"

I wanted to hear what they were saying to each other when they rounded the corner and went out of sight, because I just knew they were talking about me.

I begrudgingly reached for the magazine by extending my stiff muscles. I couldn't wait to have it in my hands. Thumbing it open about halfway through, I found an article about poaching and the penalties it carried if convicted.

Poachers always made me sick, so throwing the book at them usually gave me some satisfaction, especially if the culprit did it for money rather than for survival, or the need for food to feed their family.

Sometimes there is a fine line between malicious poaching and poaching out of a belief. Some of the older Maine natives believe they have the right to feed their families and by any and all means available to them.

Some hold the belief that it's their God-given right to kill a deer on their own property because they own the animal once it ventures onto their land. The game wardens see it differently though. I remembered coming very close to getting in trouble myself once, although poaching was the farthest thing from my mind.

It was on my first big game hunt in the midwest, about forty miles west of the South Dakota border in the foothills of the historic Black Hills Mountains...

40

THE YEAR WAS 1992. Moses and I were making our way along the rim of a dusty canyon, on our way back to camp after a successful mule deer hunt. His old white Ford was covered in bentonite and looked like a camouflaged military vehicle fresh out of an Afghanistan desert.

We had already filled both our deer tags and each possessed only an antelope license that wasn't legally valid in that region.

We wanted to get back to the tent before sundown, so we could hang up our deer before it got too dark but mainly to show off our harvest to the other guys when they drove in, especially Cuckoo.

Something up ahead of us caught our attention, so Moses leaned on the brake and slowed us down in an instinctive response. As we got closer, we could see what looked like a fresh deer carcass leaning high up against a cattle ranch's barbed wire fence.

It was evident that it had become entangled in the fence while trying to jump it, and I figured it must have died either from shock or from starvation. But as we got closer, I was sickened to realize what had really happened.

The good-sized doe tried to jump the fence—and had gotten her two front hooves caught in the wire, about four feet up I'd say. Like a caught fish on a baited hook, her hindquarters dangled just inches above the ground, leaving her cruelly defenseless to the predators below.

"The poor thing was eaten alive," Moses said. "Look at the butthole... just the butthole was eaten. The coyotes like to start there. It's the best place to start, you know."

I had seen that method of consumption on dead prey before, particularly in Maine, from red and gray foxes feasting on roadkill, or from the wild dog packs on Block Island that run down a sick or wounded deer until it drops from exhaustion.

Most animals have a tough hide and thick fur over most of its body; however, the genital area is normally more hairless and tender, making it a prime nibbling area to enter the body from.

Although disgusting to observe, I had accepted this method as a fact of life and a necessary survival technique for wildlife predators to use. But, the thought of it being eaten alive? Well, that really bothered me.

"Bobby, look at all the little tracks around that deer," Moses said. "That means that the coyote had pups with her. Lots of them, too."

Our pickup slowly crawled past the sad sight until only the mental image remained. I sat back, took off my cap, pushed my hair back, and put it back on again.

"Moses," I said. "Look at that gully running alongside the base of the fence line. It's an old dried up riverbed. That's why the deer couldn't jump the fence. The gully's lowland makes the fence that much higher, therefore making it harder for the animal to clear the top with its hooves. This whole stretch of fence line looks that way."

"Yeah, you're probably right," he said, as he feathered the gas pedal just enough to keep it slow.

We continued along the rim of the canyon for another five or six miles, while the sun began to paint its daily masterpiece on the big sky's new canvas. Out there, the sunset popped with colors, like Crayola Crayons, and held you captive by gazing humbly upon its ever-changing creations.

Another anomaly got our attention up ahead of us, but this time movement accompanied the scene.

"Hey kid, I think there are some mule deer up ahead of us," Moses announced.

"I think you're right, Mose, but something is hung up on that fence wire up there also. It looks like another deer carcass," I said.

As we got closer, the herd didn't seem to scatter. Instead, they looked like they were, as we say, "posing for Animal Crackers," standing motionless in one direction, while looking back at the deer they left behind.

Moses stopped the truck just thirty yards from the group, bringing all the details clearly into view. It was a herd of three muleys, consisting of a mother with her two fawns clinging closely to her side. Four to five months old, I'd say.

The wide-eyed little ones stood firm in our presence, while their mom stomped her front hooves, kicking up dust and dried sagebrush, while never taking her eyes off the deer on the fence.

Our eyes quickly shifted to what we expected to be a carcass hanging on the barbed wire, but were startled to see that the stranded deer was in fact alive and kicking!

"Oh man! That deer's alive!" I said, as I grabbed onto the dashboard to pull myself forward for a better look.

It was one-third of the triplets. A little doe I thought, and she had her right front leg and hoof tangled up in the top rung of the fence wire. She seemed so miserable, hanging up there by just one of her four hooves, yet she wriggled back and forth, looking like she had lots of life left in her and not willing to give up just yet.

I say she, because I could usually tell the difference between young does and bucks. Well, I could with the deer from back home anyway.

The whitetail buck in New England has a slightly wider band of white hair around his nose, and most of the time he trailed in the rear, stepping more cautiously through the woods than his bolder sisters do.

When Lauren was seven or so, I taught her a little tidbit about fawn birth rates by gender. She could rattle off nature's rule about it by heart and proud, I think, to share a hunting thing with me, just like her big brother Derek.

"Hey Dad, guess what," she'd say.

"Yes, poopy-face," I'd answer her.

"If a mother deer has just one fawn, it's always born a doe. And if a mother deer has twins, she'll have a boy and a girl. And if a mother deer has triplets, then it's always two girls and a boy. Always! Did you know that, Daddy?"

She was so proud to share her contribution to our love of the sport. I'm glad she never knew the sad side of life's food chain.

The doe's leg seemed broken in more than just one place, leaving it looking horribly twisted and facing the wrong way.

The other leg dangled in midair and could have been broken too, but there was no way to tell.

Looking skyward, the fawn's little head lifelessly flopped from shoulder to shoulder in its feeble attempt to set itself free. Its two hind legs squatted awkwardly on the ground, forcing them spread apart and leaving its tender, white underbelly fully exposed. My eyes began to fill up with pools of tears as I looked on.

Even with our windows tightly closed, we could hear the blood-curdling, bleated screams from the helpless yearling as it called out for its mother.

With her veined neck outstretched like a point setter, the mother deer snorted profusely at her young, as if to scold it for being so bad.

I don't think she cared one bit about our presence, nor did she worry about the siblings standing motionless behind her. She just focused on that fawn and refused to leave her behind.

"Moses," I said. "With that mangled leg stuck like that, she'll never get herself free. She will surely be coyote bait when nightfall comes. Hand me my rifle from behind the seat, will you?"

I fished out one bullet from my zipped jacket pocket and opened the door to let myself out of the truck.

"Where the hell are you going, Bobby?"

"I'm not going to let that deer suffer like that. I'm going to put her down. Blow the horn to scare the other deer away for me."

Moses grabbed my arm just as my foot left the truck and hit the ground.

"You can't do that!" Moses yelled. "You don't have a deer tag left!"

"The hell I can't. I'm not going to let that thing be eaten alive by a pack of mangy coyotes! Especially in the way she's trapped in that barbed wire. And, with just her butt hanging out like that? No way!"

The cries were louder now that the door of the truck was open, and the mother continued to paw the ground in protest to it all.

"I can't listen to that and do nothing, Moses! It's cruel to let her die like that. Let go and let me out!"

The mother snorted more frantically as the baby kicked in place but went nowhere. Moses squeezed my arm with a death grip. He was always a strong son of a gun—an ex-marine and *tunnel rat* who fought courageously in Vietnam.

"Listen to me, Bobby, just listen. Close the door and hear me out." I got back in and looked directly into his intense eyes.

"If you shoot that deer, it will be considered a crime. You don't have a tag for it, and if a game warden comes by, he will not only arrest us, but he'll confiscate our truck as well. It's illegal, period. Anything shot without a tag is poaching, no matter the circumstances. They don't care about your reasons out here. But more importantly, you need to understand how nature works." He took a deep breath and then continued.

"You look at that deer as coyote bait. But nature looks at it as food for those pups we saw evidence of back there. Don't forget, the coyote pups have to eat too. Is letting them starve to death any less cruel? Is it?

"Why is it less humane to let those coyote puppies die a slow death from starvation? Is it because they're not as cute as 'Bambi'? Mother Nature has provided for all of her creatures, and here is perfect evidence of that. Just remember, the coyotes have to eat, too. Understand, Kid?"

"I never thought about it like that," I said, as I stared at the crazed mother, feeling such empathy for her.

"I guess you're right, Moses. It's just hard to leave that fawn here to die a horrible death like that. It really bothers me."

"It bothers me too," he said. "But Mother Nature has provided for that, too. She has given most of her prey animals a defense mechanism to help deal with such attacks from their natural predators.

"Did you ever see a gazelle being taken down by a pride of lions and then eaten alive? It seems awful, doesn't it? Well the gazelle doesn't feel the pain you'd think it does. Here's why. As the lion sinks its sharp teeth into the gazelle's flesh, the gazelle's brain sends a signal to the nerve endings to numb that area, greatly reducing the pain that it feels. It's kind of like getting a shot of Novocain."

"Wow, Moses, you know something? I do remember when Tuffy's veterinarian showed me how to give him a painful shot of sedatives in order to trim his hooves.

With my two fingers, he had me flick my horse's shoulder muscle three or four times just before injecting the needle. The vet said spanking the muscle allowed it to defend itself against pain by numbing the nerve endings before the needle went in. The vet explained how most herd and grazing animals possess the same defense mechanism for pain. "Even humans," he said.

Moses nodded in agreement, "That's right."

I sat there in deep thought, flicking the swivel at the end of my rifle sling.

"Do you think the mother will finally leave her young one behind?" I asked.

Through squinted eyes, Moses looked out to the trail ahead of us before answering.

"She will leave. She has two other little ones to take care of and nature will force her to accept the fawn's fate and abandon her baby for the good of the others. She needs to get those young ones in a safe place before nightfall and she knows it. She will leave. Okay, Kid?"

Moses and me.

"Okay, you're right, Moses. You're right. It's just so hard to leave it like this, but I know we have to. You're right. The pups have to eat too."

————

I BROKE AWAY FROM THE remembrance and threw the hunting magazine back down on the tray table, put my head back on my pillow and closed my eyes to the memory. It was time I got a clearer picture of just what was going on with my damaged spinal cord in an attempt to repair things with my mind.

41

ENVISIONING THE NERVE endings in my legs and feet, I summoned them to move. *Complete the chain,* I told myself.

I imagined energy flowing from my brain, down through pathways and side streets, only to stop abruptly at my waist while bouncing off all sorts of obstacles.

The energy simply had nowhere to go. It was like backed-up water in a clogged drainpipe. The interruption upset my plumbing system and my nerves were working overtime to bypass the clog.

My brain was accustomed to sending messages down through the nervous system, signaling select nerves to fire on command and flex the muscle chosen to move the desired body part.

Abruptly stopping these signals in their tracks was like closing the floodgates on a dam, except the dam was built to withstand a force and the human body was not. I knew this couldn't be good for me.

I had overheard scraps of information from the hospital staff and tried to remember it all, so I could recall it and hash it over later.

Bladder infections were common with paraplegics, and the antibiotics would eventually learn their way around the infection. Then what? Is that when I die? Is that how I die?

Blood clots are a concern too, so I heard. The thought of a clot of blood stuck in my bloodstream really grosses me out. My imagination ran wild with visions of clots forming in my veins and arteries, choking and restricting the blood supply to my brain, and I knew I wouldn't feel the pain until it was too late.

Just when would I know, when my legs turned blue? When my lungs filled with fluids and I began gasping for air, or drowning in my own fluids. What a way to go!

I opened one eye and made sure that the poinsettia plant was still there. It was, thank God.

I practiced long meaningful breaths and noticed that I could slow down my heart rate, which in turn produced what seemed to be nerve pulses that pulsated slowly but powerfully down my left leg.

They originated from my left groin area and ran all the way to my toes. I envisioned my leg as an electrical wire, with low, pounding volts traveling downward and out my little toe.

I savored every "feel" and every sensation and tried to replicate them over and over again. The more I concentrated on them the more I could feel them—that is with my mind, of course.

Then it came: my first itch. Not the crazy morphine itch, a real itch. It was on my right side, at the top of my rear end and about even with my navel. The area was about the size of a quarter and emanated a wicked intense tickle!

Irritated, I quickly reached to scratch it. No relief though. Again, it itched and tickled, and again I scratched.

Am I missing it? I kept my finger on the spot because by now the itch was constant. But as I scratched, I couldn't feel my skin, and I was sure I was on the right spot. It was as though the itch was far beneath the skin, yet I had no sensation on the area itself!

How weird, I thought. *I've got an itch but can't feel the scratch! How the heck will I ever walk again if I can't cure even this one small thing?*

In dealing with the insatiable itch, I began to notice a tickly, quirky, tingle thing that erupted under my armpits. It was brutal right off the bat! The sensation immediately made me nervous, and I can only describe it this way.

Being super ticklish under my arms, I could never stand anyone touching me there and would laugh my head off at just the thought of it. That's why the new sensation bugged me so much. My mind was off the itch now and totally on the tingle under my arms. I tried to squeeze my arms down to my sides but couldn't stop it. It was nerve-racking!

I rang for the nurse and explained *my new thing* to her. It was like one thing after another. She administered my morning meds a little early to try to get me to fall asleep and kill the condition. It worked, I went out like a light but as midmorning came, I was disappointed to feel that my new thing was still there. My squirming must have alerted my roommate, because a gruff-sounding throat attempted to clear and then ended with a deep, stern and no nonsense, "Morning, Bobby!"

The low drill sergeant-sounding voice recently started greeting me each morning with the same, gruff bark. I tried to return the gesture with a comparable one but was not as good at it.

His bed remained fixed at the opposite side of the room and we faced each other at about twenty feet apart. We didn't speak right off, but after days of staring at each other, we found a common bond. The nurses that came and went were from the outside world, while we lived in our own.

His name was Jack Walden.

Annie was one of the third shift nurses from Narragansett. She told me of the reputation he had earned in that seaport town.

"Jack Walden is somewhat of an icon down in South County," she said. "Or I should say, Captain Walden, that is."

It took me some time to work up the nerve to question him on his livelihood, and when I finally did, I wished I had done so sooner.

42

CAPTAIN WALDEN WAS a magnificent storyteller and began captivating my imagination each morning as we both waited to be sponge bathed.

Being unable to sit up, I couldn't see him most of the time, yet his words painted the most elaborate paintings in my color-starved mind.

The man was from the old world. With large paw-like hands and a leather-like weathered face, the World War II veteran made his presence known wherever he was.

He made his own fishing nets as a young man, and as an elder, he built each one of his four sons their own boat—by hand.

The father of five made a living fishing for yellowfin tuna from his wooden trawler, *Elisabeth*, named for his only daughter.

The Captain spent six to seven weeks at sea and only two to three weeks at home with his wife, Evelyn. Fishing off the George's Bank was something that he had done many a day, despite the dangers that lurked in those remote, deep and stormy seas.

The United States Naval Intelligence agency counted on Captain Walden and fishermen like him to report sightings of Soviet fishing vessels operating in waters off our coast during the cold war. He explained that most Russian fishing trawlers were actually Soviet spies, gathering intelligence for the notorious KGB. He described how he spent many a day mapping and transmitting their positions to our nation's secret agency.

I asked if he was ever compensated for his time, but he just laughed and said, "No lad, not a dime." Even if they offered, I don't think he would have taken it.

One day on a routine fishing trip, the *Elisabeth* was trawling for tuna 110 miles off the coast of Point Judith, when suddenly something shook the boat with godlike proportion.

The steel-webbed fishing net had snagged something huge, stopping the *Elisabeth* in her tracks, and throwing everything that wasn't bolted down end-over-end and violently forward!

Like a trophy striper hooked on a bending bass rod, the stretched steel scraped along her rusty hull, first from the stern, then to the starboard side of the boat, splintering the side rail along the way and tipping her over sideways while spilling the cold, gray waters over the wooden banister and into the belly of the boat.

Whatever the great serpent was, it had caught the *Elisabeth* in a death grip, dragging her sideways, not *with,* but against the grain of the sea. The bilge pumps worked feverishly to keep up with the spillage, but to no avail.

The *Elisabeth* had a crew of eight, including the ship's salty old mess cook. And, most were experienced sailors, yet they had no experience in a catastrophe such as this.

All eyes were on the captain for guidance, who was up in the wheelhouse, overlooking the emergency through cold steel-blue eyes. He contemplated his options as he watched the gigantic sea pour its frigid waters onto the deck of the tiny vessel.

Awaiting the captain's words, the crew looked up to the bridge for their orders. Their skipper looked like the fisherman on the label of the Gorton's Clam Chowder can, or better yet, that famous painting of the seaman in the yellow rain suit, battling a drenching hailstorm from behind his ship's mahogany boat wheel.

Captain Walden ordered all hands to 'man' the fire axes and hack through the steel cables that made up the netting. Knee deep in icy waters, and clinging to each other's cold and wet clothing, the crew swung their axes in a dire frenzy!

The *Elisabeth* was listing to one side now, and at about a 45-degree angle, her starboard banister railing was even with the water's edge. Black smoke poured from the over-worked engines before they suddenly seized up with a low moan and a grinding halt.

Hacking at the tentacle-like cables, two sailors severed the main outer cable, and then more inner strands snapped wildly in unison under the extreme pressure of the heavy load, just missing cutting one of them in two at the waist!

Suddenly, the few remaining nets' cables lost their grip on the anomaly, and the *Elisabeth* was slingshot over to the other side, throwing crewmen violently to the other side and allowing sea foam to enter her belly from her port side. Then she rolled back to her starboard and again slowly to her port until she settled quietly in the middle.

The captain ordered her torn and frayed netting raised from the sea without delay. As the crew brought it up from the deep, they couldn't believe their eyes! The heavy gauged steel fishnet was reshaped into the form of a spiraled screw! The yeoman then yelled up to the bridge in an excitable report.

"She was tangled in a prop, skipper! A submarine propeller it was! She must have snagged a sub!"

The captain and his crew studied the new formation in amazement and shook their icy wet heads at the sight of it all. And with rising chests and half-smiles on their wind burned faces, the crew of the *Elisabeth* passed around their smokes and stared in wonderment, then slowly returned to their stations in preparation for the next adventure.

I asked the captain if he ever found out any more about the incident. He explained that back in the sixties, seventies and early eighties, the United States Navy as well as the Soviet Union, operated their submarines in international waters in total secrecy during the cold war. Neither country would admit just whose U-boat was there on that day.

Incurring more than $8,000.00 in damages, the *Elisabeth* limped on home to her homeport in Point Judith, Rhode Island. The U.S. Navy continued to deny liability, so Captain Walden enlisted the help of John O. Pastore, a senior U.S. Senator representing Rhode Island in Washington, D.C.

It took six long years, but finally the persistent senator from the Ocean State mailed Jack a check on behalf of the U.S. government, along with a letter of apology from the Secretary of the Navy.

Speaking off the record, the senator told Jack that a U.S. sub *was* in fact in that area on that day and did indeed incur heavy damages to her prop.

Captain Jack ended his story with these words.

"To this day, I am befuddled. How in blazes did the skipper of that U-boat miss us on his radar screen? He must've been a blind man, either that or he had his head up his ass."

I was grateful for meeting Captain Jack Walden. He reminded me of the reasons why I used to cherish life. While listening to his morning tales, I was right there in that boat with him and experienced the events as if they were happening right there and then.

Not all of his stories were glorious though. One morning, he spoke of a nineteen-year-old neighbor of his whom he described as a young lad. The youth's name was Jason Townsend.

Jason approached Captain Walden at the marina one autumn morning and showed off a ring that he had purchased at a Wakefield jewelry store. He planned to give it to his high school sweetheart, Leanne, that very night.

Leanne had grown up around the marina, so the captain knew the young lady as well. Jason asked Jack for a job on the next deep-sea fishing trip and promised to work hard for his pay. He said he needed to earn a good lump sum to pay for his wedding expenses.

In the past, Captain Walden had made a practice of barring rookies from his boat, for fear of jeopardizing not only the greenhorn himself, but his crew as well. He called all inexperienced and wannabe sailors, 'greenhorns.' I got a kick out of that.

Because Jason's dad personally requested the favor, the captain made an exception and agreed to employ the young lad, although it was against his better judgment. Mr. Townsend expressed his gratitude, asked that the captain bring his boy home safe and sound, and personally invited him to his son's upcoming wedding, with a seat up at the head table, to boot.

The *Elisabeth* sailed from the port of Galilee in Narragansett, R.I., for a twenty-one-day fishing trip on Friday, July 13, 1973. *Friday the 13th*, I thought. It took her three days and two nights just to get to the outskirts of the trawling grounds.

Captain Jack kept a watchful eye on Jason from his perch, high up in the wheelhouse.

On the morning of day nine, a tragedy struck that would haunt Captain Jack Walden and his crew for the rest of their days.

The sailing crew repeatedly warned young Jason of the dangers surrounding the ship's old trawling equipment. The powerful winch, sometimes called the drum, wrapped and wound the steel fish net around it and resembled a large barrel lying on its side.

The drum could spin in either direction to reel out, or haul in the vast chain-linked steel net. A four-hundred horse-powered diesel engine ran the winch, so once it started turning, nothing could stop or slow it down.

That morning was exceptionally windy, yet it produced one of the biggest harvests of yellowfin tuna of the season. The crew scrambled to bring the catch on board with the help of the mighty winch. Jason was standing close to the drum as the fish spilled over the bow and onto the slippery deck.

Amazed at the site and enormity of the catch, Jason leaned in to get a better look. And although he was warned many times not to do so, he got dangerously close to the spinning powerhouse, and his loose-fitting poncho which was unbuttoned and blowing in the gust, brushed against the cog-toothed monster and was snagged by the churning beast, drawing him into the spiraling net of steel chains.

The captain could only watch in awe while he frantically pulled the lever on the power switch, starving the powerful motor of its energy, but doing nothing to halt the churning drum until it was ready to stop on its own.

As instructed by the U.S. Coast Guard and after recording the incident by radio, the crew diligently removed the remains from the machinery and placed the young boy in the ship's hold, down with the ice and fish.

The trip home took three long days to complete, and in those three days, the crew of the *Elisabeth* spoke only when it was necessary to do so.

43

SHE APPEARED OUT of nowhere, looking like a lost puppy on a damp and rainy night. Her aura was noticeable, more youthful, probably mainly because of the elderly patients that surrounded her, highlighting her presence like a bright shining star among darker celestial bodies.

Even so, her head hung low, making the wheelchair appear as her jailer and depriving her of any liberties she may have once had.

Mocha brown, grown-out bangs hid most of her face, yet I sensed she was a lot closer to my age than the other patients were.

She looks so sad, I thought. *I don't think she can use her arms; she's being pushed by an aide. I wonder what happened to her?*

As I wheeled past across the gym floor, she lifted her head just enough to reveal her striking dark eyes, almost black I'd say. Her distant stare met mine and quickly locked onto my friend-starved eyes, and for that brief moment, we connected. Then she was gone.

"Mike, who is that girl they just took away?" I asked, as we headed back to my room from the rehab gym.

"I don't know... she's new here," he said, with a hint of curiosity in his tone. "I think she's in the Army or Navy or something. One day she woke up paralyzed and unable to call for help. From a recent head injury or fall, I think."

I waited for him to ask me why I was asking but was thankful he didn't. I don't know what he was thinking. Maybe nothing at all...or maybe he knew.

Lined with wheelchair-bound patients, the long, narrow corridor ranged from stroke victims to amputees, with most having looks of despair on their pale and sun-starved faces. They looked to the floor rather than make eye contact with us, and things like flimsy johnnies and paper-made slippers made it easy for them to assume a role of unworthiness, despite their previous life's stature.

I emerged from the wheelchair gauntlet to discover Mrs. Cornell, an older woman I had met a few days before, sitting patiently outside of her room, waiting for her escort to push her to the gym for her daily armchair workout.

She thought that her urine bag remained tucked away in secrecy—under her seat and out of view, but in fact, it hung out in plain sight for all to see. I found myself unconsciously examining the level of the urine, as if I were in charge of its overfill detection. It was in plain sight and three-quarters full. I'm glad she didn't know.

As I rolled past room 5450, shortened by the nurses to room 450, I looked in and observed three nurses conversing with Bernie, the newest attraction to the Rehab Unit.

Three nurses in one room meant that either there was a problem with a patient or a much-needed moment of comic relief, and Bernie was surely that.

Everyone loved the boisterous, seventy-three-year-old war veteran from Warwick, along with his semi-dirty jokes and positive outlook on life. Because this was his third stay on the unit in less than a year, Bernie knew every staff member by not only their first name, but also by their likes and dislikes. He sang songs—old-fashioned songs, while flirting and schmoozing all the ladies on the fourth floor.

Bernie made it his business to learn what made each person unique and, oh, did I mention that Bernie was blind? Bernie was blind.

He yelled out a big "Hello" to me as I wheeled past his semi-private room. Maybe he heard my squeaky wheel tires on the floor tiles, I'm not sure.

Bernie's wife Mary arrived early each morning and stayed with him until well after dark. I can't say for certain if he broke a hip or had a stroke or something else, because as time went on, and unlike my initial arrival, I didn't care enough to ask. I continued on, back to my room.

Totally surprised, I grabbed my tires to stop them at my door's threshold, but skidded in because Mike's force was overwhelming

Waiting for me in the big chair by my window and poinsettia plant, sat my friend Eddie, looking so serious and somber. I locked onto the plant for a split second before he jumped up and then scrambled to put himself anywhere but in the way. He tucked in his shirt while adjusting his pants.

"Hey," I said, not knowing what else to say.

"Bobby!" Eddie hollered, talking with his hands. "Do you know how long I've wanted to come and see you, brother? I was told you didn't want to see anyone, so I honored your wishes, for a little while anyway. You know I would have been here a lot sooner if they'd let me. Hey, you lost weight huh? You look good though."

"Yeah right," I smirked. "I'm okay..., I really am." I looked over at the poinsettia plant again. "What's in the box?"

"What do you think they are?" Eddie said, proudly and loudly. "They're cannolis!" he said even louder, tossing them on my lap.

"From The Hill?"

"Of course, from The Hill." Federal Hill was the only place to get real cannolis.

"Eddie, I would have been happy with just one you know..., they're expensive."

"Well, ya got a whole box!"

"Thank you," I said, with head hanging low. "The nurses will love them."

We talked for a while and Eddie assured me that I would be walking again soon. He sounded so convincing and guaranteed me that I'd even walk by the summer. I really think he believed it.

We shared a cannoli and talked for a while longer, and then he left. I wondered if it was the last time I would ever see him again. I was glad that he came but seeing him reminded me of home and my previous life. My morale was sinking lower by the minute. The tips of the poinsettia leaves were beginning to curl too.

I'll have to ferment them before they dry out. Soon.

I sat motionless for a while, listening to my breathing with my mouth closed. My jaw hurt, so I focused on that. Then I was startled! Startled to something nasty! It seemed like the entire floor began to reek! It reeked of poop! Strong, diarrhea type…, stinky poop! I quickly checked to make sure that it wasn't coming from me. I was safe.

I knew that it was bad and felt sorry for the nurses but worse for the culprit. I prayed that the perpetrator be kept anonymous in order to preserve their dignity, but because the fumes had reached my room, I knew there was little hope of that.

I made doubly sure it wasn't coming from me by doing a quick body search. I was still okay.

I pray to God it's not that girl, the new one. The one with the bangs in her face. God, I hope not.

The laundry room was in clear view right across the hall from mine. As the nurses ran nervously in and out with arms full of clean, white bath towels, I could pretty much gauge the scope of the situation, and I gauged that it was huge.

Roseanne, one of my favorite nurses, looked up at me from across the hall as she turned the corner before coming through the laundry room door with towels heaped in her arms.

I shouted out to her before she was out of range.

"Hey Roseanne." She looked up. "Code Brown?" I yelled out.

"Yup, code brown!" she answered back.

"Sorry! Hang in there!" I hollered. "I'm thinking of you! You're my hero!"

"Thanks!" She answered again with a chuckle.

I got a kick out of the term 'Code Brown.'

The hospital has different color codes for different emergencies. I'm not sure but I think a respiratory emergency is Code Yellow, heart failure is Code Red, and death is Code Blue, etc. Something like that.

The nurses affectionately called a messy bowel accident, "Code Brown," but were not allowed to let the patients in on the joke. However, they told me. They trusted me not to tell. Oops.

I couldn't stop thinking about the girl in the wheelchair. *I wonder if she needs a way out too.*

The poinsettia plant was in my reach now and no one suspected a thing. After being transferred from the wheelchair to my bed, one of the nurses thought the plant was getting too cold sitting next to the window, so she put it on my tray table right next to my bed.

I methodically plotted each step of the fermentation process and calculated the amount of plant leaves I needed to do the job. I knew that warm water (heat) would speed up the process, so I had to get rid of all the ice in the water pitcher first.

If I started soaking the leaves tonight after the second shift left, I could be sure that before the first shift arrived at seven a.m., the cocktail would be ready to drink. Tomorrow night would be a good night. It'll be ready in case I need it.

I ended the day back in the gym with Martha, my occupational therapist who taught me living skills. I was able to wheel myself this time. The exercise dictated that I park my chair in front of an opened refrigerator door, which was used for training purposes and full of food and condiments. It was supposed to teach disabled people like me to live independently.

As Martha called out the food item, I had to reach for it on the shelf, grab it and hand it to her. I hated the silly task but didn't let on. Martha was a good person, but it was so degrading.

"Ketchup!" she commanded.

I reached into the fridge and handed it to her.

"Good job!" she said. "Okay, now salad dressing!"

I reached in and gave her that too.

"Outstanding!" she praised. "Now the can of Coke!"

I gave her the can of coke.

"Great! Great!" She gloated. "Maraschino cherries!" she said.

Poinsettias, I thought.

44

A s I LEFT the gym through the open door, I skidded to a stop just before crashing into an oncoming wheelchair. It was being pushed by an aide and ridden by the girl with the bangs in her face.

It's her! I said to myself, backing up quickly to let her through the doorway. Her companion pushed her forward and parked her chair alongside mine. I knew she was tiny, but she looked so much more petite up closely. She was toned and muscular too, without much body fat at all. An athlete, I thought. She spoke to me right away, and I thought that was cool.

"Da-da-da-did," she struggled with her speech, while shutting her eyes tight and slowly articulating every letter.

"Ya-ya-ya-you...," she paused, "haaava, da-dood, da-day?" she asked, with a one-sided flirtatious smile.

Her face seemed somewhat paralyzed and her vocal cords sounded affected, too.

I was afraid I wouldn't understand her and embarrass her by bringing attention to her speech, so I zoned in on her eyes to get the whole picture. She spoke with her hands, even the bad one, so that helped.

Her left hand was closed so tightly that her nails dug into her palm, about a sixteenth of an inch deep and leaving the surrounding tissue on it looking pink and raw. And using the back of her clenched fist, she continuously wiped her chin, but it wasn't wet and she didn't need to.

Tipping her fragile head back, she attempted to speak to me again.

"Mmm...my, nnn...name," her pauses between words looked schooled and seemed to gratify her each time she took them.

"Um," she closed her eyes tight and swallowed with a long, hard gulp. Then nodded. I held my breath until she got it all out. "It's, Ti..., Ti..., Tina!" she spat out, with a mini-eruption and a sexy half smile. She looked at me with a sense of triumph. Her deep dark eyes told a story that her vocal cords couldn't, and I knew immediately that she had a lot to say. As we talked, her speech impediment became less evident, and after a while, I didn't hear it at all. Not at all.

"And this is my friend, Linda," Tina said.

"Hi Linda, I'm Bobby," I said, informing them both, then glancing back to Tina who was already my favorite.

"Does your hand hurt, Tina? Closed tight like that?"

"I don't know, I can't feel it," she smirked, illustrating her sculptured white teeth and risqué mouth.

I, above all should have known that, I thought. *She sounds like me and a jokester too.*

Tina suddenly waved her closed fist past my face and then back again.

"Smell!" she said.

"What?" I asked, as I leaned back a little.

"Smell!" she repeated with a chuckle, while looking up and back at Linda.

"Smell your hand?" I asked.

"Yes, smell it!" she said with a grin.

"Okay, I guess," leaning forward to get in closer. She pried open her fingers by uncurling them one at a time and held them all back so they wouldn't spring shut. Then, with her right hand, she presented her left one to me, palm open, with fingers bent way back.

Then, the girl with the bangs in her face leaned forward as if to cup my mouth and nose with her opened hand. And don't ask me why, but I leaned into it and took in a long, deep breath. Way too deep I might add.

"Oh my God! Holy crap!" I hollered, leaning back as far as I could go without falling out of my wheelchair. "What the hell is that smell?" I giddily laughed aloud.

Tina cracked up laughing hysterically while leaning over in her chair. Linda walked right out of the room, screaming as she walked. "I don't believe her! She's crazy! She is crazy!"

I never would have guessed that what I assumed was merely dead skin, could actually stink the way it did. It was unreal! I was laughing so hard. I mean really cracking up! The more I looked at her, the more I snorted through my nose and waterlogged eyes.

Instinctively, I reached for my sore ribs, anticipating they'd hurt me through it all. And I think I had forgotten how to laugh because it felt so awkward to do so. But I did laugh. I laughed like someone having nervous convulsions. And it had been so long since I had even grinned, my facial muscles felt tight and unable to stretch to a real smile. But Tina made them try.

I went to bed that night with that smile and the nice memory of the girl with the bangs in her face.

45

BERNIE DIED IN the middle of the night last night. I don't know why, no one will tell me. I awoke to the sight of two orderlies rolling Bernie past my doorway. He was strapped to a gurney and zipped up in a body bag.

I imagined myself in that body bag, dark with silence and with no more hurt. *No—more—hurt. I hope someone waters my poinsettia plant this morning.*

46

I SLIPPED BACK INTO a deep morning sleep, with only an hour before I had to wake up and face the monotonous grind of another day.

Suddenly, my bed shook with a bump! Then another! Bump! Too groggy to open my eyes, I incorporated the bump into a dream and weaved it into one of riding bumper cars with Derek and Lauren at Rocky Point Park. Bump!

"Hey you wazy ass! Wake up!" Bump!

Still semiconscious, I grabbed onto the bedrails and held on tight.

"Hey wazy ass!" Bump! Bump!

I opened an unexpected eye to that girl with the big brown eyes and the smelly hand. She crashed into my bed with her wheelchair, then backed up and then wheeled forward into it again! Bump!

"Get up you wazy ass," she pointed without her fingers. "You gonna sleep all day?"

My God, I thought. *This girl is forward.* But I liked her. I liked her a lot. Bump! Bump!

"Okay, okay!"

"I got you a coffee, you wazy ass. Get up and have a coffee with me!"

Wiping the sleep from my eyes, I did most of the listening. I was right; she had a lot to say. We filled each other in on what was needed but didn't get into specifics. I think we were both sick of that. I held the button in to raise the top of my bed as I became more comfortable. Actually, I hadn't felt more comfortable in weeks. We talked, I laughed, and we sipped on coffee until she had to leave.

I forgot all about watering my poinsettia plant that morning.

I OPENED MY EYES TO Dr. Lucas from Rhode Island hospital standing at the foot of my bed, with my nurse Jean, hovering over his shoulder. I hadn't realized that I fell asleep after Tina left. Seeing Jean's face made me happy.

"Hey, Dr. Lucas!" I blurted out. "Boy am I glad to see you! Thank you for coming to Kent Hospital?" I thought you had abandoned me.

"Hello Robert, how are things going?"

"Great, now that you're here, but no feeling yet. Still waiting."

"Well let's see what we have here," he softly said.

He pulled the sheets back and picked up my left leg by its ankle. Standing directly in front of it, he positioned my foot by planting it flatly on his inner wrist.

"Can you push your leg for me?" he asked.

I could only push with my mind but I tried anyway. And as I pushed hard, really hard, I became very nervous and short of breath.

"Feel me pushing?" I asked in a high-pitched voice.

"Well, let's try the other one," he said.

I began to sink. My whole body began to sink into the fabric of that bed and away from the solids of the outer world. I needed to get out of my body again.

I pushed my right leg with all I had and could have easily thrown up if I allowed myself to. *Am I pushing?* I asked myself. *I really don't know how to do it anymore!*

Dr. Lucas put my leg down and mumbled something to Jean. I couldn't hear it.

"So, did you feel any resistance at all?" I asked.

"There may be some trace there, it's hard to tell," he said.

"Do you think my spinal cord is still swollen?"

"Oh sure," he responded.

"How long will it be swollen for?" I asked. That was my way of asking how big the window of opportunity was. The window of opportunity to regain any feeling back. After that, it wasn't coming back.

"Oh, I'd say three months," he said. He knew what I was really asking.

Jean stood next to him and looked at me with a face of disapproval. I knew what she was thinking too. She felt I'd never walk again and it was written all over her face. And she was angry that no one had told me yet.

Hope is a funny thing. If you hang on to it too long, it *can* hurt you.

Dr. Lucas checked out the long incision on my back and asked if I'd had a shower yet.

"No," I told him. "Can I? I would love one."

"Oh sure," he said while looking up to Jean.

"I'll put it in his order for you to sign, doctor," Jean said, then winked at me as if to say, "good for you." Jean was my protector. Jean was the nurse that hummed that soothing hum when I most needed it. Jean was my angel.

Doctor Lucas shook his fist in the air as he parted for the door. "Be a fighter!" he said. "Be a fighter!"

"Thank you so much for coming!" I said. "And I will!"

Jean tidied up the room and began to speak without looking up. I knew it was coming. The look on her face was one of pent up anger.

"What exactly are they telling you, Bobby?"

I tilted my head to one side in a thoughtful gesture. "About what?" I asked. I knew what she meant and she knew it.

"About your prognosis," she said.

After a short pause, I spoke. "They say they just don't know."

She didn't say another word. She already said it all.

47

THE TIME WAS finally here. I was going to get a shower. My body craved, longed for, yearned, and screamed for a shower. Two nurses showed up right at 8:00 a.m., with bath towels and a big bottle of pink body wash in hand.

Elsa and Denise dropped me into a wheelchair, rolled me into the bathroom and parked me alongside an ugly old shower chair. It was made of discolored plastic and stood on rusty metal legs. It was actually a commode and used for dual purposes. I couldn't help but think how many people used it before me. The thought of that grossed me out, so I tried not to think about it.

From there, they undressed me, slid my chilly body onto the unsanitary looking seat and dragged the wheel-less chair backwards across the outdated bathroom floor, scuffing and scraping the floor along the way. And without a footplate, my lifeless feet towed behind us, dragging across the wet tiles as we went. That really bugged me too.

I struggled to keep myself from falling out; no way was I touching that nasty old floor with a body part that had feeling. The dead parts I didn't care as much about. I wonder why? Maybe I was discarding my lower half and treating it like a foreign object that didn't belong.

We reached the shower stall and tried to figure out what to do next. The yucky smell of disinfectant cleared my nostrils with a sting-ing zing, and a cold draft swirled around my upper body like a dust devil.

Elsa and Denise positioned my chair over the dirty floor drain and under the shower spigot, which was mounted behind me on a half-brick, half-tiled wall. The call button also hung on the stained tile, with a waterlogged and soap scum slimed pull-rope dangling from it.

"The shelf is right here," Elsa said. "It's to hold your body soap, and I'll be back to check on you in a few. Right is hot and left is cold. Oh, and the call button is right behind you, I'll put the pull-cord down here on the armrest, okay? Pull it if you need help."

"I will, thank you, Elsa," I said with a shiver.

Until the water heated up, turning the faucet handle up and to the right still dumped cold water on me with nowhere to run. I shut it down quickly and shivered uncontrollably.

I tried to let the water trickle out a little bit, in order to let the cold water out of the pipe before landing on me again. But there was no "little bit." The cold water hit me and took my breath away, I just had to take it, but it made me work quickly and methodically without thinking about falling.

After a minute or two, the temperature slowly began to rise and the warmer water reached me and began to calm me and sooth my soul. Just warm and still not hot, it was a sense of tranquility—and it felt good. Really good.

But as I slowed down my movements, I noticed a "pins and needles," tingling sensation coming from my left foot, yet the warm water rained down on my right.

My wires must be crossed, I thought. And when I pushed the washcloth down on my right thigh, I felt tingling on my left foot.

I lathered up my face, neck, and chest with the cheap, latherless liquid soap, and with my eyes shut tight, I leaned forward a bit to reach for my legs. I guess I didn't remember my lack of trunk muscles because I just kept going, falling forward right out of the chair until I hit the hard tile floor with a quiet wallop!

"Shit," I moaned, as I looked over my knees and shins, expecting to see bumps and bruises all over. Just a little blood leaked from one knee though and quickly melted into the water like a snowflake landing in a cup of hot coffee.

The water felt colder down on the floor, and the breeze I created quickly got me shivering again.

As I rested the palm of my hand on the icy tile floor, I was grossed out again from the loose and gritty texture of it. It was thickly wet with slime and hair, and the rusty floor drain had scum particles caught in its semi-plugged holes. All I could picture was a stream of warm pee, flowing sporadically to the drain by a dirty patient with a dirty disease.

Reaching for the call button cord was impossible, it was too high! It was laying on the seat's armrest which was way too high and out of my reach!

Here I go again. Why don't they make the cord longer so it reaches the floor? Isn't that when you might need it? When you're on the floor?

I just sat there, naked and in total repulsion, while the not so warm water poured over my face and lowered head. And as that foul bathroom floor touched my germ phobic skin, it brought back a memory of another foul floor, back when I could walk....

48

I WAS IN BOXBORO, Massachusetts, attending a Polaris Snowmobile Dealer Show with my two sales people. The evening began with a public showing of the new models of snowmobiles.

As we waited for the doors to open, my sales rep introduced me to a new dealer from Connecticut. He was the salesman and unfortunately my new competition.

The tall businessman had meticulous fingernails, with a gigantic college ring weighing heavily on one of his pale and thin fingers. With his white buttoned-down shirt and black, creased dress pants, he looked nothing like a snowmobile dealer, and I knew that snowmobilers wouldn't appreciate his Wall Street style. My customers wanted to deal with guys who knew what it was like to skin your knuckles on an engine head, while changing a spark plug on the side of an ungroomed snowmobile trail.

"I'm Alex," he said proudly. "And it is a pleasure to meet you, Robert."

"Hey, Alex," I replied. "How're you doin?"

He asked if I had ever met his boss, Donald Nickers, the principal owner of Nickers Power Sports.

I told him that although I had never met him, I had heard his name plenty, as we now competed for the same customers on the Rhode Island/Connecticut border.

I didn't let on, but Don Nickers was known to be a conceited blowhard, with a ton of money and a giant ego. I had been a dealer for 14 years and had seen guys like him come and go.

"I know Mr. Nickers is looking forward to meeting you here at the show," he said. "He has heard a lot about you as well, Robert. You sell a substantial amount of units, and some of them in our Windom County market area as well."

"With all due respect," I responded. "We consider Windom County to be our market territory. And, yes, we do alright."

He looked up to the ceiling and laughed a goofy laugh. "I'll be happy to make the introduction when Donald arrives soon," he said.

"I look forward to it," I said. *Asswipe*, I thought.

I decided to hit the men's room while I still had the chance, so I excused myself and off I went. Two glasses of cranberry juice weighed heavily on my bladder and the long walk to the lobby stimulated things even worse, so I picked up the pace.

After pushing the bathroom door open with my elbow and avoiding the door handle, I took a whiff as I entered the public restroom with my usual trepidation. My shoes stuck to the floor just a little but enough for me to notice. The urinals were unoccupied and I was glad, but as I approached the porcelain statues, I sensed someone in the stalls behind me.

I had to go worse than I thought.

As I faced the wall and did my thing, I began to hear kind of a struggling, low vocal sound, coming from one of the stalls behind me. Then, bumping and banging clamor began to erupt against the inner metal stall walls, along with more muffled and grunt-like vocal noises.

I realized that I hadn't made any sound when I entered the men's room, so I probably wasn't detected yet.

It was tricky, but I managed to look back over my left shoulder, (without spilling a drop) to check out the scuffle and to see who was making all the noise.

I had a clear view of the opening under the first stall, the one closest to me. As I examined it, I was able to see a pair of dress shoes planted squarely on the floor, and facing forward, towards the door.

Standing in those black leather shoes, was someone with dark hairy legs with a pair of unzipped dress-slacks dropped down around his ankles.

Then, facing the dress shoes, just inches away, stood a pair of white, Nike sneakers with the black checkmark on the side. And a pair of straight-legged blue jeans were dropped around those sneakers as well, with a knapsack or backpack lying beside them.

"What the hell," I whispered to myself while my face heated instantly.

Is there a kid in that stall too? I thought, with total disgust.

I stood at that urinal, stared at the tile wall just a foot away from my face and replayed the images that I just saw.

Everything happened so fast as my mind and heart began to race! The bumping of the inner stall walls continued. *Bang! Bump! Bang!!!*

Within seconds, I devised a plan to break down the metal door and save that kid inside.

It had been a while since I used my karate, I thought. *I'm out of shape! And these dress shoes that I'm wearing, will they give me the traction I need to throw a sidekick to that door without slipping on this tile floor? I doubt it.*

I pushed my bladder down harder to speed things up, but there seemed to be no end to the stream!

Will the stall door break open from just one kick? I wondered. *And will it hit the kid in the back when it swings open?* I pushed a little harder. *Man, how much did I drink?*

More movement and grumbling swirled from inside that stall, so I nervously backed away from the porcelain, dripping pee droplets over the front of my khaki-colored Dockers, and charged the stall in a fury, without fully tucking things back in.

As I neared the chrome-hinged stall-door, a defensive instinct dropped me to the floor for a quick peak under the stall, also to better assess their position before kicking it in. But when my right hand and knee sensed contact with the soggy floor, my fingers quickly retreated to form a fist, in an attempt to keep just my knuckles in touch with the germ-ridden floor tiles.

From that level, I could see the dried stains and smell the god-awful stench that was embedded in the tile grout of the public latrine. I then became even more angry at the predator for making my pant leg absorb a wet and putrid stain on my knee—but mostly for abusing whoever he was abusing in there.

Just as I peaked in and under the door of the stall, it flew open with a bang, just missing my face by inches!

And there, gazing down at me, as I stared up at him, stood a startled man, wearing dress pants and clutching Nike sneakers and straight-legged blue jeans against his stomach and unbuttoned shirt. His backpack hung open from his arm, ready to receive the change of clothing.

He was the only one in the stall!

He..., was the only one in the stall! The guy was changing out of his casuals and into his dress clothes!

"I can explain this!" I announced. "This is not what you think!" I announced again, as I pitifully looked up at him from the dirty floor.

"It's not?" he blurted back at me, pushing the door open the rest of the way.

"I thought a kid was getting molested in there!" I said, as he plowed right through me, tipping me over onto my other side, forcing my other knee and hand to make contact with the wet and disgusting floor.

"Whatever," he said, with his back to me, as he headed for the exit door.

"I can explain this if you'll listen to me!" I hollered. "I thought someone was being molested in there! I saw two pairs of shoes with pants and belts, and I heard grunting and the sneakers and stuff, it just sounded like, it sounded like, do you believe what I'm saying?"

He was gone.

Funny, he didn't wash his hands, I thought.

Later on, back at the show, I stood amongst the dealers with my water stained khakis, hands raw from scrubbing until I couldn't scrub any more, and a big pee spot for everyone to see. Khakis show pee spots like a neon sign in the middle of a pitch-black desert.

Alex "tight-ass" tapped me on the shoulder. As I turned, he spoke in an annoying and announcing tone.

"Hey Robert, this is Donald Nickers, of Nickers Motor Sports," he said, and then turned to his boss who was standing over his shoulder. "And Donald, I'd like you to meet Robert, the dealer from Rhode Island."

As my eyes locked onto his, in a duel of surprise and disdain, his brows pursed below his over-tanned forehead, while he answered in a stuffy and unfriendly tone.

"Yes," he muttered. "I think we've already met." ....

———————

STILL LYING COLD AND NAKED on the shower stall floor, I watched as the water swirled unevenly down the cloggy drain, picking and choosing different holes to drop into while it bounced off the ones it couldn't.

I wondered how I was going to get back up onto the shower chair. I still couldn't reach the call button cord, nor could I drag myself over to the bathroom door to call for help. I was way too weak.

Much colder than before, the water ricocheted wildly off the seat and continued to rain down on my scalp—splashing me in my face and forcing my eyelids to flicker rapidly with each assault. Just inches from my face, I stared at the floor drain through the water droplets and thought about killing myself again. *Is this how it's going to be? Like this?*

I tried to shift myself away from the rusty drain, but was stopped by the bone-crunching sound my butt made as it pressed against the floor. Due to the atrophy of my glute muscles, it was bone against tile with no cushion in between.

I just lay there on that bathroom floor and stared at the drain...

Elsa appeared above me, and that's when I noticed that the water had long turned cold. I didn't care anymore.

"What are you doing down there?" Elsa hollered, over the hum of the running water. She then hopped right in the semi-enclosure, getting her smock and pants soaking wet, yet she never flinched.

"Oh, Bobby, what are you doing on the floor? And this water is freezing! Why didn't you call me?"

"I couldn't," I said in a soft voice.

She reached out for the pull-cord that was high above me and summoned the nurses' station. "I need help in here right away!" she yelled out, drenched from head to toe. "Room 450, stat!"

As I waited with nowhere to go, I thought about that day in Boxboro—and my previous life.

I went from throwing sidekicks, to this, I thought, as I sat on that skeevy floor. Naked, vulnerable and without hope.

49

THEY ORDERED A round of x-rays of my hips and legs because they said they looked a little swollen from the fall. No bruising though. I never did bruise very easily.

The activity did increase my back and nerve pain quite a bit, enough for me to complain to Shirley about it when the second shift arrived. I wanted to tell her about the girl I met too.

The smell of processed foods filled the halls and drifted into my room without invitation. My supper was coming but I couldn't care less.

Shirley sat at the edge of my bed with both feet planted firmly on the floor and her chiseled chin held high. She was a classy lady.

"Shirley, today is my son Derek's birthday, and it hurts that I'm in this place. Tonight, we're going to have his party in the patient's gym," I sighed. "And I'm sick over it. I love Derek, more than life itself, Shirley, and I miss being with him the way it used to be. I miss him so much."

Tears ran down both my cheeks. I tried to hide it but couldn't so I looked away instead.

"I know it's hard, Bobby. I can't imagine what you're going through. But I do know this. You made a new friend, Tina? You need her and she needs you. Do you understand?"

"You know that we met? How?" I asked.

"I know. We all know. We have been expecting it. You need each other to get through this. And, if you both draw strength from each other, you'll both beat this. Maybe you *will* have to live like this for the rest of your life, maybe you *won't* walk again, but you can still live with whatever life you're left with."

Ahhh... There it was. My stomach filled with butterflies, and I felt queasy and nauseous all at once.

It was the first time anyone had ever said it. It was the first time ever! No one was supposed to say that I might not walk again. It had been so long, so long since the truth was spoken, and it hurt. It hurt a lot. My defenses went up to repel the truth.

Shirley had hurt me without knowing it, and I was embarrassed that her words could do that to me so easily.

Hearing what I already knew was extremely painful, yet at the same time, a sense of relief overcame me with a euphoric sensation. I can't explain it; I didn't like what she said, but I was glad that she had said it.

"So, Shirley, you don't think I'll ever get return of any sensations?" It scared me so much to even say those words. I was so afraid of her answer. It was like, if she said it, it might come true.

"It's not for me to say," she answered. "I just know that life is too short to wait and see."

I stared down at my hospital I.D. bracelet. I had worn it so long it was a part of me. Derek and Lauren had each taped something personal of theirs to it, tiny swatches from their favorite play shirts to remember them by and to have them always close to me. Derek's was from his hockey jersey and Lauren's was from her soccer's. I fiddled with them while we spoke.

I knew it was against hospital policy for Shirley to be saying that stuff to me, and that made it more meaningful. She put *me* before her job and I will never forget that.

That night, I think I took my first steps toward my way to recovery.

50

TINA SLAMMED INTO my bed again and sent me about six inches into the air. Bump! I awoke trembling uncontrollably but did not want her to see. So, I scratched and stretched, and did everything imaginable to try to cover up the tremors.

I first noticed those tremors when Lauren was stringing Christmas cards and hanging them from wall to wall behind my bed.

I remembered how Debbie stood on a chair and handed Lauren my med-chart clipboard to use as a hammer and drive in the purple pushpins.

She accidentally dropped the clipboard and it landed flat on the floor with a tremendous whack! Surprised by the sudden noise, my legs began vibrating with electric-like pulses, which were so intense, it reminded me of being shocked by a live wall outlet.

The electrical shocks doubled me over in a fetal position and left me squeezing my thighs while begging them to stop. It felt as though high voltage was shooting down my legs, from my hips to the tips of my toes and then back again, causing my abdomen muscles to go into continuous convulsive-like spasms. All from an unexpected noise!

The nurses were summoned that day and took notes on it all as the condition slowly subsided. The next day, Dr. Toms visited me and tried to explain what was happening to me.

"Holy cows, Doc! It was like the sudden noise scared the heck out of my legs! Like they had a mind of their own!"

"That is exactly what happened, Bobby. We all have involuntary reactions that we are born with. Did you ever see a baby that was startled or about to fall? They instinctively throw up their hands with their fingers spread out widely. They're protecting themselves from harm. It's an involuntary movement, voluntarily controlled by the nervous system. Your nervous system is working on instinct."

"Okay, I get that, but why the electrocutions?"

"Your nervous system has been damaged. You've got a lot going on in there."

"Yeah, my wires are crossed, I do know that."

"Why do you say that?"

"Because, when I pull on my right ring finger, I feel it on the left one. And if someone squeezes my left hand, I get a far away feeling in my right. Stuff like that."

"Well, just be thankful you're still here with us," she said.

I didn't answer then and now I wished that I did. I wished that I had addressed everything I was feeling a lot earlier. Shirley taught me that.

Tina had a coffee for me. She added two of her little containers of cream while I dealt with my shocked legs, undetected.

"Holy crap, Tina, you get up so early. What did you have to do this early, milk the chickens?"

"Ha ha. Just get up and smell the coffee, wazy ass. Hurry up, cause I need you to take me outside for a cigarette. We have to sneak off the unit."

"Who, me?" I asked.

"Yes, you. You are stronger now, Bobby. I saw you wheel down the corridor yesterday. You can do it."

This girl makes me laugh, I thought. *She is so wacky, but I love her. She's full of life.*

"Come on wazy ass, I can't sneak out alone. I need your help. This hand won't work well enough to wheel my chair, so I need you to help me. Come on let's go, I'm dying for a butt!"

"I can't now because I have therapy, but after the first shift goes home, I'll sneak you out. The second shift is more relaxed. Okay?"

She didn't want to but gave in and returned at the end of the day, around 4:30, just before dark. She flew into my room, speaking to me even before she got through the door.

"Let's go, wazy ass!"

"You know, Tina, smoking is gonna stunt your growth."

"Mind your business and help me get out," she said, as she bumped my bed with a smirk. "Now, get your coat and let's go."

"What coat?" I laughed.

"I know, I don't have one either," she laughed. "Well, zip up your johnny," she snickered.

We headed down the corridor toward the nurses' station, giggling like two little kids on Christmas morning. Picking up speed, we coasted past the countertop with our heads ducked low, just keeping below it. Tina couldn't keep up so I pulled over to let her catch up.

"You're all over the road, Tina," I laughed in a whisper. "Can't you drive straight?"

"No, I can't," she chuckled, smashing into me, never touching her brakes.

"Ouch!" I complained, shaking off the pain she caused from pinching my fingers between our wheels.

"Oh, stop being a baby and just go," she giggled.

"Yeah, yeah, yeah," I told her, while looking over my chair frame for a way to tow her. "I think I got it. Hook your foot under the back of my wheelchair, Tina. Hook it under this frame bar. We'll be like a train. I'll tow you and you can be the caboose. Now, let me do the pulling and you just steer."

Because of the brace on her leg and foot, her shoe fit and locked stiffly under my wheelchair's rear crossbar, so I leaned forward and strained ahead, first veering way to the side, then eventually straightening out as I got the hang of it.

"How you doing back there?" I yelled out.

"You are crazy," she giggled.

"Want to go faster?"

"Go ahead," she laughed, nervously.

"Hold on then!"

I really put my back into it and yet the pain didn't faze me. The slight wind we created exhilarated me! It felt so good to be alive again!

Voices sounded from around the upcoming corner, so I picked up the pace again and sped past the intersection, glancing down the right hallway as we flew by with our heads ducked low.

A fleeting image of Mary-Lynn and Michelle came and went. Mary-Lynn was Tina's speech therapist and the expression on her face as she looked up at us spelled nothing less than surprise.

"Uh, oh! We got caught!" Tina yelled out.

"Do you want to go back?"

"Hell no, escaping is a blast. Keep going," she nudged me ahead, "keep going!"

The elevator was in full view with its eggshell chipped door and its control buttons looking too high to reach. The intersecting corridors looked so confusing too, and I feared that I might not find my way back. We had both arrived by rescue and came up by the service elevator. It was the first time either of us saw the hospital's layout. But on we went.

We skidded a little sideways as we reached the door. Tina hit the down arrow button and the door opened immediately, surprising us by exposing the tiny elevator car inside.

"Are we both going to fit in there, Bobby?"

"Maybe if we go in and turn sideways. You go first."

"Jesus, don't let the door close on me," she said.

"I'll hold it open, go ahead in," I motioned the same with my head.

"I'm in, hurry up and get in here, you, before someone spots us," she whispered with more giggles.

"Okay, Tina, I'm in. Push the close door button, come on, hurry up."

"I can't reach it! Plus, you're not all the way in!"

"Well move in some more, you nut," I chuckled and added, "How can I get in with you sticking out this far?"

"Shut the hell up, you pecker head, I'm trying!" she scolded with a smirk.

"Nice talk, typical sailor talk," I said, as I pushed in harder and against her left wheel and tire.

"I'm in the Army, not the Navy…, pecker head."

"Whatever!" I announced, looking up.

"Shhh! Bobby, I hear someone coming. Hurry up and get in. Move your arm so I can reach the door button. Okay, I got it!" she grunted.

The half doors closed seamlessly together, making a tight seal and providing quiet in the small elevator car. It was funny to hear ourselves breathing after all that noise.

"May I help you!" a woman's voice suddenly asked, from the intercom above us on the button panel somewhere. She sounded much like a telephone operator's monotone voice from an old AT&T pay phone.

"Shhh!" I laughed, while snorting out my nose. "Tina! You must have hit the help button, too! Unbelievable," I whispered.

Tina covered her open mouth with her unopened hand. "Oops… Sorry!" she whispered back, looking up at me with those dark puppy-like eyes.

"May I help you!" the nasally voice from the intercom demanded again.

"Shit!" Tina replied without thinking. "I mean, no thank you!" she followed up, while looking up at the ceiling to the invisible authority, with a squint.

"Oh jeez, we're busted," I said softly. "I can hear her calling security on us right now."

"Should we go back, Bobby?"

"No way!" I said. "Hit the button for the lobby. Hurry up, push it."

Slowly the elevator began to move. While holding on to our wheels, we looked at each other and began to giggle again. We were having a ball.

The elevator slowed and we slid sideways when we landed, making us both dizzy from the lack of motion we were used to.

The doors opened to the hustle and bustle of the busy lobby—with visitors, doctors and nurses walking briskly by, as if they all had somewhere important to go.

Before the doors closed on us, we jockeyed and bumped our way out of the elevator and headed up the long concrete ramp toward the main entrance of the hospital. Because of the dead weight towing behind me, it was really hard to pull Tina up the steep incline, so she tried to help pedal her wheel with her one good arm, but ended up turning us aimlessly sideways instead.

"Just hold on Tina, let me do it. Make sure your foot is hooked well under the back of my chair..., just hold on." I leaned forward and gave it all I had up the steep incline.

Unaware that we were escaping without permission, a young nurse that was coming from the other direction stopped us halfway up to offer a helping hand.

Adding to our small train, she got behind Tina and pushed while I pulled, and with spectators rooting us on with smiling eyes, she got us up and over the top of the ramp with a synchronized "yoo-hoo!" from all three.

"Thank you!" hollered Tina, becoming the caboose again.

"Yes!" I said without stopping. "Thanks for the push!"

We passed through the electric eye that tripped open the exit doors in the lobby, exposing us to the chilled air of the lifeless winter eve.

"Wow, can you smell that fresh air, Tina? It smells sweet, and it tickles my chest if I take it in too fast!" I stopped wheeling, parked us outside the entrance for a moment and breathed it in deeply. "Mmm, it's been a long time," I said with savor. "It's been so long."

"Bobby, over there, bring me over there, that's the smoking area. Bring me by the benches and the ashtray!"

Dressed in just sweatpants and johnnies, neither one of us seemed to be bothered by the 40-degree air temperature. We were just happy to be out.

"Okay," Tina said, "Now you have to get me a cigarette."

I stared at her in disbelief. "Are you kidding? You don't have any cigarettes? Where am I going to get you a cigarette?"

"Bum one from somebody for me," she said, through sparkly and smiling eyes.

"Are you alright? Bum one from somebody?"

"Come on, Bobby, please? You have to ask someone for me, they'll never understand me if I ask! I'll stutter all the way through! Please? Hurry up, before they come looking for us."

Mumbling under my breath, two teenagers walked past us when one of them glanced over at me just in time. I motioned to him by lifting my head and then hollered out my request. It was way too easy. I got her a butt on the first try.

"Thank you!" said Tina, stuttering a bit, but not too bad, as they threw me one while they walked past.

"It's not my brand but it'll do," she said.

"Well, I hope you enjoy it, Tina."

"Okay, Bobby, now you have to bum a light for me."

"You're kidding me, right?" I forced one eyebrow up and the other one down. "You're driving me crazy, girl. You couldn't tell me you didn't have a lighter when I asked them for your cigarette?"

"I didn't think of it," she said with that devilish smile.

"Mmm," I shook my head from side to side, and it should have aggravated me, but it didn't. I got a kick out of her, and I must have asked six or seven passersby before I found her a light. But it was good to see her looking so happy, glancing up at the stars and massaging that cigarette like it was her last.

We sat out in that sweet—bitter air for almost an hour, sharing feelings and well-kept secrets. And as we made our way back to the unit, we brought back with us something special. Something that would tie us together until the day we die.

I think every nurse, therapist and patient on that unit heard of our getaway that night. The nurses smirked at us because some thought the two of us had something going on, but it wasn't like that. We shared something that no one else could know, and I felt blessed to have found her, as my lifelong friend.

I totally forgot about the poinsettia plant that night.

51

THE NEXT MORNING, Michelle came in to ask me about my primary goal, meaning, the one thing I wanted to accomplish during my stay in rehabilitation therapy. After some careful thought, I gave her my wish.

"I'd like to know about leg braces. Am I a candidate for braces? How do they work? Could *I* ever walk with them?"

Michelle tilted her head to the side and pondered on my question. "Leg braces are good mostly for standing. They lock your knees so they don't bend, then you throw your hips forward so you can balance yourself in a standing position. Not many can walk with them though. Most cannot. It depends on what you're left with and your ability to control certain hip muscles. If you can thrust a leg forward using your hips, you may be able to take a step with them. But, this is done with either a walker or Canadian crutches. Those crutches band around your wrists rather than under your arms. They are hard to use and require great upper body strength to do, like a body builder. Both methods expend a huge amount of energy, exhaustive energy. If that is what you want, then I will arrange for an orthopedic tech to come in and measure you for a pair. But we have a lot of work to do before you even think of strapping braces on. You need to have super human upper body strength and that requires weight lifting, along with intense physical exercise to build greater muscle mass. Are you up for it?"

I imagined myself wearing leg braces, hidden beneath my jeans, and walking normally, unassisted, because I would be the one that would not have to use a walker or even crutches. I'd be the one to learn how to walk on my own. I'd be the one.

"Yes, I'm up for it! When can we start?"

"Well, you need to start eating better and putting on some weight along with muscle mass. I can put together a program for the staff to follow, along with your regular daily therapy. We can start on Monday," she said.

"Thank you, Michelle. This means a lot to me. Even if I can just stand for a minute without taking a step, I would like to try it. Now I have something to look forward to. Thank you so much. Thank you."

As Michelle left the room, I glanced over to my right at the poinsettia. It looked so old and withered. The red leaves weren't red anymore and the brown tips curled upward to a crusty point. *I wonder if the dried-up leaves could still ferment now. I don't think they would. I don't think they could.*

Bang! My bed shook with a quake and I never saw her coming! "Hey wazy ass, you gonna stay in bed all day? I have a Nerf football, see?"

Tina was holding it up with her opened hand and balanced it with her closed one. "Let's go play catch in the gym while there's no one in there to stop us, before therapy starts. Then later you can take me outside for a cigarette. Come on!"

Yeah, I thought. *Those brown leaves are way too dry now.*

52

DAYS PASSED AND Tina and I became inseparable. We spent every spare moment together, pushing ourselves through the exercises and training. Debbie loved her as much as I did and our families became friends. Her spirit inspired me to go on.

53

TINA WENT HOME unexpectedly today...most of the patients did so, because of Christmas. I was devastated.

54

Tom took me to the gym this morning because the rest of the staff left early for Christmas. He and Carl transferred me up onto the mat and laid me in my usual position, flat on my back.

A group of nuns from St. Theresa's Church were ushered in to sing Christmas carols to the few remaining patients on the unit. There were about four patents there, all over seventy. I missed Tina so bad but kept it to myself. I was back to keeping *everything* to myself.

Listening to the nuns just a few feet away, I enjoyed their angelic voices and jingling bells while Tom worked on range of motion to both my legs.

Just when I was thinking that the sisters sounded very good for nonprofessionals, I thought I felt something! I thought I felt some feeling down at my left leg!

With my back to the mat and my eyes facing the ceiling, I remained perfectly still, and with an eager mind, I focused on that spot. *There it is again!*

It was a far away, tingly, vibrating feeling—somewhere down by my left foot.

"Tom!" I shouted, with my head still flat on the mat pillow. "Did you just touch my left leg? Way, down..., down below, did you touch it?"

Just then, the singers ended their song, so I could hear Tom clearly, as he shouted back.

"I was squeezing your right ankle, Bobby, why?"

"Holy shit! I screamed. I felt that! Holy shit Tom, I did! I really did! Shit! I felt that! Shit! Shit! Shit! Holy Shit! After a deafening silence, I called the two nurses over that were standing by the door.

"Tom, do it again! Watch this everybody!" I concentrated on that area, and when I thought he was squeezing me down there, I yelled it out. "I feel it!" I hollered. "I feel it on my left foot! Is that where you're squeezing me, Tom?"

"I'm squeezing your other ankle!" he yelled back.

"I don't care; my wires are crossed. It's the first time I felt anyone touching me, even if it is the wrong ankle! Holy shit!"

The nuns were just standing there, quiet, staring at us.

Oh boy, I thought, too embarrassed to look at the sisters. *How many times did I yell the words, "Holy shit?"* I wondered.

I thought I'd better say something, so I yelled straight up to the ceiling without looking side to side. "I'm sorry everyone..., for yelling!"

What I really meant was, I was sorry for swearing in front of a bunch of nuns, but I was too embarrassed to say so. So, I pretended that I didn't realize I had sworn. *Boy, am I going to hell,* I said to myself. I lay back with both hands interlaced behind my head.

"Tom!" I hollered. "Can we do it again?"

Tom lowered his voice down as the nurses giggled. "We sure can, Bobby, only this time try not to swear in front of the nuns on Christmas Eve, okay?"

55

I TRIED TO MAKE the best of it today but I was lonely, and I was constantly thinking of my kids. I missed them so badly. But it was Christmas, so I tried to be thankful, thankful for having them.

I loved them both so much, that it hurt.

They were to arrive at noon, so I put on a good shirt and a nice pair of pants, well, the only ones I had in my room closet, and laced up my sneakers instead of those flimsy hospital slippers that I usually wore. I had learned how to dress and tie my shoes that week and wanted to show them what I could do.

All day long visitors came and went, bringing me loads of home-made goodies and chocolates...lots of chocolate.

I was so touched by the precious time everyone gave up to see me, and on Christmas day too. I knew what a pain it must have been to fit me in.

We opened Christmas presents in front of the poinsettia plant that Lauren had decorated with a few strands of tinsel. *How ironic,* I thought. *If they only knew.*

Derek brought a bridge table from home and set it up with some chairs in front of my bed. Captain Walden got to go home in time for Christmas, so I had no roommate but that made it easier to rearrange the room the way we wanted. I was happy that he got to go home but missed the company.

Mom asked if she could bring over a pan of lasagna for us when she visited that morning and instead brought enough food to feed the whole hospital. Derek had to make at least four trips to her car and carry up overfilled boxes of everything under the sun for our Christmas dinner in room 5450.

In tradition, Mom cooked Christmas dinner for the rest of the family at her house, so I told her not to come that morning because she had so much to do. But it was like talking to the wall. She, my father and Irene came to see me every single day since my accident, and on day 27 she was not about to miss that one.

The nurses that weren't lucky enough to get the day off popped in and out of my room all day long, tasting a different Italian specialty each time they stopped by.

It was a tough day for me, but nobody knew.

Mom left for home but returned at 8:00 p.m., after her company had left her house. Visiting hours did not pertain to patients on my unit; the nurses didn't worry about things like that. They were too busy caring for us.

"Mom, why did you come back, it's late, and you must be exhausted?" I knew she came back because it was Christmas.

"No, I'm fine. Jim is reading the paper in the car. We are going to go to the ten o'clock mass tonight. How are you feeling, Bobby?"

I knew she was fishing. Because it was Christmas, things must have bothered her more so and she must have figured that it bothered me as well.

"Mom, I'm fine," I answered her, with my eyes looking for a place to go.

Without planning, and maybe because it *was* Christmas, I blurted it out.

"Um, I have a question, Mom." My legs started to vibrate when they realized my inquest, so I grabbed my thighs and rubbed them down, as I continued with trepidation.

"Um, when I had that operation at Rhode Island hospital, when I had the accident, what did Dr. Lucas say to you? I mean, remember when I woke up in the middle of the night, after the operation I mean. Didn't you tell me that the operation was a success?"

I felt bad that I was putting her through this. I rubbed my legs faster.

"Did I misunderstand you, Mom?" I asked, my hands soaking wet.

She nodded nonstop, as if to say, "I knew this was coming and I have practiced this response for quite some time."

"Bobby," she stopped nodding and took a deep breath. "The day of your operation was very scary for us. We didn't know if you were going to live or die. Auntie Carol, Auntie Norma, Debbie, your father and your brother Ricky were all in the hospital waiting room. Dr. Lucas took some of us into a conference room, put up your x-rays, and tried to explain the procedure to attempt a reconstruction of your spine. We were so nervous Bobby, we couldn't think, so we relied on each other to remember all the details so we could talk about them later."

"Did he say *then* that I would or wouldn't be able to walk again, Mom?" She started nodding again. I hated doing what I was doing to her.

"Well, it was kind of understood, well at least it was on our end. We... we did ask that question, yes. But, we were also concerned about him saving your life. Yes, we did ask that question."

"And, what did he say?"

"He said he would know more when he got inside there to look. We can't remember exactly." Right then I knew that my family had talked about this and tried to figure out the confusion as well. I wanted to stop pressuring her but I needed to know. She started to continue. "We just can't...,"

"It's okay, Mom. It's okay. I just remember waking up after the operation and someone saying that the operation was a complete success. I took that as, well, that I would be able to walk again after rehab." I tried not to look down with any disappointment.

"I know, Bobby, I know you did." This time she was the one looking down.

"Bobby, I..." she lifted her eyes, showing me their changed shape and softer projection. "We cannot thank Dr. Lucas enough for what he did for us. When he came out of that operation room six hours or so later, he announced that the operation was a success and, Bobby, I am not sure we heard anything else he said after that. I know, Bobby, I know," she said softly. "We just didn't want you to lose hope."

"I won't, Mom. It's okay, I won't lose hope. You know, I think this bothers other people more than it bothers me.

"It's just that when I was told the operation was a success, I thought it meant that I would walk again. I believed it and hung onto that. It's not that bad. Thank you. You had better get going if you're going to make the ten o'clock mass."

We both pretended that everything was fine as she leaned over the bedrail to kiss me goodnight.

"Merry Christmas, Bobby, I love you."

"Merry Christmas, Mom, I love you too."

56

THEY SENT A shrink in to see me today. And I don't know who authorized it either. I didn't expect it.

The nerdy looking guy bounced in right at lunchtime and made my macaroni get cold. I was looking forward to the ziti that day too, although the meatballs were another story. They were always horrible.

"Hello Robert, I'm Dr. Doolyle!" he said, (or a name something like that) and with a tone that was a little too cheerful, I thought. And way too loud. "How was your Christmas, Buddy!"

Why does he have to yell when he talks? I asked myself. *Plus, that name of his, Dr. Doolyle?* As he began to speak, all I kept picturing was Dr. Doolittle and his "Push-me Pull-you llama."

He slid a chair over to my bedside, bumping the footboard on the way over, oblivious to doing it.

"I hear you need to talk to me, Robert!"

He spoke just like Mr. Rogers from that children's program. You know, that condescending tone that drives you up a wall, when they pronounce every single syllable as if they were talking to a kinder-gartener? I got caught staring in disbelief when he repeated himself.

"I hear you need to talk to me!" he said.

"Um, no?" I said in a sarcastic tone and wanted to scream it back to him at the same volume level but didn't.

"Well, they sent for me to meet with you. Surely, you asked to speak to someone in my capacity. They said that you are seeing people that aren't there?"

"Who's they?" I asked. I did not like this guy one bit, nor did I like the way he enunciated his every word to me.

"Hmm, I'm not sure who exactly requested my services, but your doctor wrote the order." He skidded his chair in a little closer and scanned my legs that were just bumps under the white hospital sheet. "So, what happened to you, Rob?"

I let more than the average amount of time go by before I answered. "I fell out of a tree."

"Hmm..., tough break," he said. "Where and when do you see people that aren't there?"

I didn't like these questions or the way they were asked. I answered him.

"I saw people off to the sides of me sometimes. Out of the corners of my eyes, I guess."

"Do you see people in the room with us right now, Rob?" he said, slowly, as if talking to a child.

"What? No!" I snapped back. "It's not like that. That was like 35 days ago! I'm not crazy. It was the medication or fatigue or something! No, I don't see people now!" I said, in a mimicking way. "I'm fine and thank you but I don't need a psychiatrist. I'm all set."

I reached for a forkful of soggy macaroni and filled my mouth up. And I think he got the hint because he sprang up and reached into his jacket pocket.

"Okeydokey, Rob, I'll leave you my card, so don't be a stranger now! Here you go! And stay out of the hot sun!" He hollered more things on his way out, but I'd already tuned him out.

"Thank you," I answered.

As I chewed on my cold ziti, I whispered under my breath. "Rob, I'll give you Rob...asswipe."

57

DAY THIRTY-SOMETHING. IT was fifteen minutes before the Y2K, New Year's Eve, new millennium scare. The world's computers along with North America's electrical grid were predicted to shut down and begin the countdown to total world chaos. The hospital had been testing its generators all week in anticipation of the dire apocalypse. The first test showed that they didn't work correctly.

I sat by the television in the Rehab Unit's kitchen and worried about my family.

Hospital janitors were called in that night and forced to work overtime, in case of a power outage on the unit. Armed with a flashlight in hand, each floor had assigned one janitor to stand guard over it. Our guard, armed with *his* flashlight watched for the Times Square ball to drop and ate leftovers that visitors had left behind.

As he and I made small talk, I kept thinking of Derek and Lauren and how they needed their dad home with them.

A nurse from another unit came flying into the Rehab Unit's kitchen and began nervously ransacking the silverware drawer. She held a corked champagne bottle and a stack of plastic cups under her arm.

"Do you guys know if there is a corkscrew in here?" she hollered without looking up at us.

"I'm sorry, I don't. Would you like me to see if the nurses have one at their station?" I asked.

"There is no time!" she answered with a shaky voice, while rattling through the forks and knives. "I have to get back right away! We have a patient on the third floor that may not make it. He wants to see and toast the new century before he dies. It is important to him! Here's one! I'm gonna take it with me and bring it back later, okay?"

She left the drawer open and skidded around the corner as she sped past us on the slippery floor. She ran down that corridor so fast, I thought for sure she would collide with someone.

The ball dropped and the new millennium began without incident, so the janitor went home with his flashlight. As I wheeled back to bed, I paused to the sound of the open intercom, hissing and crackling before it began its announcement.

"Attention, attention!" the voice over the loud speaker warned. "Code blue! Respiratory to third floor, room 3460, stat! Code blue! Respiratory to room 3460, stat!

As I positioned the transfer board to scoot across and into my bed, I prayed that whoever it was, had made it in time and got to see the new century. Then I prayed for their soul.

58

THE NEXT MORNING, New Year's Day, Mike had me wheel to the gym and into the big room, where the rectangular floor mats lined a lot of the floor. He unbuckled my seatbelt, asked me to face one of the floor mats, and walked out, leaving me quietly sitting alone in the safety of my wheelchair.

Thinking he was going to tip me back and teach me to do a wheelie or something, I grabbed the wheel's hand rims and held on tight, but instead, he snuck up behind me and pushed the back of my chair forward, rough and fast, spilling me out of it, face first and onto the floor with a wallop!

Mike then jerked the chair forward and then pulled it back, as if he was dumping a wheelbarrow full of dirt and had to shake out every last drop. He held on to the chair handles as I flew ahead with my legs and feet going in all different directions!

I landed hard. You would think that the floor mats would be a little giving, but it was like hitting bare pavement and rocked the fillings in my teeth!

"Now, get back up into your chair," Mike ordered, with a puffed-up chest and the hint of enjoyment.

I couldn't talk just yet. I was still dizzy from the sudden shock. I couldn't see my legs either, but I did spot them going the wrong way on the way down and was worried that I looked like Gumby to the spectators I had now drawn.

"Mike, how am I going to do that?" I asked, with quite a pissy tone.

"Not my prob, Bob. What would you do if you were out with your friends and you fell out of your chair? Would you just lay there forever?"

"Um, no Mike..., I'd ask them to pick me up and put me back in."

"That's funny, Bobby. Real funny," Mike said, standing with his arms crossed and legs spread wide.

"Mike, my pants are down in the rear and everyone is looking at my bare ass. And I'm pretty embarrassed right now. Do you want to get me up now and...," I stopped talking in midstream because as I was speaking to him, he was mimicking playing a violin to me, slowly, with long bow strokes. I got the sentiment. He was pretending to play the blues while I cried them.

"Mike, get me up please. I don't like being down here. Plus, you hurt my back when you pushed me out like that."

"Okay, Bobby, but you can't leave rehab until you're able to get back into your wheelchair on your own."

"Yeah, well, not today," I said.

Every day after that, Mike dumped me out of my chair and onto the floor. He taught me a way to get back in, but I just didn't have the strength to achieve it yet.

Each time I got close to pulling myself back up into the wheelchair, he taunted me miserably, always just before I fell back down to where I started. And, if I were dumb enough to complain, he'd play that stupid invisible violin again. It would get me so mad, that I would almost find the strength to climb all the way into that chair. Almost.

59

Day Forty-Three
January 10

"HAPPY BIRTHDAY, WAZY ass!" Bump! I opened one eye to see Tina, sitting in her wheelchair at the edge of my bed! I don't know if my family called her to come and visit me or she came back to the hospital on her own. All I know is I was happy to see her. We talked for an hour but it seemed like just minutes, then she had to go. I really missed her.

60

I WENT TO THE gym with lots on my mind that morning. Michelle and Carl strapped the try-out braces on my legs and wheeled me between and under the gym's parallel bars. My mom came early that day to watch me stand and walk. I couldn't wait.

They locked my knees and created two stiff limbs out of my limp legs. I liked it.

"Okay, Bobby," Michelle said. Grab on to the bars, pull yourself forward and up out of your wheelchair. Carl will keep your heels dug into the floor. Ready? Pull up when you're ready."

I pulled on the bars and raised my butt about two inches off my seat, only to quickly fall back on it. Looking over at my mom, I grabbed the parallel bars again and tried to pull myself up again; this time Michelle put her hand under my butt for the extra lift. My arms were getting bigger from the daily weight lifting but nowhere enough to manage the job without help. Sweat and trembles showed just how exhausting the seemingly easy task was.

As Michelle pushed me up to a three-quarter stance, Carl grabbed my waistband and pulled me up the rest of the way. I was standing. I was swaying and shaking but I was standing! What a feeling it was to be eye level with Michelle for that brief moment before my burning arm muscles gave way and dropped me back against and into my depressing wheelchair again. I immediately tried to lift myself up again to get far away from the despair but couldn't. I tried again and again. I failed. I tried two or three more times but couldn't do it. It reminded me of being on the forest floor that day, trying to get up but falling helplessly back to where I began.

More determined than before, I grabbed those bars and gave it all I had. Overheated and red faced, I turned my head just in time to lock onto my mom's tearful eyes. That broke my concentration and I finally gave up and plopped back down into my wheelchair.

"It's not what you expected is it!" Dr. Toms hollered out from just outside the doorway. "It expends more energy than it's worth sometimes! And if you are able to stay standing, you then have to throw your hips forward with a heavy leg attached to it in order to take a step, all the while holding yourself up with a walker. Do you still want braces?" she asked.

"Yup!" I yelled out in exhaustion. And someday, I'm going to come back to visit you Doc, hobbling down that corridor to the nurses' station all by myself, on braces!"

"I hope you do, Bobby. I hope you do," she said with a smile.

61

MICHELLE TOOK THE anti-tip bars off the back of my wheelchair today. She says that although they stopped me from tipping over backwards, they also prevented me from doing a wheelie when I needed to.

Learning to do a wheelie was paramount if I wanted to travel independently over sidewalk curbs, small step-ups and even threshold bumps in most doorways. If you don't do a wheelie over thresholds, your smaller front caster wheels can spin sideways and stop you in your tracks, throwing you out of your wheelchair head over heels.

Michelle had taught me to balance with my front wheels just a little bit off the ground, and now, without the anti-tip bars, she made me lean back even farther to find my balancing point. It was scary. I fell over backwards at least six times, and each fall happened so fast, that I would whack the back of my head on the tile floor if I didn't throw my hand back fast enough to protect it. Eventually, I got good at it.

Michelle then asked me to tip back and do a wheelie without touching down the front wheels, for three long minutes. Then she had me do it while spinning in small and then larger circles.

The last test took me to the nurses' station and positioned me at a starting line where all the nurses watched and cheered me on. I did not want to fall backwards, not because I'd crack my head open, but because I didn't want my legs going in two different directions in front of the staff, or even worse, visitors.

From there, Michelle had me pop a wheelie, roll down the entire length of the main corridor and take a left at the intersection toward the staff's elevator, the one Tina and I had escaped in. It was a lot harder doing a wheelie while rolling myself forward than I thought it would be.

I was exhausted by the time I reached for the elevator door button and almost lost it when I took my hand off the left wheel.

"Here is where most people fall backwards," Michelle said, as the elevator door opened. "Take your time going over the threshold; the bump is going to throw your balance off. Getting tired of holding yourself up, Bobby?"

"Yeah, but I'm okay. What happens if my front wheels touch the floor?" I asked.

"You have to start all over from the beginning," she chuckled.

I tried not to smile as I entered the elevator and then reached for the door button and closed the door.

She asked me to push the lobby button too. I pushed "L." It surprised me as to just how far she was making me go. She was so competitive. I liked the push though, so I kept balancing myself with my front wheels off the ground.

Going down in the elevator wasn't bad, but I almost lost it when we hit bottom. I teeter tottered until I regained my balance, still able to keep my front wheels from touching the floor.

After about thirty seconds, Michelle gave me the go-ahead. I took my hand off my wheel rim and reached for the up button and pushed. Going back up was harder, especially when the elevator lurched upward from a dead stop. My front wheels managed to stay up though.

The elevator stopped at the top with another small jolt. The door opened and I went back over the threshold again and headed for the turn. My wheelchair rocked and jerked as I turned the corner for the homestretch. With the finish line in view, I was drenched in sweat and ached in my arms and back muscles. I couldn't do it again if I lost the wheelie and my front wheels touched the floor, not that day anyway.

The sight of nurses at the finish line was all I needed to push on and cross it. They were *my* nurses.

I did it! I began to feel good about myself and my new accomplishment.

62

Day Fifty

THE DAY FINALLY came. I was going home. Mike was meeting me in the gym that morning to throw me out of my chair and onto the floor again. He said I still couldn't go home until I was able to get back up—but we both knew that the insurance company was sending me home no matter what.

They said that I was rehabilitated. I still don't know what that meant. I do know that after 50 days in two hospitals, I thought I couldn't wait to go home. But it wasn't so. I was petrified to leave the safe, daily routine and the loving nurses and therapists that took care of me.

A team of occupational therapists went to my home two weeks before and evaluated it for handicap accessibility. My father and Derek built some ramps and installed a few grab handles in the bathroom. The idea of it all bothered me. I was afraid to go home.

As I sat and waited for Mike, he snuck up behind me and tipped me out of the chair extra hard this time. I felt it was unnecessary. My legs flew out in all different directions and my pants and underwear fell down to my hips. I landed on my side, hard too. He was trying to prove a point and it pissed me off. I had the trip home on my mind and I was in no mood for his violin lessons.

"Get up this time," he said cockily, looking down at me with a determined look on his face. "You're not going home until you do."

"Mike, listen. I'm spent. I didn't sleep all night and I'm worried about leaving today. Plus, my pain level is high because of it. I need a break today, okay? I appreciate all you have done for me."

Instead of Mike pushing my chair closer to me and helping me back up and in, he pulled the chair a foot farther away and this time he tipped the chair over! It looked like a car accident! My backpack had fallen off the back of the handles and opened wide, spilling personal items across the gym mat that I wanted kept private.

"Stop your crying and get back up," he teased, with that damn violin-playing motion again.

That was it! I had enough!

"Mike, what are you an asshole? Do you think I'm gonna let you screw with me like this? How's about I knock you the hell out!"

With effort, I rolled over onto my stomach, well the top half of me anyway, then reached down and crossed my legs over to follow. I crawled with my arms toward him and my wheel chair, dragging my lower half behind me like Hugh Glass after that grizzly bear mauling.

Imagining myself grabbing him by his untucked polo shirt gave me the adrenaline I needed to get over to it fast. As I reached out for the chair frame, I noticed my right bicep pumped up more than ever. By grabbing a handle with one hand and anchoring myself by gripping the floor mat with my left, I flipped the chair over on all four wheels and faced it towards me in no time. A sense of pride overtook me when I realized my strength and took my mind off the pain. I was still pissed though and could not wait to get my hands on him.

Faster than I had ever done in practice, I positioned both knees under me and placed both elbows on the wheelchair seat with my face buried in its cushion. I could see his pant legs beyond the chair and as he got closer to me, I thought about punching him in the groin right then and there. He was still playing that stupid invisible violin and saying antagonizing stuff to me but I couldn't hear what.

Lifting my head, I quickly threw my elbows out and landed both hands with palms down onto the seat cushion. Mike was still jabbering away while I grunted into a pushup position, then a midair twist, and landed in the seat on my right butt cheek. From there, I squirmed the rest of the way in and sat back in my wheelchair totally out of breath.

Mike was standing over me when I looked up. He had his arms crossed with a huge smile coming from his leaking eyes. He put his hand out for me to shake it. I looked up at him for a second and then reached out with mine. We held that shake longer than usual.

"You are ready to go home now," he said softly.

"Thank you. Mike," I said, even more softly. "I won't forget what you did for me."

Before I leave this subject, please let me fast forward a few months later.

I was back working at my business when my manager and I locked up shop for the night. It was dark and I didn't notice that my van, equipped with hand controls, wasn't parked in its usual space. Jim must have put gas in it for me and left it parked in the unlit alleyway around the corner. By the time I realized it, Jim was out of sight.

I probably should have fetched my Maglite from my backpack attached to my chair, but it was cold and I wanted to get in quick and warm myself up. That's why I rolled into that dark alley faster than I should have.

When the front caster wheels hit the small crack in the tar, they turned sideways and stopped the wheelchair in its tracks, throwing me forward into the dark night and onto the cold, hard ground, chafing my leather jacket and scraping the palms of my hands.

To make matters worse, the wheelchair kept rolling past me after I fell out of it. I watched it roll away into the dark, about fifteen feet away I would guess.

I lay on my back with mixed emotions, looking up at the countless stars in the clear sky. Maybe I began to feel a little sorry for myself, I can't remember for sure. But I do remember thinking about Mike and the tools he taught me to take care of myself.

I could picture him saying, "Flip over on your stomach, drag yourself over to your wheelchair and pull yourself up! Do whatever it takes! You have the skills. And don't complain!"

So, that's what I did. I got up and went home. Thanks again, Mike. I'll never forget what you did for me.

63

BEING HOME WAS hell. Well, for the first two months anyway. Reminded of the daily things I couldn't do, I became depressed because it was always right in my face.

If I couldn't reach a drinking glass, it bugged me. If I had to use my reacher, it bugged me. If I put a few glasses on the counter so I could reach them, it bugged me to see them out of place.

So, I stopped drinking, became dehydrated and even more depressed. There were a million things like that which bothered me.

In the beginning, I stayed in bed, avoiding obstacles by immersing myself in television in order to escape reality, all the while well aware of my deterioration. I learned that antidepressants couldn't solve problems by themselves, only help fight them. I had to talk to myself constantly to climb out of the hole that I had slipped into.

I immersed myself in TV shows that were upbeat and without violence. I couldn't bear to watch anything else, especially anything with bad connotations. They made me nervous. I was never like that before.

To help with the nerve pain, I arranged to get Cranial Sacrum Therapy from Bess when I left the hospital. She helped me in the hospital and agreed to have me come by her house one night to see if I could get up onto her massage table. I was able to, so I went back the next night for pain management and energy treatment. Plus, because of the still opened window of possible return, I was still waiting to walk again.

She had a small, but nice cape house, filled with eclectic furniture and new age decor. I was surprised at her strength as she pulled my wheelchair and me backwards up the three steps and into the kitchen.

It was a tight fit, but I squeezed through the door jam and into the massage room without scraping any new skin off my knuckles. With Bess's help, I shimmied up onto the narrow table and settled in the best I could. It was painful to lay on my back but I had no choice, so I watched her light the row of mismatched candles and bit my lower lip as she did.

Bess stopped to comment on my legs when she helped pull my sweatpants legs down and viewed them for the first time.

"Bobby, that's a good sign you know."

"What is?" I asked.

"The hairs on your legs are."

"The hair on my legs is a good sign? Why?" She didn't answer, instead started deep tissue therapy right away, just above my rear end. That's the spot I complained about the most. It worked! I immediately felt relief in that area as it was soothed by localized heat from her hands. Both of our eyes remained closed while we chatted quietly about the energies we were both sensing.

"Hey, Bess, how did you get into this stuff anyway?" I asked.

"Oh, I've been into exploring things like this all of my life. I'm just a free spirit, I guess. I just got back from a life-changing experience too, down in Miami, swimming and communicating with dolphins."

"You communicated with dolphins? What do you mean? Are you psychic, Bess?"

"Yeah, I am. The Florida trip was a gathering for other psychics to meet each other and talk with a pool full of chatty dolphins. Do you believe in mental telepathy?" she asked.

"I've always been interested in the subject," I said. "I believe that we are born with more than just the five senses; we just don't know how to use the others. So, tell me Bess, did you really *talk* to the dolphins?"

"Honestly? I spoke rather easily to them. They are amazing and they have a lot to say. They complained to me though, about the size of the pool and the overcrowding it created. All in all, they were eager to talk with me."

"Hmm," I said, with my eyes still closed; then, her voice rose slightly.

"While I was getting out of the pool, my guardian angel showed up with eleven other angels to observe the event. Twelve of them in all. They were senators from ancient Greece. It was so awesome!" She shifted her hands a little in order to dig into another spot in my back.

"They did? What did they look like?" I asked. "What were they wearing?"

"Togas," she said. "They always wear togas." Then she suddenly lifted her head and opened her eyes, while looking down at my feet with a puzzled stare.

"What's wrong?" I asked.

"Bobby, you have a tear in your energy field, and a small amount of energy is escaping out that hole."

"I have a what?"

"Your energy," she repeated. "Your energy flows throughout your body like the way your blood flows through your veins. It's like..., you're bleeding."

"And what do you do for that?" I asked her.

"I can try to zip it up. Let me try," she said.

She shut her eyes, and with her head still facing down to my feet, things became quiet, so quiet I could even hear the clock in her kitchen stove ticking. After a minute or two, she opened her eyes and smiled.

"All set," she said. "We sewed the tear and sealed it up good. It shouldn't leak anymore. Your energy should flow evenly throughout your body now."

"We?" I asked.

"I fixed it with the help of my guardian angel," she said. "They come in handy at times."

"Wow," I said with surprise. "I wonder if I have a guardian angel," I said half joking.

"Of course, you do. Everyone does," She replied. "In fact, you have two of them you know."

"How do you know that I have two?" I asked her.

"I always saw them standing by you, Bobby, when you were in the hospital at Kent. They never left your side."

"You did? Do you see them now, Bess?"

"Now? Let's see," She answered, lowering her head and closing her eyes again. About fifteen seconds went by. "Here they are..., okay. They are here."

"They are where?" I asked.

"They are standing by your left side."

"Oh boy," I said, and felt obligated to say something more. "Okay, then. Bess, can you ask them something for me?"

"I'll try," she answered. "What would you like me to ask?"

"Umm, what are their names?"

After a moment of silence, Bess spoke again.

"Their names are David and Jason," she blurted. "And they said they have been with you since you were a small boy."

"Wow, were they with me when I fell out of the tree?"

She bowed her head in thought before answering. "Yes, Bobby, they were," she said.

"Okay...," I said slowly and a little too loud. "And you're talking to them right now? Wow. Unreal," I whispered. I wasn't sure what to make of it all.

"Whoa," Bess said, as she stared down toward my feet again, only this time speaking a little louder.

"What?" I asked. She didn't answer right away, so I asked again. "What Bess? What's the matter?"

"Umm, Bobby...are you religious?" She looked downward again and slowly closed her eyes.

I wasn't sure where things were going, so I thought out my answer really carefully before answering.

"Religious?" I said. "Yeah, I'm kind of religious, I guess. I'm Catholic. I mean, I believe in God. Why do you ask?"

"Well, Bobby, uh," she exhaled out her nose and then paused for a brief moment before going on. "This is just so...I don't know exactly how to say this, but."

"What is it, Bess... just tell me."

She exhaled again before parting her lips in a lopsided smile.

"Alright, Bobby, um..., Jesus," she paused, this time inhaling deeply. "Jesus is standing at the foot of your bed," she blurted out.

I didn't say anything. I couldn't. I didn't know what to say.

"I wasn't sure if I should tell you or not, Bobby, but he's standing right there by your feet. I just couldn't ignore him."

"He is?" I finally asked and this time opened one eye to peek. "He's just standing there?"

"Yes, he is," Bess replied. "And you know what? Now there are six angels hovering above him. Three on each side. They're looking down on you, Bobby. Is it okay that I told you this?"

"Um..., yeah," I replied. I didn't know what to say next. I had to wait a second before doing so. But I did.

"Are you religious, Bess?"

"No, not really,"

"Oh," I said meekly, in trying to keep the conversation awkwardly going. "He's really standing down at my feet? Jesus is?"

"Yes, he is," she replied.

"Can you ask him something for me?"

"I'll try. What is it?"

"Does he still care about me?"

"Yes, he does," she came back quickly. Rather too quickly, I thought. "And very much so," she added.

Okay, I thought. *Now she can't say that she tried but can't communicate with him. Jesus answered the first question right away, so he'd have to answer my next one just as fast.*

I felt bad that I was testing her because I truly liked her, but I had to know. *She opened the door,* I said to myself, justifying it.

"I'm glad he still cares about me, Bess. Thank you. Now ask him if I'll ever walk again."

I figured if she told me that Jesus answered yes, then it would have to come true. Otherwise, if I didn't walk again, it would mean that she really didn't see him after all.

And if she said that Jesus answered no, that I wouldn't walk again, and by chance I ever did, then that would also mean that she was making it up.

I was curious to see how she would answer it, so I waited. And you know, it's funny. Throughout it all, I imagined seeing Jesus Christ quite vividly, presiding over my legs with his arms raised high, and his palms facing heaven in a conduit-like stance.

He wore a Greek-style toga too, loose fitting and wrapped haphazardly around his tall and slender body.

And the angels? They were all wings. Huge, with cream-colored, soft-feathered wings. In fact, too much wings and not enough body I'd thought.

"I'll ask him," Bess said, bowing her head a little lower, as if to fine-tune the frequency. "Will he ever walk again," she repeated softly. Then she listened.

"Yes," she said, aloud and proud as a peacock.

Wow, I thought. *I didn't really think she'd answer it. She truly believes either that I will walk, or she just threw that out without thinking about the consequences. Better yet, maybe Jesus really is standing by my feet. That would be something.*

But if she did just throw that out without thinking, then she'll have to backtrack pretty quickly, I thought.

No sooner did I formulate that opinion, then Bess decided to append the answer.

"Just not in the same way," she added.

"What?" I asked.

"Yes, you will walk again," she said. "He says just not in the same way. You will walk again in other ways."

Good save, I thought.

I mean, I wanted to believe her, and I could almost see Him standing there. It's just that, I don't know. I just don't know.

64

L AUREN CONFIDED IN me today. She said that when I got hurt, she was never told that I wouldn't walk again. And although she was just thirteen, she said she was embarrassed for being so naïve.

She said she couldn't understand why so many teachers in school would say how sorry they were for her dad, at which she would always reply that I was fine. She thought that rehab was for getting better and that's what I was there for. I can't blame her, I did too.

I asked her who finally told her, and she said, "nobody did, as time went on, I just figured it out myself."

I wish I had known.

Slowly, I regained my strength and began archery hunting again. Never thinking I could do it, the first time out was filled with mixed emotions and lots of flashbacks, especially with all that time to sit and think. I was both exhilarated and saddened at the same time.

As I sat in my wheelchair on my first hunt, I couldn't see more than 20 feet in front of me over the tall and thick briar patches. I didn't see a deer that day but didn't care.

After that, my brother Ricky built me a ladder-mounted tree stand that would get me off the ground. It was awesome! With the help of an electric winch, it carried me on a seat, up between two rails and about 14 feet in the air while leaning against a smooth-barked oak tree. I could finally see above the briar patches and as spooky as it initially was, I was back in the air again! Yes, I wore my safety strap.

At first, it was hard to shoot my bow while in a sitting position, mostly because it was hard to pull the string back until my bicep muscles increased in size.

Something began to happen as I delved back into the sport that I loved. I didn't notice the nerve and back pain as much. And as months passed and I kept my mind occupied, I was able to push the hurt further away. I was distracted.

Charlie Lindsay had called from Canada back when I was in the hospital and wanted to come down just to sit with me. I talked him out of making the long trip from New Brunswick to Rhode Island by promising him that I would go back up there to hunt black bear when I got out. We both knew I didn't believe it at the time.

Charlie was such a good friend. My buddies and I had been going up to his hunting camp near the St. John's River for over 30 years. I'm not sure of the stats now, but back then, New Brunswick had more black bear per square mile than anywhere else in the world. In fact, our first year there, we were allowed to harvest two bear per hunter. I'm glad that they have such a competent and dedicated Fish and Wildlife Department to manage the bear population. It ensures the species' survival for our children to enjoy for years to come.

My family and I enjoyed bear meatloaf, meatballs, bear steaks, stew meat and bear hamburger, and I had shot lots of bear but never in a wheelchair. Talking my family into letting me go back up there was hard, but I think they knew they couldn't hold me back. I had to try it and try it I did.

Cuckoo flew in from Wyoming, while Moses, Ricky and Little Charlie joined me in my first bear hunt as a paraplegic.

We threw the motorized tree stand in the back of a pickup and away we went. It was just like old times, almost. No one wanted to leave me alone in the woods and tried to baby me all the way, but it didn't work very well so they finally gave up. I sat in that elevated stand for four days and shot a bear on the fifth. I was on my way back and appreciated what I had!

We went up north again the following year and almost every year after that, while I perfected my skills as a paraplegic hunter. Only now, I had ditched the stationary tree stand for an ATV that I could get around on as I pleased. I got my independence back too.

I carried a camouflaged netting in my backpack and threw it over the 4-wheeler when I parked in a good spot. I had to learn to stay on a 4-wheeler by holding on with just my arms because I couldn't squeeze my legs into the sides of the seat. I fell off at least three times before I mastered it. I broke both ankles 3 times each and one foot once, both legs and a toe. Now, I never fall off. I couldn't help it in the beginning because I got so excited, I would forget that I was paralyzed and drove as fast and dangerous as if I wasn't. I try to remember now.

I'm right-handed and because I couldn't turn my body very far without slipping off the seat, I had to learn to shoot my rifle left-handed in case a bear came towards me from the left. Initially, because Old Betsy was a little heavy, I had to hold myself up with my elbows planted on top of the handlebars, but the more I sat on that ATV, the more my stomach and torso muscles strengthened and eventually I could bring the rifle up to my face and hold it there without falling forward.

We hunt bears by sitting motionless in full camo clothing for up to six or more hours without moving. We would go into the woods at 2:30 p.m. and come out at dark after 9:30 p.m. Sundown is around 9:00 up there that time of year.

Most times, I would go into an alpha brain, trance-like state and the hours would just fly by in what seemed like minutes.

During that second hunt, of the five hunters, two shot their bear, and I was proud to be one of them. I teased them to no end on the way home that year too.

"How could a paraplegic beat the pants off you hunters?" I asked. "Maybe next time I should give you all a handicap because you guys certainly need it!" The following year all five of us shot a bear. After filling our freezers with meat, we donated the rest to a local gun club who distributes it to the needy.

65

A COUPLE OF YEARS later our good friend Moses passed away. It was heartbreaking. We believe he died from the Agent Orange he was in contact with when he fought in Vietnam. That spring, Cuckoo and I decided we needed to get away once more, so we swiped the small marine flag that was stuck generically on Moses' grave and headed back to Canada with it as a symbol of his presence.

As always, it was great to see Charlie's family. His mom cooked the best food and his dad told the best stories.

Charlie's good friend and hunting guide, Jerry, has become a good friend of mine as well and sometimes visits me in Rhode Island when he and Charlie go to sportsman shows in the United States.

Jerry and I usually almost pee our pants in laughter when we get together. He makes fun of my Rhode Island accent and I make fun of his Canadian... everything.

The area that I was hunting in that year was too thick for an ATV to maneuver in, so Charlie Lindsay talked me into hunting from my wheelchair. He also saw some huge bear tracks and really wanted me in that area rather than a rookie. There were other guys from Pennsylvania in the camp that year, and I guess he considered me more qualified even though I was handicapped. I thought that was weird but I didn't argue. Big tracks meant big male bears and big male bears are smart just for surviving so long. I relished the challenge.

The plan was for Jerry to drive me out past the area they called Down River, which was about 30 miles from camp. We frequently hunted between 5 to 15 miles apart from each other but not usually this far out. We called this area, No Man's Land.

Jerry and I were to leave early, just after lunch, and Charlie and Dennis would shuttle the other hunters to their designated locations at their normal times. We wished each other luck and away we went, sharing stories all the way. Whenever Jerry would zing me with a dig, I'd wait until the laughter stopped, shake my head and say, "friggin' Canadians."

He'd usually reply with a straight face and that slight New Brunswick brogue, "fockin' Americans."

We got to our destination and quietly stopped the truck on the desolate one-lane logging path, which skirted a newly formed beaver pond. I hated the idea of hunting in that wheelchair right off the bat but didn't complain about it to Jerry. Besides, we had spotted a bald eagle perched over the beaver pond, and I couldn't have been more grateful to be there.

With my rifle across my lap and my backpack hanging off the chair back, Jerry tipped me back on two wheels and pushed my chair forward by its handles. I did my part by pushing the wheels to take the load off Jerry as best I could but it wasn't good enough.

As we entered the soggy swamp, the sunlight dimmed and the rough terrain gradually slowed us down to a sinking stop among the skunk cabbage.

"This isn't going to work," Jerry said, out of breath and shooing the endless swarm of blackflies from his hat bill. "I'll have to carry you on my back and come back for the wheelchair later. We have a long way to go and I thought it would roll better than it does. Come on, get on."

"Are you crazy?" I answered. "I'm not letting you do that! No way! Let's just skip the hunt today, it's no big deal."

"Here! Give me your rifle!" he whispered. "Set her down here on the ground and I'll come back for her later. She won't go nowhere," he said. The Canadians called inanimate objects "her" or "she" and, of course, I teased them for it. I would ask them how they knew that the object was a girl and not a guy? They would usually answer back that it was because they liked girls better than guys.

Jerry knelt down with his back to me and whispered loudly, "get on my back and I'll hear no more of it!"

I didn't fight it. I knew better. I clasped my hands around his muscular neck and pulled myself forward. The six-foot-four Canadian stood up almost effortlessly with me dangling from his rock-solid back. I couldn't raise my legs, so they dragged on the ground until he reached down and grabbed each one behind the knee.

I haven't weighed myself since 1999 but I think I must weigh at least 165 pounds.

"You are one tough bastard," I grunted quietly in his ear, hanging on for dear life.

"No tougher than you," he whispered back and trudged silently through the cedar swamp and skunk cabbage. I begged him to take a break but he wouldn't. I was exhausted for him.

A good five minutes passed before we reached the spot with torn-up roots and bear-claw-marked tree trunks. Bears sharpen their claws by scraping them down the bark of limbless trees, sometimes stretching six feet high and into the wood an inch deep.

Jerry threw me down on my butt atop the pine needles and ran back to the get my rifle and chair without taking a breather. *This guy is the strongest guy I've ever seen!* I thought. *And, he's not a kid either. He's older than me!*

I felt bad he had to do that for me, and I worried that he might hurt his back. Rarely do you get to experience such a selfless act, and I was reminded of all my friends and how lucky I was to have them. I hoped they all knew that I would do anything for them as well.

He returned with Old Betsy slung over his shoulder as he dragged the wheelchair over the downed branches and sporadic underbrush.

I could see her bald eagle embroidered sling and it looked good from a short distance, hugging someone else's shoulder.

We mouthed gestures and used hand signals at that point and I had already determined the wind direction for placement of my chair in front of a huge-trunked pine tree. I was in *mossy oak* camouflage clothes and once I put my facemask on, I knew I would meld into the backdrop behind me. I motioned to Jerry to my choice location and he gave me the thumbs-up.

I tried to help myself into my wheelchair but with all those clothes on, I just couldn't. It bothered me to have Jerry pick me up again. He saw that in my eyes.

Once in, I positioned my feet on the footplate, and he dragged my chair backwards to the big pine. But as he backed me up against it, I was left leaning forward because of the pitched ground at the base of the trunk.

"I can't sit tipped forward like this for six hours," I whispered.

"I have a ratchet strap in the truck," he whispered back. "I'll go and get her." He was gone before I could object.

Jerry returned with the nylon strap in no time and I gave him a look of appreciative disapproval. I had put some pine needles and dirt under my front wheels to help level myself off, in the meantime. He fed the ratchet strap through the back of the wheelchair and around the tree, then ratcheted up the strap with the winch buckle until it began to pull the top of my chair backward toward the trunk, leveling me off where I could sit comfortably. I was glad he did it for me; because I would have been miserable tilted and leaning so far forward for all those hours.

"Do you have your radio?" he mouthed.

Yes, I nodded.

"You're so far out, you won't reach me until I get within five miles of you on my way back tonight. I'm going to pick up you up last, well after dark."

Yes, I nodded again and gave him the thumbs-up. He returned

the gesture and mouthed the words good luck, then away he went, quietly tiptoeing around the blowdowns until he was out of sight. I appreciated that too.

I methodically went right to work. First, I loaded my rifle, something I learned to do years ago after realizing that wild game can appear out of nowhere, at any time, no matter how much noise was generated from the initial settling in period. Besides, I wasn't hunting prey animals that day. I could be the prey on this one.

Three rounds of ammo was my number, two in the magazine and one in the rifle chamber. That was a safety measure I implemented over 30 years ago. Loading the same number of rounds in every rifle eliminated the guesswork in determining how many rounds were in the firearm before and after each shot.

I then rechecked the rifle's safety, raised the rifle to my cheek and tested the scope sights in all directions. I couldn't turn to my right with a raised rifle and hoped that the bear would come in from my left, so I wouldn't have to shoot left-handed.

Next, I threw my head net on because the black flies and mosquitoes were atrocious. We had to tape up our pant legs to our boots and our coat sleeves to our gloves, because their sole reason for living was to find a way to your skin and then inflict a bite that far outweighed the size of their tiny bodies. The few welts that were already swelling on my neck weren't a big deal, so I ignored the itch and began reaching for saplings and brush to plant in front of me to help break up my outline. I did this all in an ever so slow and deliberate motion. Animals can pick out a quick motion immediately, but it's harder to detect a slow movement because it may mimic the natural swaying of tree branches on a windy day.

After constructing my little blind and repositioning myself for a long sit, I did a mental check on everything, settled in, melded into that tree trunk and imagined myself as invisible.

Uh oh, I thought, as I tried to look over my right shoulder but couldn't.

If I had to get away, I asked myself, *can I reach around the back of this pine tree and release the ratchet button to unstrap myself from the strap that is tying me and my wheelchair to this tree? I remember that tree trunk being wide, but I can't see just how wide it is!*

Trying to look over the other shoulder, I began to worry and still couldn't see the release buckle button on the strap. *Did I just let Jerry tie me to this tree? What if I want to turn my chair? What if I should have to roll away? Are you kidding me?*

Without looking down, I reached down with my right hand and felt for my buck knife that hung in its leather sheath on my belt. I pulled out the knife and tried to reach it under the nylon strap, but it was cinched too tight against the tree's trunk behind me. I couldn't cut the strap if I wanted to, so I sat back to think.

I can't blame Jerry; I didn't think of it either. I've only had one close call with a bear in all these years. I'll be okay. I can't believe I did this! I'll be alright tied to this tree!

I made a mental note of the number of bullets I loaded into my rifle, reached down again and tapped my knife after dropping it back into its sheath.

A lot of planning went into that bear hunt, but sitting in my wheelchair, in the middle of the woods and tied to a tree was not part of it.

We hunters planned our trips weeks in advance by removing unnatural scents from our clothes, pores, and hair. We used unscented soap, shampoo, and deodorant, washed our camos in scent-free detergent and stored our gear in totes filled with dirt and pine needles before spraying them down with human scent neutralizer.

Some hunters even stop eating meat when deer hunting. It is believed that prey animals can smell the meat on your breath and pores and associate it with a meat-eating predator like a coyote, wolf, big cat or bear. A deer can distinguish between 10,000 different scents at a distance of hundreds of yards and a bear can smell for a distance of over two miles, even more powerful than a bloodhound.

I began to forget about my predicament. As I sat back and drifted toward my usual daydreams, I recalled some of my thoughts and feelings in that hospital bed not that long before. I took a swig of the clear Canadian air, while briefly shutting my eyes to my surroundings.

I never thought I'd ever be doing this again, I thought. *Never in a million years.*

Cedar and wet leaves stayed with my nostrils before I stopped noticing, while patches of sunlight followed the sun as it moved from my left and then my right. Hunters don't look at their watches, they watch the sun and moon. Another way I could tell how much time had passed was by the soreness in my stiff back and neck.

By the drop in temperature and the fading sun shadows, I figured it must have been approaching 8:00 p.m., which was *prime time* and just before dark. That's when most animals are on the move.

The peep toads peeped louder as the dark became evident, but I still had a half hour until sunset and could legally shoot a half hour after that.

I figured I must have sat for about five hours or so but didn't remember the time passing at all. We usually go into an alpha brain state, kind of like a trance when we hunt sitting motionless, and I was surely in one. It's like driving home from work in deep thought and not remember doing it when arriving.

I always try to sit completely motionless, moving only my eyeballs when alerted to movement or sudden changes from light to dark. You see more wildlife that way.

Suddenly, about 50 yards out and straight ahead, something quickly caught my eye and honed in on it, like a heat-seeking missile locking in on its target. I stared with intensity, adjusting my site like a pair of binoculars.

There was no more movement but I was sure there once was. My eyes had caught too many culprits to be wrong this time. Therefore, I waited..., then, between the brush, there was dark where there was once light..., then there was light—then dark again. It was moving slowly.

I calculated the height of the shadow in comparison to the spruce trees that stood by it.

It was a bear.

I instinctively thought to turn my wheelchair to the right for a sideways shot, stance shot before remembering that I couldn't move!

I improvised by leaning on one butt cheek and swiveling my hips to the right instead, not knowing if they followed me, because I wouldn't take my eyes off the partial bear.

It was closer now and coming into view, yet it still made not a sound. Bears have padding under their paws like cats do, and surprisingly for their size, they prowl easily along in stealth-like silence. This one was exceptionally quiet. *A male*, I thought.

Now, about forty-five yards away and still sneaking slowly, I had the entire bruin in my view. I observed jet-black fur that blended well into the oncoming night and a big head with ears that looked too small for its scull. This told me that it was indeed a big bear. Its snout was wide too, indicating middle to older age and again, probably a boar rather than a sow.

It walked..., it stopped..., and it smelled the air above. Then it started walking slowly toward me again. And the peep toads stopped peeping.

I raised my rifle and pushed forward on the safety with my thumb, all in the same deliberate and fluid motion. My cheek found the gunstock and my right eye found the scope. I had the scope turned down to 3-x power for close range viewing and because it was getting dark, then quickly found the crosshairs inside.

However, as I locked on the target, I detected movement from behind the big bear. I dropped the rifle a few inches in order to see over it while pulling the safety back towards me in a safe position. I looked, squinted, and honed in with my strained eyes. It was another bear!

This one was smaller and that immediately concerned me. It was too big for a cub but too small to be an adult. Possibly a yearling.

Cubs are about the size of a football that time of year and wet sows are considered sacred to every hunter that I have ever met. Although unlikely this time of year, shooting a mother with cubs is something we do not do.

Yearlings are usually weaned off and long gone by late spring, but I couldn't be sure if the big bear was a male with a sidekick or a sow with a late-leaving teenager. I was almost certain that it was not a wet sow, but I wasn't taking any chances and decided to pass up the opportunity, even if it meant giving up a big bear.

Lowering my rifle and breaking my stance was tough but I knew I did the right thing. I decided to watch undetected and maybe learn a tip or two from them for the next hunt. I lowered my posture, melded back into the base of that pine tree and just watched. I marveled at being so close to those wild creatures without being detected.

The big one grew in stature as it wandered within 40 yards, while ferociously standing sideways to me and looking in the direction of the smaller one.

Without warning, the fern plants lifted from the ground moss and a small hint of wind blew through the swamp and slightly changed the northwest direction that I so cautiously set my ambush on. No sooner did I think the word "upwind" when the large bear, still standing broadside, snapped his head in my direction with lightning speed and locked his sights on me.

Oh shit, I thought. *The wind has shifted direction and now I'm sitting upwind! And, I'm tied to this tree like bear bait!*

It couldn't have been worse. It didn't know what I was, but it knew I didn't belong there and I was beginning to feel the same way. We were in a staring contest to see who blinked first, and believe me I was dying to be the one.

Oh no, I thought, again and again.

I wondered how long it would take me to slowly raise my rifle from my lap, but I didn't want to give myself away. With its ears pinned back like a tiger about to bite its prey, it lifted its nose high in the air and smelled deeply into the wind. I thought I should raise my rifle while it looked away but it was too late. It dropped its head fast and stared back at me again.

Don't move a muscle, I told myself, *stay completely still,* but my chest was already beginning to rise steadily. My heart began to pound loudly too, and I was sure it could hear it.

Seeming as if it were looking me in the eyes, I kept telling myself it still wasn't sure I was a man, just trying to provoke a move from me in order to prove it.

That's what predators do; it's like playing bluff poker. *Don't even blink!* I told myself.

I did not like the tuft of thick black hair that was standing straight up on the back of its neck. My vibrating legs and feet told me they didn't like it either. Raising its nose to the wind once again, it took in a lungful of air, then dropped its head to the ground and pretended to nibble on a piece of fern.

Uh oh! I know what that means! Fake out! Get ready!

I raised my rifle to my face and flicked the safety off as the bear suddenly raised its head, turned and charged me at an unbelievable speed! Loose dirt and live foliage kicked up from behind it as it made immediate traction on the soft, swampy, fern carpet!

The ears were pinned back even farther as it charged, while its mouth flew open wide, flashing bits of pearl white teeth against its pitch-black silhouette! My crosshairs bounced from its front shoulder to its humped neck as I tried to steady my rifle on the moving target. It wasn't working! I had nothing to rest the rifle against and was aiming freestyle; something I wasn't good at from a wheelchair and really hated to do.

Without slowing, it suddenly hit the brakes and skidded to a stop about 25 yards from me, almost flipping over, end-over-end, due to its shorter front legs and the massive weight behind it.

With both front paws dug into the ground, it stood motionless and stared me down in what felt like a Mexican standoff! Then it slowly turned its massive head away and cumbersomely walked back from which it came. I kept my sights on it as it approached its starting point but my rifle was getting heavy. I kept it on it just the same.

What an adrenaline rush! I screamed in my head. *What...a... rush! Wow!*

The weighted gun barrel was swaying and lifting with every breath and my steadying turned to a tremble. When I had my legs, I used to crouch down and lift up a knee and use that for rifle support but that was out now.

I took my eyes off the big bear for a split second in a zero attempt to locate the smaller one. Two bears against a guy without legs and tied to a tree was a challenge I didn't relish.

Oh, crap! It's turning around!

Facing me head on, it jumped up with both front legs off the ground and pounded its clawed paws down hard in an attempt to unnerve me. I felt the ground's percussion in my butt and through my lower back, enjoying the rare sensation in a welcoming yet perverse way.

Dropping its head to the ground telegraphed another charge, and I was right. *Here it comes again!* The massive bear ran at me in another full-speed charge, only this time my crosshairs lost it entirely! It was too close for my scope to see and it was moving in and out of it too fast! At the last second, I locked onto its left shoulder and held my breath!

This time the big bruin slid to an abrupt stop just 20 yards from me, skidding violently, tearing up fern plants and creating a cloud of dirt that changed parts of its black fur to brown! It jumped up and down and began pounding its front paws again just feet before a small gully. At that distance, the thumping was like earth tremors but I kept telling myself not to flinch. It was a showdown and we both knew it.

I got a better look at its long claws as it spread them wide each time they left the ground. The claws were jet black but the tips were silver, advertising the razor-sharp points that ran shivers down my spine. Old Betsy felt like she weighed a hundred pounds and my arms were killing me.

Again, the bear slowly turned its giant head and again walked back to where it came from; only this time it opened and snapped shut its jaw repeatedly on the way back. When bears fight, they sometimes create a very loud snapping sound with their teeth to intimidate their opponent. I was intimidated.

I estimated the ground gully to be about 10 to 12 yards away from me and decided that if it crosses it, I'm going to shoot. That will be my line in the sand.

Convinced I could not hold my rifle up for another second, I shifted my weight by switching from my right butt cheek to my left—and did not care anymore if it saw me move. It knew where I was.

I was in a bad shooting stance and needed to turn my wheelchair. It's really hard to look down a rifle barrel almost straight on but I had no choice!

It stopped walking away from me but kept on snapping its teeth! With its back end to me, it raised its nose and sampled the night air above.

Suddenly, it lowered its head, quickly turned and charged me a third time! Only this time it looked as though it was coming all the way! I was amazed at how fast it was moving! I brought the rifle up again but my ability to keep the crosshairs on it was failing and they briefly left the target altogether!

Suddenly, the black bear skidded to a stop just inches from the gully! It was as if he knew where the line in the sand was and purposely did not cross it! I didn't trust it though and refused to drop my rifle.

My heart was pounding so hard it was moving me, my rifle and my wheelchair with every beat and it took all I had to keep still!

The other bear suddenly came into view behind the big one and that concerned me. I feared the ruckus could send the two of them into a frenzy and allow them to feed off each other's frustration, further escalating the turmoil. Two bears charging at the same time would be impossible to hit with a bolt-action rifle, especially at such close range.

The other bear began thrashing about in that small opening and its lasting presence meant either innocence or arrogance. Either one was dangerous and worrisome.

The big bear monitored the other one this time as it headed back again to the starting line. This time its pace was faster, and I knew it was more agitated, so I managed to watch both bears with both eyes, one eye in the scope and the other one out, but I concentrated more on the big one. Its body language told me it was highly pissed off!

I gripped my gunstock tighter with semi-numb fingers that moved involuntarily due to cut off circulation. I tried to shift my hips but couldn't. *I cannot believe I'm tied to this damn tree!*

Highly agitated and with ears pinned back, the big bear slowly continued back to the starting line. He didn't make it halfway back before it suddenly stopped again!

Oh boy! Here we go! I can almost smell the fury! It was running toward me at full speed even before it turned all the way around! This charge started in a different way and this time I knew it was serious!

With its mouth opened crookedly and its head shaking wildly, it was within 15 yards from me within seconds! It was moving fast! As it picked up speed, the vegetation flew from its hind legs like a rooster tail, and I just knew it wasn't going to stop as it crossed the gully and my line in the sand! *It's going to run right over me this time! It will be on me in seconds and I'm tied to this damn tree!*

All fears were put aside as I went into an offensive posture and a fighting mode. I squinted hard in the dim light while the crosshairs lost their mark for a split second, landing on a dark corner or a tree trunk or something; then they instinctively found and stayed with the bear, as it tried to bounce in and out of my scope and pounce upon me and sink its sharp incisors into my soft, throbbing neck!

I don't know how close it got to me, before I squeezed the trigger in a calculated yet surreal instinct. But—"Bang!"

Before the rifle's barrel settled down to its level position, I had the bolt open, the spent casing ejected and had another round slammed into the chamber, ready for a second off-the-cuff shot.

My first shot hit it good and knocked it back and to the left, so I held off on the next one.

The sunlight was all but gone except for some sky above the tree canopy. This, I saw as I looked up to the sky as I leaned way back in my chair to take a much-needed breath of air. It was weird because I didn't remember sitting so far forward.

I lost sight of the bear against the dark and didn't hear it drop! It all happened so fast! I knew one thing; I didn't feel good about the shot.

I sat quiet and listened. Glancing at total darkness to my left forced my pupils to dilate but not quickly enough. I couldn't see a thing!

A sporadic, 'crashing through branches sound' resonated and remained long after the episode began to subside within my din-filled head. I couldn't see the other bear and wondered which one was crashing and thrashing.

I wounded it. I thought. *I know I hit it good but I wounded it. I didn't want this to happen.*

There is only one thing worse than an agitated bear, and that's a wounded, agitated bear.

What am I going to do now? I can't get up and go after it to put it down! I can't even turn my wheelchair to see what's behind me because I'm still tied to this damn tree!

Total darkness was upon me now as I tried to listen for its position. I wanted to put my flashlight on but couldn't. I had to become invisible again. I couldn't see my hand in front of my face so I slowly felt for my radio in my backpack and whispered for Jerry.

"Hey Jerry, you got a copy?"

"Hey Jerry, you got a copy?"

I tried once more with no luck, so I decided to keep quiet and wait for the 10:00 p.m. pickup time.

The sound of snapping twigs surrounded me at 365 degrees. The peep toads started up again, loud, making it harder for me to listen or hear myself think, let alone two ticked off bears. Walking sounds behind me were interrupted by running sounds out in front of me. Still, I couldn't see my own hand in front of my face. I sat silently, tied to that tree.

"Hey Bobby, was that you?" Jerry's voice broke through the dark silence, sending something crashing through branches off to my left side and scaring my legs and feet again. They were already vibrating with irritating pins and needles-type feelings, caused by the bear charging me. I didn't like that Jerry's voice gave away my position but was happy to hear from him just the same.

"Yeah, it's me, Jerry," I whispered. "I got charged by a bear and wounded it. I didn't want to shoot it because it was with a smaller one, not this year's cub though. I thought it was a boar but didn't want to take the chance of it being a wet sow, so I wasn't planning on taking it until it charged me. I wounded it, I think. Oh, and by the way, Jerry, did you know I'm strapped to this tree and I can't reach the release button? Of all times to get charged by a bear! Do you copy, brother? I said I'm tied to this damn tree! Over!"

A long pause followed. I knew he was thinking about the ratchet strap and it was cracking me up inside. I loved torturing him when I could. It was actually my fault too, but I'd never tell him that.

After a while, I heard the Chevy pickup off in the distance and relaxed my grip on the rifle a little. My arm and shoulder were throbbing from holding that rifle across my chest for so long.

Jerry's tiny Maglite lit up his pathway like searchlights in deep space. I saw him coming a mile away.

"You okay?" he yelled out, still about 100 yards out.

"Yeah, yeah, yeah! You want to untie me from this tree, please?"

"Shut up or I'll leave you out here for coyote bait! he answered in a trot. "Where's the wounded bear? Did it run off?" Hollering in the forest like that seemed disrespectful.

"Yeah, but I'm not sure where. It could be laying right out there to my left, close, alive! I heard some crashing sounds but can't be sure which bear it was, I had two of them in here."

Jerry shined the Maglite out about 60 yards and we both saw the other bear at the same time before it bolted out into the darkness.

"There goes the smaller one, Jerry! Why is he hanging around? That's not normal at that age is it?"

"Yeah, I saw it, Bobby. That's not a suckling in my opinion. It's too big. You could have shot the bigger one right off. No problem. I don't think it's a wet sow. I don't know why the small one is hanging around though. That's unusual. Give me your rifle and I'll see if he's not laying right out there dead."

"I hope it is a *he*," I replied, as I checked the safety and handed him the rifle. "Be careful, Jerry."

"I will."

Jerry's flashlight beam searched for sign between the gully and me and quickly found some blood. I watched him walk briskly along the blood trail, yelling to me there was a lot of blood to follow, until his light dimmed out of sight like a burned-out match. Total darkness again. I reached for my Maglite, turned it on and listened. More crashing erupted off to my right and startled me enough to jump..

Wait a minute! I thought. *Is something wrong with me? I have a wounded bear here somewhere, I can't see more than 20 feet out in front of me, even with my light, I gave Jerry my rifle and I'm still tied to this damn tree!*

Crashes erupted again off to my right, so I pulled my knife from its sheath and placed it on my lap. My thumb scraped its blade to test the edge. It was sharp.

I sat in silence again, detecting every little noise around me while the sounds behind me bugged me the most. Then I heard a gunshot that made my legs jump and tingle with vibration. Then I remembered.

That was two bullets. I thought, as I fumbled for the radio.

"Jerry!" I shouted with urgency in my voice. "You only have one bullet left in that gun! It just dawned on me! One bullet left! Do you copy?"

He found his radio in his back pocket and radioed me back about a minute later.

"Hey Bobby, you got a copy?" He was out of breath.

"Go ahead, Jerry."

"I walked right up on that bear! He was wounded all right! I never did see him until I was right on top of him, too! He waited until I was right up to him when he stood up on his hind legs and scared the bejesus out of me! I dropped my flashlight and it shut off when it hit the ground. I had no time to raise the gun either, but I managed to shoot from the hip and knock him down before he ran off again!"

Jerry took a deep breath and thought for a second before continuing.

"Well, if I only got one bullet left in this gun, I ain't going after it. Let's let it lie down, die, and come back for it early in the morning. We'll take the 4-wheeler so you can track it with me. Over?"

"Ten four. Come on back and untie me from this tree, will ya? Please?"

"I'll have to think about that," he chuckled.

Because Jerry dropped his flashlight in the dark, I had to whistle for him until he found his way back to me.

While my good friend carried me to his truck, he paused a moment as I hung from his back.

"Hey, Bobby, how come you didn't tell me there were only two bullets left in that rifle when you handed it to me?" He then shook his head, as he mumbled miserably under his breath, "fockin' Americans," he said.

With Uncle Tony. Enough meat to feed my family for two years.

"Hey, Jerry, how come you tied me to that tree, I replied, mumbling cheerfully under mine, "friggin' Canadians."

POSTSCRIPT

We went back the next day and retrieved the bear. Thankfully, it was a mature male. Just the right age to be harvested. The meat helped feed my family and friends for nearly two years.

66

I BEGAN FLYING. I mean, I began to board airplanes again with flights to Wyoming, Florida, California etc., all alone and totally independent. Deb and I were divorced years ago but have remained friendly for the sake of the kids. The airplane experiences are not so easy though.

Airlines put themselves out there as being special-needs friendly. They're not at all. Wheelchairs cannot fit down most airplane aisles to get to their coach seats and certainly cannot fit in the onboard bathroom even if they could get to it. I cannot bring and leave my wheelchair on a plane, no one can. It has to be stowed underneath. What good is that?

If I board an aircraft and am not able to reserve or afford a first-row seat, which is always the case, they must first strap me into a "straight-back" in order to bring me on board and then down the aisle to my seat.

A straight-back is an embarrassing, uncomfortable, least thought out, humiliating, L-shaped two-wheel chair that resembles a freight dolly or a hand truck. It's just centimeters wider than my butt is, and they strap me in it using four harnesses: one across my ankles, one across my lap, and two crisscrossed on my chest. They then tighten the straps down by pulling way too hard on the harnesses, as they loudly quote the regulations in my ear when I complain about it. Then, they tip me back on its two wheels and drag me backwards;

that's the only way it goes, backwards, down the plane's aisle. I look like Hannibal Lecter without the mask.

Usually, they drag me past the already seated passengers, because either they forget to board me first, which I always ask for and are supposed to, or the contraption doesn't arrive, even though I request it ahead of time. I always have to remind them to board me first, and they usually forget and start calling rows to board; by then it is too late. When I first get to the check-in counter at the gate, I always have to ask the following questions:

"Did you know I was coming? I am a paraplegic and I called ahead." They did not.

"Do you have me sitting in the first row, like I asked?" They never do.

"If so, will my chair fit through to get to my seat?" They never know the answer.

"If I'm not in the first row, my wheelchair won't fit past the first seat, so do you have a straight-back chair coming?" They usually don't ahead of time, even though I purchased the ticket with special instructions stating that I'm in a wheelchair—and the first check-in counter person assured me that the notation would be on every connection. It never is.

As they drag me onto the plane backwards, tied in the straight-back dolly contraption and past the seated passengers, I usually bump my elbows against other unsuspecting elbows on the way to my seat. The straight-back, resembling a hand truck, doesn't allow me to see where I'm going, and I'm usually the one yelling out, "Excuse me, watch your elbows or sorry about that!" By then everyone on the plane is usually staring at me.

As I arrive at my seat, they untie me and I ask the flight attendants if the armrest goes up on the aisle seat. They usually ask me "why?"

"Because I can't stand up," I say, embarrassed in front of the other passengers. They never know if it does or doesn't go up, and almost always, and after *I* fiddle with it, it does not.

The two straight-back attendants and passengers wonder how I am going to get over the armrest and into the seat. No one knows but me.

I ask someone to open the overhead compartment, stretch up like heck to grab the opening of it, and with one arm, I pull myself up high enough to sit on the metal armrest on the first seat for a second. It's skinny, so either it goes up my butt a mile or I balance desperately on it not to fall off.

Everyone watches as my legs fly out in all different directions while I let go of the overhead opening above, slide off the armrest and land headfirst onto the lap of the passenger in the next seat, pleading for forgiveness.

Before the attendants leave with the empty straight-back, I remind them to remember to put my wheelchair in the plane's cargo hold and please do not tear the seat cushion off it because my wheelchair does not fold up. They all try to rip it off, probably because wheelchairs used to fold up years ago.

As I settle in, I can still feel all eyes burning on the back of my neck and pray to God that I don't have to go to the bathroom in flight, because I can't go "just" anywhere!

I pass up all drinks, nuts and crackers and just sit there and worry. Worry that I don't get a stomachache or need to use a bathroom.

Starved and thirsting by the end of the flight, when the last passenger exits the plane, at least one attendant usually forgets that I can't walk and yells to me that I must get up and get off the plane with the rest of the passengers.

One time, I was the only one left on the plane, and I was waiting for them to fetch my wheelchair from the cargo hold when the conversation with a flight attendant went like this:

"Sir!" she hollered to me from about 15 rows ahead while applying blush to her cheeks, "rules require that you must disembark the aircraft when all passengers have left!"

"I can't get up; I'm waiting for my wheelchair!" I hollered back over the seat in front of me, just managing to stretch just my eyes over the top of it.

"Excuse me? Your what?"

"My chair!"

"I'm sorry, what chair?"

"I can't get up! I'm paralyzed!" I stuttered. "I'm a paraplegic, you know?" I just hate saying that.

Another attendant emerged from the cabin kitchen area and whispered in her ear right in front of me.

"Oh, okay sir, your straight-back and wheelchair will be arriving soon, sir!"

"Thank you!" I lowered my head and repositioned myself with nothing to do but wait and think. *I can't wait to climb up on this seat's narrow metal armrest again, only to be tied up in another straight-back. I'll bet they didn't order me one yet, and I'll have to roll like crazy to get to my next gate and flight connection before I miss it. Then I get ready to do it all over again for the next two connecting flights.*

I'm not trying to put the airlines down, but they should know better. And I can take it, but I always worry about the elderly men or women that may not get the respect or consideration they deserve. It's not fair. Bathrooms on the ground have to be handicap accessible, why not in the sky? Why should I worry and be embarrassed every time I fly?

When will we require airlines to design their aircraft with aisles that are wide enough for wheelchairs to get to our seats and bathrooms that are accessible?

"Hey Boeing, make your aisles wider please, a few inches or so, so we can get to the bathroom like everyone else. And when we get there, make the doorway wider and the bathrooms bigger, so we can then get inside. It may not be a law, but it's the right thing to do."

67

I RECEIVED A FRANTIC call from Wyoming—it was Cuckoo. Our good friend Roy was heading home on a dark dirt road, when two mule deer shot out ahead of him, causing his pickup to swerve into a culvert, flip once and land hard on its side.

Cuckoo said the paramedics found Roy crunched up with his head jammed under the emergency brake. He was instantly deemed a quadriplegic.

Isn't it strange how fast things can change? What are the chances of two friends in a small group of hunters ending up being paralyzed?

Roy is the type of guy that most men aspire to be. A Wyoming cowboy to the core, his large stature and strong body contradicts with his gentle manner and generous nature.

I remember hunting with Roy out of a 19th century prairie cabin in the middle of nowhere. It was located out on the desolate but beautiful Hell n' Back Ranch. At somewhere around the age of 62, Roy would get up early each morning and do about twenty-five pull-ups from the open doorframe that separated the two-room log cabin. Then he would finish up with a half dozen one-armed pull-ups, rotating between arms after each one. I looked on in amazement. At many years his younger, I don't think I could beat him in an arm wrestling match, even if I used both hands.

We all enjoyed that cabin, especially at the end of a long day's hunt. The owner of the ranch joined us for steaks and beans one night and told us a cool story I have never forgotten. Cuckoo, Chipper, Glen, Roy and I sat by the old Franklin stove, sipping on black coffee and chewing on pieces of dried out venison jerky that got stuck in my teeth.

Glen and Roy sat off to the side, sharpening their knives after dulling them up on antelope hides earlier in the day.

The rancher explained how the cabin was once used as a hideout by a murderous outlaw back in the eighteen-hundreds, before being found there by the infamous Deputy Marshal, Joe Lefors of the Pinkerton Detective Agency. We all listened intently as the rancher paused to light his cherry tobacco-filled pipe, before continuing with his captivating story. I inhaled the pipe smoke that floated my way, as I picked stubborn jerky from my teeth.

"How did the murderer get caught?" Chipper asked.

"The outlaw sipped whiskey from a bottle while sitting on a barstool in a nearby saloon," the rancher explained. "Drunk as a skunk, he had the nerve to wear a woman's gold wedding ring, which the bartender recognized as the ring owned by the wife of a young couple they found robbed and murdered in a small farmhouse the week before." The rancher took a deep breath and shook his head in disgust before going on.

"Joe Lefors had been the tracker that led a posse and chased Butch Cassidy and The Sundance Kid halfway across the Wyoming Territory," he said, while puffing three quick puffs.

"What happened to the outlaw after Lefors captured him?" I asked the rancher.

"Oh..., well, Deputy Lefors transported him to a jailhouse right up here," pointing up and to the west with his cherry wood, pipe handle.

"Then, the sheriff conveniently went fishing, while an angry mob broke the outlaw out of his jail cell and took him to a small bend in the Snake River just outside of town. There they hanged him from a wooden bridge for all to see. They say that when the noose tightened around his neck after that drop to the crick, well, his head just popped clear off!"

I FLEW OUT TO WYOMING as soon as Roy was able to see me. The flight was as usual. Miserably un-handicap accessible in every way.

When I arrived at the hospital, Roy and I talked in private and had a good visit. I went away that day confident that he would be okay. It would take some time, but he would be okay.

His wife Gloria enrolled him in a top-notch rehab center where they both learned the tools needed to get back to their home, which is nestled in the foothills of the Big Horn Mountains and resume their hard-earned retirement life.

When I think of Roy's wife Gloria, as I do of Cuckoo's wife Debbie, I think of the old adage, "behind every good man is a great woman."

Cowboys are tough, but I think cowgirls are tougher.

68

IT TOOK YEARS for my daughter-in-law, Toni, to tell me the secret. The secret she had been keeping from me since the first time my son Derek took her home to meet the family.

Toni and I had been very close, that's why I was shocked to learn that she had a secret she was keeping that included me!

Toni works as an administrative executive for a small police department a few towns away. That is how she and Derek met. He was in the Police Explorer Program, and she was a full-time dispatcher seeking all the overtime she could get. Before that, she was a dispatcher for the Foster Police Department where she received her initial training.

After an Easter dinner and with Derek by her side, she began nervously telling me her secret at our dining room table after a deep breath and a long drawn out sigh.

"Go ahead, Toni, tell him. Get it off your chest!" Derek said. "Tell him!"

"Tell me what?" I asked.

"Tell you about my employment at the Foster Police Department years ago," Toni said, with a voice I had to strain to hear. "I have something to tell you and I don't know where to begin."

"Start at the beginning," I said.

"Okay," she sighed, choosing her words carefully while glancing over to Derek for support.

"Here it goes. This was some years before I met Derek and you. When I arrived at the police station for my first day of dispatcher training, I was surprised at the age of the building and the Mayberry RFD atmosphere that it had. I was looking for a job that I could call home and loved the small town feeling I got as soon as I walked in."

I knew what she meant. I had recently visited the station myself a few times and sort of liked the historical yet dilapidated look.

The main building sat next to a rickety old barn and rested on large and heavy-looking granite stones. Wheelchair access was through the back door, so I got to view the blatantly displayed cat dish, which overflowed with tuna-looking fish. I guessed they had lots of mice. The previous chief's duck and chicken cages still littered the landscape in the back yard.

Inside, a sixties-style blue rug spewed across an unleveled hallway floor, which my chair wheels detected immediately. I had to keep one wheel locked to prevent from drifting off into a wall.

I expected to see Otis from Mayberry, blanket covered in the jail cell, sleeping off his drunken Saturday night stint on the town.

"Yeah, I thought it was kind of cool," Toni continued. "That's why I took the job, because I felt it was a country town without a lot of action."

Toni then described her training supervisor as a veteran dispatcher who took her job very seriously.

"Right from the start, Pat made me answer all calls from Police, Fire and Rescue on my own," Toni said. "She sat by me in case I got in trouble, but it was pretty much all me from day one."

"Toni, you're a quick learner," I said.

"Thanks, but don't give me too much credit yet, not until you hear what I'm about to tell you," she continued. "It was on my second day of training when Pat told me that I'd be working all alone the following day!" Toni's eyes widened as she tried to make me understand.

"I was really nervous and didn't think I was ready—and I told her so! Pat said that I'd be fine because I knew the procedures inside and out. Plus, she said an officer would be available in case I had a question. That didn't make me feel better because I knew the officers knew less than I did."

"It must have been scary, Toni, being on your own for the first time. I know I couldn't do that job."

"I was very nervous," she nodded, then continued. "Well, just before Pat left her shift, she pulled down a thick, heavy manual from the overhead shelf and plopped it down on the desk in front of me.

"Oh yeah," Pat said. "Believe me, you will probably never use this thing, but you should know about it anyway."

"What is it?" I asked her.

"It is the landing zone coordinates for a helicopter medivac unit. In case of a serious accident, we may be required to guide a helicopter into a landing site to airlift a badly-injured victim. I have been here for fourteen years and have never had to use it, and you probably won't have to either Toni, but it's good to know and it's there just in case."

As Toni told her story, things began to click.

"*You* were the dispatcher on duty that day?" I slowly asked. "Toni, I didn't think you worked there in 1999."

She nodded twice with her head down. "I was there."

I grabbed my left side to hold off a neuropathic pain spasm but it was too late. It took my breath away, so I paused for a moment before speaking again. "Okay, sorry to interrupt," I said. "Go on, Toni."

She slowly continued.

"With one officer on the road and the lieutenant inside, the morning started slowly with one or two license plate checks and a telephone call asking for information about recycling dates or burning permits, I think.

The 911 call came into the station on the designated 'black phone' as I was about to head to the ladies' room; I had to pee so badly! They requested Police and Rescue to a cow pasture on the southeast end of Foster Center Road."

"Who did, Toni?" I asked.

"The caller on the 'black phone' did with the 911 operator listening in. He said he found a hunter in the woods that had fallen from a tree stand. The caller was frantic—and described the victim as having a broken back and fading in and out. He said it appeared to be serious. The lieutenant bolted out the door while I dispatched Police and Rescue to the scene, leaving me completely alone on my first real day on the job!

"A few more radio transmissions came and went, and then it was quiet for a while, so I felt that the initial urgency of my job was done. Then, the rescue unit on the scene radioed me, said the hunter was critical and requested a helicopter medivac unit to be dispatched to Foster and land at the Captain Isaac Paine school parking lot! Then I really panicked!

"Pulling down that heavy manual from the shelving above, I began searching for the telephone number for the medivac unit and quickly called the number listed on the inside cover. It was a Connecticut phone number for the Norwich Hospital Trauma Unit. When the operator answered the phone, she requested the landing coordinates from me!"—Toni explained, while holding her chest and exposing her wedding ring on her wide opened hand.

"Those book pages were filled with random numbers that made no sense to me and seemed to go on forever! That was the first time I even saw coordinates! I put the operator on hold before picking up again and explaining my situation. I told her I was new and the only one in the station right then! "Actually, I told her it was my first day alone and asked her to walk me through it! The operator was as cool as a cucumber and dispatched the helicopter, then asked me to find and read the coordinates to her, which I did. "After a short time, I could overhear the pilot talking to her by radio when he advised her that he was approaching Foster and could see the landing site I provided. Therefore, I advised the units on the scene that the helicopter was landing.

"Just then, one of the volunteer firefighters screamed frantically over the radio! He was waiting at the Captain Isaac Paine School for the helicopter and it wasn't there nor was it anywhere in sight!!

"I wanted to run out the door and never come back! How could the pilot see the landing zone, hover above it, yet the rescue worker couldn't see the helicopter?

"Then, the pilot radioed the operator and reported that they were hovering over a grassy field next to an old cemetery! I reread the coordinates section and found that there were more coordinates and another landing zone on the back page! I had sent the helicopter to the North Road cemetery instead of the school! I sent the helicopter to the wrong place, wasting valuable time!

"With my voice trembling and my hands shaking, I relayed a new set of coordinates to the pilot and waited for the next transmission. It was too late. He was already landing at the cemetery. Another volunteer firefighter had spotted the helicopter hovering over North Road and marked the landing site by laying down a huge X in the grass with silver duct tape.

"So, I rerouted the Rescue and all personnel to the cemetery instead and had the pilot complete his landing." Toni stared down at her fidgeting hands a few seconds before continuing.

"After it was all over, I was so afraid I may have seriously delayed the process and prevented them from transporting you to the hospital on time. When Sergeant Moony came back to the station, I saw the look on his face and was sure you were dead. He said you were still alive, but didn't look good, and I knew it was all my fault! I called my mom when I got home and broke down crying, still not knowing if you were going to live or die.

"After a sleepless night, I called Pat the next morning and told her I just couldn't come back to work. I'm sure she already knew the story, but I explained how I had caused a big delay in getting help and didn't belong doing that job. She begged me to reconsider, and I don't know why, but Pat talked me into coming into the station that day to speak to her and the lieutenant. I went back to speak to them but had no intention of staying.

"They sat me down and Pat told me that the job I did that day was highly commendable. She said that not many people could have continued under those circumstances, and as far as she was concerned, I was a darn good dispatcher that should be proud of seeing things through that day, especially without the proper training in that particular scenario. I did not think of it that way at all," Toni said, as she looked at me with approval seeking eyes.

I nodded my head in agreement. Toni continued, "The lieutenant told me that I actually saved them time because the coordinates that I sent to the helicopter pilot actually landed them closer to the accident site. I wasn't sure how true the lieutenant's statement actually was. I'm still not. I eventually went back to work after that pep talk and gained the confidence I needed to get through many more tense situations but never forgot the mistake I made that day. And, I want to say...that I am sorry."

———

AS SHE FINISHED HER STORY, I reached out and held her hand.

"Toni," I said, pulling her hand in closer. "It wasn't your fault. You did the best you could with what was thrown at you, at the time. If you hadn't dealt with my accident that day, you may never had gotten the confidence needed to continue and realize your true calling! You could have quit that day, but instead you became a good dispatcher—good enough to earn a better job at a larger department where you eventually met my son. You two kids may never have fallen in love, gotten married, and made me a grandfather.

"So, you see, things happen for a reason, and I wouldn't have changed falling out of that tree for one minute, if it meant not having you and Nevaeh in my life. I feel it was the best thing that ever happened to me—if that is what in fact brought you to me. Do you understand, Toni? And by the way, thank you for taking care of me that day."

Nevaeh crawled up the wheelchair and onto my lap as she sensed the raw emotions. I didn't know it then, but soon I'd be blessed with another little one, Olivia. Both girls were born into this world with my wheelchair included alongside my image. They didn't know any different. It took Nevaeh about two and a half years to notice that I couldn't walk before she asked me why.

Most children stare at me and smile with curiosity, and I encourage their questions, as it's usually just the parents that are uptight.

Toni seems to have ridden herself of any guilt and the subject doesn't come up anymore.

And, did I mention that I got to choose the name for my first granddaughter? It's Nevaeh. Nevaeh is *heaven* spelled backwards. When I proposed the name to Derek and Toni there were only 5000 children with that name, now there are over 50,000.

And if I may jump ahead, my children (or kids) Derek and Lauren have gifted me with four beautiful grandchildren, Nevaeh and Olivia, Scarlett Rose and a boy, named Sam.

69

LOTS OF TIME has passed since I've written anything in my journal. My family urged me to dig up my notes, start writing again, and finish it this time. I am ashamed that I haven't done it sooner.

Chapter 69. This is where I suggested that the reader skip right to if they or their loved one suddenly finds themselves in a predicament like mine, searching for answers to some of those terrifying questions.

When I was in that hospital bed, I remember thinking that I should write a book if I ever made it out of there. I promised myself to keep a journal and then publish it in order to reach at least one person in need of answers, but a busy, rich and chock-full life got in the way.

I shouldn't sugarcoat my life though, there are still plenty of struggles, but nothing of what I imagined on the day I lay paralyzed under that oak tree on that cold winter morning.

Do you remember when I wrote about lying there on the ground, imagining myself like that paralyzed boy, Kyle C?

I said, "I pictured him, not in a wheelchair, not in a therapeutic pool and certainly not in a rehabilitation center, but flat on his back, helplessly looking up at the ceiling, 24 hours a day, 7 days a week, 365 days a year. I imagined him battling insanity minute by minute—and wearing baby diapers, with matronly looking nurses spoon-feeding him like an infant."

But it's not like that; it's not like that at all. I do more now than I did before, "only in a different way." In those first few days following my accident, I needed hope and I needed answers. I'm not blaming my family or caregivers for any of that. They just didn't have anybody to ask the right questions to. Plus, they certainly don't know the crazy thoughts that go through one's mind when you realize that you are suddenly paralyzed and that your life is turned upside down. How could they know?

But those dark days are behind me and sometimes I feel that I'm happier now than before my accident. Mostly because I notice the little things—and, the things that were important to me before are not so important to me now.

I'd like to think I have learned patience, some wisdom, and an appreciation for what I have. If you find yourself in the same predicament, then I believe you can do the same.

My early log entries were quite dire and depressing. Family, friends, caregivers, and hope got me through it and I want the reader to know, "that it really *is* only temporary." That's what my mom told me over and over again. She was so right. It is only temporary, the dread and hopelessness are, I mean.

If only I had someone I could have talked to, back then. Someone to tell me what to expect in the days ahead, besides the heartache and misery. If only I knew then what I know now.

Maybe I should bring the reader up to date on my progress before I go any further.

I am still unable to walk, but as my granddaughter Nevaeh said to me at age four, "You can't walk Grandpa, but it's okay." Then, I always reply, "but I can do other things, right?" Her smile to my question helps me to remember that as long as there is hope and a will to do so, I *can* do other things—"only in a different way."

My fear under that oak tree was that I wouldn't be able to walk Lauren down the aisle when she got married. I'm still determined to do so when the time comes, only I realize now that it will have to be by sitting on four wheels. I'll do it. "Just in a different way."

Some sensation has returned but I don't want the reader to compare me to another SCI person. Please keep in mind that everyone is different. The person you know may get return that I have not, or vice versa, but we can all learn new things to replace the things we have lost.

And, just as Jesus predicted through Bess, that day on her massage table, I *am* walking again, "just in a different way."

70

I SPENT THE FIRST five years visiting patients in hospitals with newfound paralysis, even some amputees. I was asked to go in and show them that there is what I call a "huge light at the end of that dark tunnel."

Sometimes I would meet with just the family because the patient didn't want to meet me. They didn't want to identify themselves with a Para. I get that. I did that too.

Usually the first question from the wife of a paralyzed husband is—"Will we be able to be intimate with each other again?"

My reply is always the same. "Absolutely. And it can be better than before."

"Why?" they ask.

"Because you'll appreciate each other more."

One couple asked me if I had an aide.

"An aide for what?" I asked.

"An aide to get you dressed in the morning," the husband replied.

"Why would I need someone to dress me?"

"Well, I mean, will I be able to dress myself," he asked.

"If you want to. You have your arms, right?

"Yes, but how..." I stopped him from speaking by putting my finger up as I looked down to view my lap in the wheelchair. Then I lifted myself up by pushing down on the tops of my wheels to straighten myself out.

"I'll show you." By reaching behind me to hold the back of my seat with my left hand, I stopped myself from falling forward and bent over to grab my ankle with my right hand. I then lifted my leg straight up in the air about six inches from my chest. I wished I were that flexible when I practiced karate.

"This is how I take each shoe off," I said, and then did it.

"Oh, wow, how do you change your pants?" the curious wife asked.

Without thinking, I removed both shoes and put my feet back on my footplate. Then, I unzipped my jeans, pushed off on both wheels with my hands and lifted my butt off my seat. Dropping my right arm to land on my wheel, allowed me to pull the right side of my pants down with my fingers, while still keeping my right butt-cheek off the seat. I collapsed into the seat to take a quick break, then lifted myself up again and collapsed my left arm to land on its elbow—and again pulled the left side of my jeans down with my fingers.

After I landed with both butt-cheeks on my seat, I did a little hop while sliding the rest of my pants past my thighs and down both legs to the ankles. I finished by lifting an ankle again and pulling the pant leg up, away, and off the leg. I did it all very fast and it was a good thing I had clean underwear on too!

"You're not wearing a brief or diaper of any kind?" the perked-up husband asked. "Will I be like that too?"

I looked at them both before answering. "Who knows? Everyone is different. But if you work on it like I did and get some return, you may be surprised."

I hope they are both happy today.

Two years after my accident, I was invited to speak to doctors and nurses at Kent Hospital on the subject of "hope." I was wicked nervous to do so in that packed auditorium. To make matters worse, eight days before the lecture, I was on an elk hunting trip in Wyoming when my hunting party became stranded on a mountain top in an unexpected snow storm. Our chainsaws were out of fuel and we barely had enough wood to warm our tent. We had only drops of gas

Stranded on a mountain in a snowstorm for eight days.

in our four-wheelers to make it down the mountain when the storm subsided. The trip was only supposed to last four days. In addition, our canvas tent roof caught on fire and I thought for sure that I would miss the lecture. But I made it back in time, told my story, and spoke of "hope." Not knowing exactly what to speak about, I just began like this. "Even though we patients may not always communicate with you all, most of us watch your every move as you scurry about during your daily tasks. We watch you like hawks and hang onto every word. We lock onto your eyes in an attempt to capture the smallest glimmer of hope. Please try to remember that we search for hope in you."

Things surely have changed. Remember the girl I met in the hospital? The one with the big brown eyes, the bangs in her face and the smelly hand? The one that called me wazy ass? Well, Tina met a nice guy, got married and bought a small animal farm about a quarter mile away from my house in Foster. She is so close, I can jump on my 4-wheeler, cut through the woods and be at her house in less than three minutes!

Who knew that when I teased her about getting up so early back in the hospital, that someday she really would be "milking the chickens!" She appropriately named her little farm, Tina's Funny Farm. It fits.

I began playing the drums again. I'd played in a basement band as a kid and we thought we were rock stars, so the thought of getting back into playing was exciting.

But, when I sat down to play, I realized that without my legs, I couldn't complete the entire beat. I needed to kick the bass drum pedal in order to find the missing beat that I needed.

So, I improvised. I had to learn to retrain my brain to do it. It was hard, but with practice I got better and faster. I play with my mouth.

I continue to pound away on my drum set with that pedal switch between my teeth. I look like an idiot, drool like a horse with a bit in its mouth and miss a beat sometimes, but I don't care, I'm just grateful that I can play again. I took up drum lessons again, enrolled in The School of Rock and joined a band where we do periotic gigs. I'm still a rock star! I have googled paraplegics playing the drums and found absolutely nothing on the subject. Now that I've found a way, I hope to YouTube it and share it with the rest of the paralyzed community.

I'm still able to do most things I used to do and more. I go clamming, on my butt of course, metal detecting for artifacts and digging

Halloween gig with my band, Mutiny.
From left to right: Paul LaCava, Andrea Paglia, Anne Marie Vale,
Bobby DePalo, Deanna Hanafin, Amanda Petteruto, Alex Ricciardi.

in old dump sites—again on my butt. I go swimming by lying face down on a boogie board, fishing from a boat, 4-wheeling like crazy, staining my deck, leaf blowing my yard, shoveling snow and, of course, hunting any chance I get.

I'm able to dive off the 4-wheeler onto the ground and field dress a deer, antelope, or bear—and climb back up onto the 4-wheeler to rope and drag my harvest home all by myself.

My point is this, if you were a great checkers player and now you can't reach the checkers, make a contraption to reach it. Make it happen. Don't give up what you once loved to do. Do it differently, if you can.

I have a bucket list and I'm not going anywhere until I empty it. I want to see the Sistine Chapel. I just have to hit Power Ball first.

71

Now, I HAVE agonized over whether to divulge the most personal details concerning bathroom duties and things like that. It took me a long time to reach this decision, and I have decided to spill the beans (no pun intended). I usually speak privately about these matters, but to reach more people with newfound paralysis, I think I just have to get it out there.

Please remember that I only have experience as a paraplegic and not as a quadriplegic. I have the use of my hands and arms, so things work differently for me. I don't want to speak for quadriplegics but hope I might help someone with similar challenges.

Initially I was worried that people I know may look at me in a different way after reading this book, but I want people to know my story and maybe help someone to get through those early days of fear and uncertainty.

So here I go.

Bowel Function

I started with that because it was most important to me. There was no one in the hospital who could tell me what to expect or even tell me how I was going to move my bowels. I knew that I hadn't gone in days and thought that an accident was imminent, so I asked for a bedpan to be placed under me every few hours, even though I was still lying in a prone position.

They brought it to me each time I asked without explaining anything! I don't blame them, because they just didn't know what I now know. I really needed someone to tell me the following facts:

After a physical trauma, your digestive system shuts down and not moving your bowels for days is quite normal. No one told me that.

You are not going to have to lay in a prone position with a bedpan under you, wishing for a movement for the rest of your life. No one told me that. When your system starts up again and you get your strength back, you will get out of bed and learn the bowel routine that works for you and move your bowels routinely without a worry. No one told me that. Unfortunately, I couldn't imagine anything past that moment in time while laying on that bedpan hoping for a miracle.

Today I have improved enough to consider myself very lucky in that area. If you don't get the return back that I have gotten, I believe that you may be able to use other means to be okay with it too. I don't have to wear a diaper or a brief now but everyone is different.

In the beginning, I couldn't push to go but I never stopped trying. I am not sure what I pushed with, where I pushed from, or how I pushed—but I pushed like heck, and over time, something worked.

After paralysis, I believe that if all you have left are your earlobes to push with, then push with your earlobes.

Think about it this way. Before your injury, let us say that out of billions of nerves in your body, you once used one thousand of them to push those abdomen muscles to get things moving.

After your injury, if all you are left with is just fifty nerves that you can control, use them. Use those fifty! Find them and use them! Two things may happen. Your muscles may become so strong, that just those fifty nerves may be all it takes to fire those particular muscles. Also, those fifty nerves may reconnect to others and grow more nerves down the road. Rewire your nervous system. It's worth a try! Remember, it's not what you don't have; it's what you do have after your injury. Build on that.

Some of my hip movement returned for me in that same way. The docs said it could be from the reduction of swelling after the injury, but I attributed it to the return to activity, regeneration of nerves and strong will. Maybe it was all of the above.

Back to the bathroom routine. I'm not sure which muscles I use to push when I push, maybe it *is* my earlobes (just kidding), I just know that I'll use whatever I have and take whatever I get.

That long, foldout, stimulating-stick, contraption thingy that SCI expert showed me in the hospital was not for me at all but maybe people without hand and arm control may benefit from it.

For paraplegics, digital stimulation can be accomplished by using just a gloved finger, (if you can reach.) And just because you can't reach *now* doesn't mean you won't be able to reach your bum in a month or so. The nice woman that visited me in the hospital and wanted to sell me that foldout stick didn't know that most paraplegics can reach their bottoms with their hand. The stick was for quadriplegics I guess, which is cool, but she should have known that. She also did not tell me that bowel sensation return could occur sometimes when you leave the hospital. Although she meant well, she left me feeling hopeless.

Here is how digital stim works.

Some people may stimulate bowel movement by gently circling the opening of the rectum area with a gloved finger and pushing simultaneously. There, I said it. I can hear my friends now. "You want people to do what?"

I can also hear Uncle Tony who once said to me just before he passed away, "Don't be embarrassed and put it all in your book. Let it all hang out if it means helping somebody. People are not going to judge you, besides, everyone's got one of those." Uncle Tony is right; we all do have "one of those."

Some people "empty" every day and some do not. Some people wear briefs and some do not. Some people manage just fine by themselves, without help, and some do not.

Once you develop your own routine, whatever it is, I promise you it will become as natural for you as did your previous bowel routine and you will not worry or even think about it.

I know, I know, no one could have convinced me that it would be okay, either. But when you start to live your life again, you really will get used to your new routine and lose the worry. You'll see.

I'm still called back to hospitals to speak privately with families and patients suffering from paralysis. For me, one of the most commonly asked question is the one concerning the bathroom routine. It was my primary worry as well. Maybe someday you too could help someone figure out what options they have. Maybe you could help them get rid of that pit in their stomach and realize that laying there on that bedpan right now is *not* how it's always going to be.

Pressure Sores / Blood Clots / Etc.

The care givers will put the fear of God in you concerning bed sores. They swore to me that I would get them. I haven't. I think I have avoided bed and seat sores by being active and watching what I eat. It's all about mobility and diet, my doc told me. Bedsores need a bed to get sore in, so if you are able to, stay out of that bed as much as possible. I have never had my skin break down, never, so maybe my doctor was right.

Many quadriplegics can tip their motorized wheelchairs back, in order to take pressure off their bottoms. That's just one way.

And, those old lady stocking things they made me wear on my legs that were so important at the time? Teds or Teddies? I ripped those off when I got home. One doctor told me that stockings are to prevent blood clots and another doctor told me that paraplegics are not at risk for blood clots. I should have checked on the CareCure site for the real answer but really didn't care. They're white, they're old ladyish and stand out like a sore thumb. My semi-tight, black socks work for me just fine, try it. I'm just mad at the makers for not making colored Teds.

I stopped wearing those Leonards at night too. Some of the care-givers freaked out if my Leonards were not on me just perfectly so. Those Leonards boots they put on me at bedtime were supposed to keep me from getting foot drop. Everyone freaked out about me getting foot drop. I figured, "what do I care about foot drop?" I got a terrible night's sleep if I wore them, because they prevented me from turning. I had to lay on my back all night. They also made me wear them to prevent my heel skin from touching the bed and breaking down. But if you can stay out of that bed during the day, your foot heels won't be touching the bed's surface anyway. I threw those away too.

Peeing / Urinary Tract Infections

I have replaced one of my favorite drinks, orange juice, with cran-berry juice cocktail and try to drink lots of water. Cranberry juice is supposed to prevent bladder infections. Paraplegics are susceptible to urinary infections, so I drink lots.

I can feel when my bladder is full, but I'm not sure how. Is it a learned thing or the benefit of my somewhat low level of injury? I couldn't feel any of it when I was in the hospital but have since learned to sense when I need to pee. It has developed over time. Try to tune into it and let your mind do the sensing if you can.

I know a girl who senses pressure in her bladder when she needs to go.

I sense a slight, far away burning sensation in mine.

Another guy told me he knows when to urinate by subcon-sciously keeping track of the fluids that went in and how much time has elapsed throughout the day. He said he doesn't even think about it; it comes naturally now.

Some people with paralysis empty their bladder the natural way by pushing. Just because you don't have the ability now doesn't mean you won't be able to push later on.

Lastly, some people need to use a straight catheter that takes about three minutes to get the job done. They do it themselves and it's easy. Some can push to pee but choose to use a catheter because it's less straining and quicker.

I think some people imagine paraplegics wearing a pee bag but that's not necessarily true. I think I incorrectly thought that was the case too. What did I know?

Body Strength / Exercise

If you just remain active, and I don't care how active, muscles will develop somewhere. Don't think you have to spend the rest of your life lifting weights either. Just live. Enjoy what you like to do and do it. Strength will come back and sometimes exceed what you had before.

Some improvements may come back in other forms. My family is convinced that I have developed super human hearing. I have noticed improvements there too. I attribute it to my need to fine-tune my hearing out of necessity.

I used to be able to get up and run here and there to see what was going on in other rooms or areas. I used my eyes then.

Now I am sometimes stuck in one place (laziness), with little choice left but to listen. I find myself stretching my hearing out to sounds that didn't matter before and subconsciously try to figure out what's going on instead of rolling out there to look.

I think my sense of smell and far-sight has also improved for the same reasons.

I took so many of these things for granted before.

Depression / Attitude

How could we not get depressed? I just wish I got out of my slump sooner, because I wasted a lot of time on that when I could have been enjoying the things in life that I do now.

Of course, there are still times when I get down, but doesn't everybody? Sometimes I miss feeling the grass under my feet. I fought my family's suggestion for antidepressants in the beginning and now I wish I hadn't been so stubborn.

Being independent is something I'm proud of, and most of the time I forget I'm in a wheelchair altogether. My friends and family say they forget too and don't see me in one; although it took me a long time to believe that.

Try not to get too mad when people do and say dumb things. Learn patience even when it is hard to.

For example, when the seating host in a restaurant totally looks past you and asks someone with you the following question, "Does *he* need a table or is a booth okay for *him*?" My family or friends usually respond this way: "I don't know, why don't you ask him?"

And, if the host or hostess does ask you, they usually yell at you as if you're deaf. I try to laugh it off because my son Derek usually does a great impression of them when we get to our table, anyway.

When you are able to do so, hop out of that wheelchair and sit on a regular piece of furniture, maybe the couch or armchair. It's good to get rid of that thing once in a while and I think we sometimes forget that we are not glued to it. It helps me to get the wheelchair out of my view sometimes. I try to remember that when I can.

As I am writing this, I'm beginning to feel like I'm preaching, but I'm not sure how else to relay these things. Please know that they are things that work for me. I also don't want to pretend that everything is all peaches and cream. Dealing with paralysis sometimes sucks, and I don't want to pretend it doesn't.

I just hope we can remember that able-bodied people have plenty of things that suck too.

My caregivers in the hospital told me that SCI patients have a high divorce rate. Relationship therapy might be an option too when you get home.

What they didn't tell me was that coming home would be hell

for me as well as my family. For me, it lasted about two months but your family may differ. Once I realized I needed help, I was able to get better. I used the tools that were taught to me by my caregivers, used the medication that kept me on an even keel, and used my mind to get back what I had lost.

After I started hunting again, I not only improved my upper body strength, but my spirit skyrocketed. I realized how important distraction was and how it was the single most cure-all for the chronic pain I had developed on a daily basis. Not all people with spinal cord injuries will experience pain, but if you do I have found that distraction is the best medicine. I honed my hunting skills even further, all by doing it in a different way. I was semi-successful in harvesting two bear in the years prior to my accident. But after my accident, I shot eight bear as a paraplegic by developing new methods on the fly.

When I first got hurt, one of the doctors told me that the question of a cure from stem cell research wasn't *if* they would find a cure but *when*. So, I asked him, "when, then?"

"Oh, within three years for sure," the young doctor said. Well, I hung on to that. I hung on to that for far too long. That was in 1999.

Today, I have learned to stop waiting for a cure and live my life. If it happens, then it will be a bonus, but I refuse to wait for something I have no control of. The day I stopped waiting, is the day I started living and I feel much better for it.

I left the hospital on January 16, 2000.

The internet was in full swing and I had to create a username, email address and word to identify myself in connection with the internet. It was tough coming up with a name that would correspond with my new identity, which I despised.

I remembered a get well card I'd received from my Cousin Kenny. I got a kick out of the note Kenny wrote me on the inside cover. It read, "Hey Cuz, who do you think you are? Don't you know you *can't fly*?" When I read the joke to my nurses, they loved it and started calling me "Can't Fly."

So, "Can't Fly" was taken as a username and email name but "Kantfly" wasn't. I grabbed it and have had it ever since. To this day some people call me Kantfly and like the idea of me poking fun at myself and making light of my accident. If you've read my book this far, you now know what the title of my book means. Not super climactic, just the truth.

I recently inserted and added this part.

15 years have passed since I started this journal. Whoa! Time has surely flown by!

I was just diagnosed with PTSD (Post-Traumatic Stress Disorder). I recently began waking up from a deep sleep with full-blown panic attacks. After all these years it decided to show up now, but the good news is, there is a real remedy for it, besides drugs. It's called EMDR (Eye Movement Desensitization and Reprocessing), and it is really helping me to eliminate these episodes.

When I got hurt, I have a memory of waking up in an MRI machine in the hospital. My upper half was strapped down tightly and I couldn't move my lower half. The experts say that things like that caused my PTSD, and resurrecting this book may have triggered flashbacks and memories—but I'm confident that I can beat it.

I was referred to a therapist who immediately began treating me with EMDR therapy and discovered that I was very responsive to the treatment. I'm so grateful and hope that other SCI sufferers learn about EMDR like I did. Hope it helps.

Showering / Dressing

When I first got hurt, I thought that I would need assistance to undress and dress myself for the rest of my life. Not so. I can do it sitting on the bed if I want to, but I find it easier to do in the wheelchair.

When I first tried, I flopped over like a spineless jellyfish, but in time I got stronger and stopped thinking about every move. I found that just by putting my own pants on, gave me a huge sense of accomplishment. Muscle buildup did too. Now, I wouldn't dare let anyone help me with that, nor would they even want to.

I have come a long way since I fell off that shower chair in the hospital and laid helplessly on that floor by the dirty floor drain, feeling sorry for myself. Showering can be done independently if you have upper body control. At first, you may be able to slide from your wheelchair over to a shower chair by using a transfer board. Eventually your upper body strength could allow you to jump into the tub onto an awaiting shower chair without the board.

If you don't have hand or arm control, you can certainly help your aide get things done.

Don't think that what you have to work with today is what you are going to have in the future. You'll see what I mean.

After my torso muscles came back, I was able to sit on a shower chair and steady myself with my elbow by leaning on the grab bar that I bolted to the shower wall. That left me with one hand free to clutch the hand-held showerhead and the other hand to lather myself up. It took me forever to remember to leave a dry towel in reach though. I still forget.

I sure wish that someone had told *me* that the wheelchair seatbelt was only temporary. In the beginning I never dreamed that I would ditch the chair's anti-tip bars too.

Pain

Boy, do I have lots of it. I have two types of pain. Just the normal, I broke my back and have rods in it now, type of pain—and then I have neuropathic pain. I get pain spasms throughout the day and night, and it increases its frequency if I eat certain foods, become tired or stressed, the weather changes, or for no good reason at all.

When the nerve pain meds fall short, sometimes my mind can stop the pain spasms when they get going. I'm getting pretty good at it now.

I believe that the mind can control the body and learning to do things with it has really helped me. I had a background in martial arts training, but it was nothing compared to what I now know and use.

My friend Carol, who is a Reiki Master, did Reiki on me and it helped with the pain, so I became a second level Reiki practitioner and now do it on myself as well as on others. It is amazing.

Most people don't understand how people with paralysis can experience pain. I wouldn't have either. I think my damaged spinal cord tries to fire nerve signals but instead shoots them out as pain signals instead. That's my professional diagnosis. I really don't know. I should go on the CareCure website to find out.

I do know that if I sit and think about it, the pain increases, but if I stay active and immerse myself in the things I like to do, I forget about the pain altogether.

Of all the things I have tried, I find that *distraction* helps the best with pain relief. So, I keep myself distracted with being super active, hunting and fishing, metal detecting for historic artifacts, 4-wheel-ing, hanging out with family and friends, and living life to its fullest. There is so much more I haven't tried—but will. I firmly believe that distraction is the best medicine.

Sensation

This is where the mind comes in again. Although my legs give off a strong "pins and needles" sensation most times, and I don't feel them to the touch. It's as if I can feel my legs if I see someone else touch them.

In other words, I feel the sensation with my mind. I can imagine it or maybe just remember it; therefore, I can still feel it. I can't explain it the way I want to. Let me think.

Maybe because my mind remembers what my leg felt at the moment it was once touched. Maybe it still relays that signal to my mind when I see it being touched now.

My wires are crossed too. When you squeeze my left foot, I feel increased vibrations on my right and vice versa. When I squeeze my left index finger, I feel tingling on my right foot. The left does it too.

It seems that I know when something is wrong too, like sitting on a pen or laying on one of the kid's toys.

Once, while hunting on Cuckoo's 4-wheeler out west, I instinctively reached down to touch and feel for my left knee for no apparent reason at all, only to find a swollen leg that was broken in two places at the tibia and fibula bones. Something told me to touch my leg, but what? I didn't realize I had broken it while field dressing an antelope I had shot an hour before. My mind sensed it, though. I have too many stories like that.

Driving

I installed very simple hand controls in my Ford minivan. I found them used on eBay for $60.00. My brother, Ricky, and I installed them ourselves.

I push the lever down for the brake and forward for the gas. I transfer into the driver's seat by holding onto the seat with my right hand and hold the door where the window controls are with my left. I pull myself up into the seat and throw my wheelchair through the left sliding door behind me.

I'm not sure if quadriplegics can get their chair inside without help. Remember, everyone is different, but some may be able to with the help from a wheelchair lift.

I once watched a quadriplegic drive his own minivan unassisted, by motoring his power chair up an electric ramp and into his van. He parked his chair where the driver's seat would normally go, and instead of using hand controls, he used a head pad to control the gas and brake lever. He was in and ready to go in about three minutes flat.

My point is, that guy really wanted to drive independently and managed to do it with what he had.

Sex

This was the second most commonly-asked question when I met with families, especially from spouses. I feel that the partners were not asking out of concern of their own needs but rather they wanted to know how they could help their partner feel just as adequate and as normal as before.

When I was in the hospital, my night shift nurses who were more fun than the day shift, once talked to me about sex and told me that it wasn't understood why, but most men with spinal cord injuries can last forev...,—oops, never mind, my kids are going to read this! You guys will have to find that stuff out on your own. I just know that being intimate is not an issue but I would never have thought that would be the case when I first got hurt.

If sex becomes an obstacle then urologists have lots of answers. Lots.

I met a woman at a rehabilitation center that was paralyzed from the belly button down. She explained that she still enjoys sex just as much and maybe more than before, only now it was with her mind also and not just with her body.

She went on to say that being intimate was still just as satisfying, because her mind allowed her to sense feelings and emotions on a higher level than before. Some things she could feel and some things she imagined she could feel.

I don't want to preach or give false information here. Again, there is a great website for the over 250,000 of us. It's called "CareCure Community" and the web address is **sci.rutgers.edu**. I hope by the time I publish this book, CareCure is still in business. It contains a wealth of information, along with lots of topics and message boards with SCI men and women who post their comments. The doctors, nurses and moderators are great! You can search almost any question you have.

I wouldn't spend all of your time there though, because I think you can devote too much to it searching for a cure and less time living your life. I used to just hit and run, now I just live.

Leg Braces

The radio spot ad for Kent Hospital was in my opinion a little misleading to the public. People later told me that they thought I was walking again. The ad quoted me saying, *"Several months later I came back walking unassisted in my braces and hugged all my nurses and gave an angel to Dr. Mary Eleanor Toms and her staff and told them, "you're all my angels."* I want to be clear that for me leg braces expend way too much energy for the few steps I may take. Although, at the time no one was going to talk me out of conquering the leg braces. Today I buzz around in my wheelchair and get to where I'm going much quicker.

72

RECENTLY, I HAVE been speaking to kindergarten kids about disabilities and what it's like being in the wheelchair. I really need to try to drop that phrase, "being in a wheelchair," and replace it with, "getting around in" or "doing things from a wheelchair."

Also, don't you just hate the words paraplegic and quadriplegic? They're so ugly. How can we change them? Can we start a movement to replace them with the words, umm, how about no label at all? That's my vote. What's yours?

It is so much fun visiting young schoolkids—they are so funny. Just last week I visited a class of nineteen eager and curious little sponges that left me feeling so proud of their teacher, parents and of course the little rug rats themselves. It is still fresh in my mind, so I thought I would share some of what we covered when I was asked to speak at their school. I have kind of a "*bit*" that I follow, and here are some of the conversations and details of my visit.

I arrive at the school unexpectedly, because I specifically ask the teacher not to tell them I'm coming. I knock on the door and enter the classroom with a mischievous smirk on my face, with one eyebrow up and the other one down. They are usually sitting on the floor in front of the whiteboard. The first time I saw the whiteboard and marker, I asked the kids where the blackboard and chalk were located. They laughed but surprisingly knew what I was talking about—these kids are smart.

"Morning, kids!" I say, with enthusiasm.

"Mr. Bobby, we call them friends," the teacher corrects me, but nicely and with a big smile. "Because I'm not a fan of political correctness, I make fun of the policy and get the kids going right way.

"Do you boys and girls know why I'm here?" I ask.

"To visit us?" an enthusiastic little girl responds.

"Yes, but why?" I ask, again. They don't have a clue. "I want to teach you about people with disabilities, for instance, people in wheelchairs." I then go on to teach them the words paraplegic and quadriplegic, what they both mean, and explain to them that I can't feel or move my legs and why. I also told them how I got hurt and injured my spinal cord. They knew what a spine is.

I showed them my reacher/grabber stick that I hooked on my seat back and then showed off my arm muscles, but pronounced them muskles, like Popeye does.

"So, tell me," I continue, "when you see a person in a wheelchair, say you are at Chuck E. Cheese or the food court at the mall, what do you think about that person? Do you ever think that they *can't* do things? Tell me what you think *I can't* do and I'll write it on the white 'blackboard.'" They giggle and all raise their hands high. "By the way, I would like you guys to know that I can do almost everything you can do, *just in a different way*. Okay, tell me what you think I *can't* do."

"You can't play," a little boy, says sadly, looking away as it leaves his lips.

"Do you mean like, soccer?" I ask.

"Yes," he replies. I write that on the board. *Can't play.*

"Who else," I ask.

"You can't sleep, I mean on a bed," says a cute little girl with a large blue fabric flower in her wild and wavy blond hair.

"Great!" I fired back, as I write that answer on the board too. *Can't sleep on bed.* "How old are you sweetie?"

"I'm five," she replied, timidly.

"Oh, wow. Are you married?" I asked.

The kids laugh from their bellies, as the little girl shakes her head *no* and covers her eyes with her tiny hands. "Do you drive?" I ask her. This time she laughs aloud with the rest of them and surprises me with a loud giggling, *no*!

"Good answers so far, who else? Yes?" I ask, as I point to and call on an adorable Indian or possibly Pakistani little girl.

"You can't drive a car!" she answers, proudly. I write that on the board too. *Can't drive.*

"Next! Yes, sir! You, sir!" I point to an adorable, squirmy little boy that just can't sit still. "Yes, you, the guy with the ants in his pants!" I holler out to him.

The little boy took forever to spit it out, and I make like I fell asleep while waiting, which gets he and the kids laughing uncontrollably again.

"Um..., um..., you can't change your underwear!" he finally blurts out with a serious expression on his face. Of course, the class roars in laughter again.

"Wait a minute, hold on! Do you mean that I can't dress myself? Is that what you mean, because if so, that's a great answer!"

"Yes, that's what I mean," the little boy with ants in his pants replies, ever so proudly, still squirming in place. I raise my right hand as if to take an oath. "I promise you that I change my underwear every day!

I wrote three or four more *can't do's* on the white blackboard and asked for just one more.

Now, keep in mind, I was sitting sideways, perpendicular with the board and had to hold on to the back of my wheelchair with my left hand, so I wouldn't fall out. As I stretched to try and write higher and higher on the whiteboard, I was doing my best to keep it legible but guess I wasn't doing as good a job as I thought I was. "Just one more, last one," I said, as I called on the quiet-looking, little darling in the back row. "Yes, what *can't* I do?" I asked her.

She stared at me, almost afraid to answer but finally got the courage to tell me what was on her precious little mind.

"Well," she said in a soft, sweet and much too quiet voice. "You can't..., um..., you can't write neatly."

The class didn't know what to do! I quickly looked over to my sloppy scribblings with my mouth opened wide and one eye squinted shut. Then I crossed my arms and gave out a big, "oh, really!" The smile that came across my face gave them the cue that they could erupt in uncontrollable laughter.

"A kindergartener is going to tell me that I write sloppily? Come over here and say that," I said, to the shy little girl who was as red as a beet but giggling with the others just the same.

"Okay, settle down, friends..., settle down," the teacher announces, firmly, yet kindly as she chuckled.

At that point, I show the kids how I jump on my bed to sleep at night by demonstrating transferring out of my wheelchair and onto a pretend bed, which is actually a chair that the teacher pushes over to me.

When I hop from my wheelchair over to the pretend bed, the kids are amazed and tell me it's because of my strong arms that I am able to do it. I remind them that I can do almost anything I want, only in a different way. Then, I cross that *can't* item off the list on the board too, with their permission of course.

I go down the rest of the list and come to the *can't do* that says *can't play*. I ask the teacher for a soccer ball and ask for a volunteer. By then, they all raise their hands at the same time. I choose a child that hasn't participated yet and ask a little boy in the back row to play kickball with me. Instead of my feet, I use my arms to kick the ball back and forth with him and cross that one off the board too.

When we come to the one on the board that says I can't drive, I explain that I drove there. I get them thinking by asking them to help me think of a way of how I can drive without using my legs and feet. Some of the answers they gave were hysterical and yet in the end, they had it all figured out. They invented hand controls right there on that classroom floor. I let them know that I did in fact have hand controls and they asked if they could see them. The teacher then asked the principal if they could go outside and into the parking lot to see them. We got permission to do so before I left.

———————

LAST ON THE LIST OF *can'ts* was the one about difficulty changing my clothes by myself, or should I say, underwear. After reminding them that I use my arms in place of my legs most times, I had them figure out how I could change my clothes even if I couldn't stand or move my legs. As they told me what to do, I followed their instructions. They had me reach down with my hands, grab on to one shoe, and lift my leg high in the air. Then holding it up by my left hand, they instructed me to untie my shoe and remove it with my right. To remove my pants, they decided that I could use my strong *"Popeye muskles"* because my arms were full of them and to lift my butt off the seat to drop my pants down—which I pretended that I did. They were thrilled to figure it all out. I kept reiterating that I can do everything they can do, *only in a different way.*

"Do you guys want to see me pop a wheelie?" That was a big hit. They even had me spinning in circles with the front wheels off the ground. After that, I had them try out my wheelchair, making sure they didn't try doing a wheelie, although the brave ones wanted to.

In the end, I told them a story. "When I want to do something that my friends are doing, I don't stay home and just accept that I may not be able to participate, I try to figure out how I can do it too, like we all just did. Only in a different way. Here is a for instance," I told them.

"When I was bow hunting with my friends one time, we stayed in a cabin on an island. Bow hunting means hunting with a bow and arrow, kids. Did you all know that?" Most kids did because of Katniss from the Hunger Games and Brave, the Disney movie. I continued.

"Well, we all brought our favorite snacks for the weekend. Mine are Devil Dogs. I love Devil Dogs! Do you guys like Devil Dogs?" The teacher interrupted me and chuckled. "I don't think they've ever seen a Devil Dog, Mr. Bobby." I crack up laughing and tell them to go home and ask their parents to buy them a box of Drakes Devil Dogs. Then the teacher announced, "Mr. Bobby is going to get in big trouble!"

I continued. "Well, my friends teased me one time by putting my box of Devil Dogs on top of the refrigerator, so I could see them, but couldn't reach them! Then my friends went for a ride while I decided to stay back and wax the string on my bow and get ready for the early morning hunt. We were always pulling pranks on each other like that and I guess I deserved it because I was just as bad.

"So, as I sat there waxing my bow, I kept looking up at those Devil Dogs and thinking to myself, I can either sit here and wish I could reach them or I could figure out a way to get them on my own. So, do you know what I did?"

"You figured out how to get them, but in a different way," screamed the shy girl with the flower in her hair.

"That's right, I did. But, how did I do it?" I asked. After many guesses, I explained that I had something that I brought for them and maybe they could figure out how I could retrieve that too. I reached into my backpack and pulled out two bags of Pirate's Booty veggie treats.

"I was told you kids like these, but I could be wrong," I said, teasingly. They went crazy for them! Then I had the teacher place them up over the cupboard just inches from the ceiling. I sat back in my wheelchair, scowled at not being able to reach them, and watched as they came up with ingenious ways to get those two bags of goodies down from that cupboard top.

"I know," said the boy with ants in his pants, "you could use your reacher and grab it!"

"Great answer, but it's too short..., how could we make it longer?"

Mom and me after the accident.

Another boy raised his hand up high. "Maybe you could tie another stick to it and make it long!"

"Awesome! Let's try it! Is that a broom over in the corner? Can someone bring it to me? I don't have string but I carry black electrical tape in my backpack. Let's try that!" I taped my reacher and the broom handle together and made one, super long stick. "Okay, I won't be able to push it off the cupboard because the bags need to come forward. I need to attach something that will make the bags stick to my stick. Something like magnets..., hmmm." I thought, with my finger on my chin.

"Oh, oh, I know," said a girl who hadn't spoken before. "We need something sticky to put on the end of the stick!"

"Yes!" I screamed, making them all jump back a foot or so, then falling over sideways onto the clean-carpeted floor, while holding their tummies in laughter.

"Something sticky, huh? What if I take my electrical tape again, turn the sticky side out, and fasten it to the end of the stick? Maybe we touch it to the Pirate's Booty and pull it towards us and off the cabinet?"

"Let's try it!" they screamed, on their knees bouncing up and down in contagious excitement.

The kids guided me through the sticky tape process and then I rolled over to the cupboards where the Booty was.

"Who wants to try it?"

"I do, I do!" The Indian/Pakistani little angel beat the others and stepped forward as if she knew what I was going to say. Her huge eyes lit up as I handed her the elongated stick with the sticky end. With two hands, she struggled to get the stick up and onto the closest bag. It stuck! Then she slowly maneuvered the Booty bag towards her until it reached the edge and fell over onto the desk below. The kids cheered as she handed me the stick for my turn to grasp the second one.

After I pulled it over the edge, I asked the kids to tell me how I got the Pirate's Booty. Almost simultaneously, they yelled out proudly and loudly—"You did it! Only in a different way!"

I added, "And my Devil Dogs too!"

Kindergarten class, disability awareness.

After the children settled down, I ended my bit with some final questions.

"So, the next time you see a person in a wheelchair, are you going to assume they can't do things?"

They all seemed to speak at once. Even the shy ones. "No, I won't! I won't!" I sat back in my chair and smiled.

"Do you think you'll invite them to play games at recess with you like any other friend?"

"I know, I know," blurted a little boy with both hands raised and hadn't spoken before.

"Yes?" I asked, as I began gathering myself to leave, super interested in his response.

"They can play soccer with us!" he said proudly. "They can do anything that we can do, only in a different way!"

Delighted, I smiled at him and all the children. "There you go," I replied. "Mission accomplished. Now let's eat some Pirate's Booty!"

73

I WISH I COULD end my story with the ultimate statement that would allow the person with the spinal injury to get just a glimpse into a hope-filled future.

As I withdraw my one typing finger from my laptop,—and btw, I do not type with just one finger because of any disability, it's just because I can't type.

As I sit back and try to figure out how to end this book, all I can come up with is this:

Whenever I start to feel bad for myself, I try to remember that there are people who have it a lot worse than I do. Not long after I got hurt, I spoke to a quadriplegic online. As I complained to him about something I thought was important, he responded this way.

"Bobby, you're only a paraplegic, I'm a quad! Hell, it takes me almost a minute to shoo a damn fly away if it lands on my damn nose!"

Since then, I try to appreciate what I have.

I am sure a quadriplegic wishes that he had what I have. Just as I wish that I had what an amputee on crutches has. And, I'll bet the amputee wishes that he had what the footless man has. And so on. Do you think a blind man wishes that he had what a quadriplegic has?

My physical therapists were right about the leg braces. They expend too much energy and are not practical. I buzz around in my wheelchair just as fast as if I were walking. However, I promised

Dr. Toms that someday I would come back to the hospital on those braces after she witnessed my unsuccessful initial attempts to get up and stay up on the parallel bars.

———

SO, SIX MONTHS AFTER I was released, I called Kent Hospital and tipped off a few people as to my surprise visit. I hadn't actually been back to the unit since I left for home on that scary day, day number 50.

I called Michelle and Paula when I got to the lobby, and after zooming down the steep ramp, I sat still to strap on the cumbersome leg braces. I couldn't help thinking of Tina and struggling to climb that same ramp after our "escape" that night, months before.

After putting on the braces, I unlocked the knee hinges, tucked my feet onto the chair's footplate and headed for the elevator. I scooted into the overcrowded gift shop on the way, complained nicely to the manager that the aisles were still too narrow for wheelchairs to get through, purchased a ceramic little angel with widespread wings and a halo, and headed for the elevator again.

The smells of the hospital unleashed butterflies in my stomach as I reached for the door button. The elevator door opened before me, forcing me to quickly maneuver past the exiting visitors and zip into the occupied elevator. "*Boy, what a difference,*" I thought, as the doors closed and the silence was deafening. "*It's hard to imagine how far I've come.*" "What floor?" I asked, as I reached for and lit up the other buttons above my own.

The doors opened to the fourth floor. I think I hesitated for a second when flashbacks and emotions tried to emerge, but I dismissed them quickly and bolted through the door just before it closed.

Wheeling fast around the corridor corner, I almost took out Michelle and Paula at the knees before skidding sideways and laughing into the wall with both hands out to stop.

Each girl hugged me tightly and I didn't want to let go. I kissed their necks and hung on tight, then wiped the tears away but continued to hold both their hands while I brought them up to date on things.

Michelle had a walker waiting for me by Mary-Lynn's speech therapy office. I immediately thought of Tina again.

The walker had green tennis balls stuck on its front legs and reminded me of the elderly patients that I shared my time with there.

"Where is Dr. Toms?" I asked them.

"She is doing paperwork at the nurses' station," Michelle said. "She doesn't have a clue you're coming. Lou Ann, Shirley, Mary Lou and Elsa are down there. I think Maria is there too. Carl and Tom are in the gym, and you know that Mike and Roseanne left a few months back, don't you?"

"Yes, I heard. She has no idea I'm coming?"

"No idea," they said, simultaneously.

I put my legs out straight and locked the brace hinges. Paula held the back of my wheelchair and Michelle stood in front of the walker with the green tennis balls.

"Bobby, your arms are huge! What have you been doing?" Michelle asked.

"Just living," I replied, and then pulled myself up to a standing position while holding on to the walker. It was probably sixty feet to the nurses' station but I was full of adrenaline and didn't care.

When I threw my right hip forward, my right leg followed but didn't go very far. I realized my foot had dropped farther since I practiced last and it was coming out of the brace bottom, so I kicked it up a notch and moved faster. I didn't want her to catch me coming down the corridor before I was able to sneak up on her.

As I passed the rooms on the way, I couldn't help looking in. Emotions began to tug at me again, but my mind was averted to the strain and struggle of the long trek.

"Good thing I wore short sleeves," I whispered to Michelle, who was now behind me with Paula. "You guys always have the heat set on cremate in here."

As I got close to the station, some of the nurses looked over at me with big smiles and surprised stares. Before they gave me up, I took my hand off the walker, put my pointer finger to my nose to shhh them, and in an off-balanced shuffle, almost went flying before catching myself. I was drenched in sweat.

The nurses parted way as I stopped at the small opening at the station. Dr. Toms sat with her back to me as I breathed heavily when I spoke.

"I told you that someday I'd come back to visit you by hobbling down that corridor on braces, all by myself."

Startled, she jumped up, turned to me with her hand on her chest and looked at me with the most compassionate eyes! Then came the tears.

I pulled out the angel, which was wrapped in tissue paper and tucked in my waistband, and began my unprepared, choked up speech.

"I want to thank you, and all the wonderful people here at Kent Rehab, who were there for me when I needed you most." I spoke through water-filled eyes because wiping them dry would risk letting go and falling down in front of them all.

"You all helped get me through a horrifying experience and I wouldn't be here today if you hadn't. Although I am handing this angel to you, Dr. Toms, I need everyone to know that you are *all* my angels. I think of you all every day and know that I will remember you all until the day I die. Thank you all so much," I said, this time looking down in time to see a tear fall off my face and land on the floor. "Thank you."

I have gone back many times to visit patients and staff over the years, and the first thing I do as I enter the nurses' station is glance over at the desk shelf where Dr. Toms used to sit. And there on that shelf, still sits my little ceramic angel with the widespread wings and the gold halo.

This was supposed to be the ending of my book but something awesome has happened to me. Thank you for letting me share it.

74

Y EARS HAVE PASSED since I found myself under that oak tree, lying on my broken back, imagining my daughter's wedding day and heartbroken over the thought of not being able to walk her down the aisle.

Last Christmas Eve was an unusually cold one. I had just hopped into the seat of my minivan and had thrown my wheelchair up and in through the sliding door behind me in the dark. I quickly started the engine and set the heater on hot to make my date in the passenger seat more comfortable. Then I pushed on the hand-controlled brake lever with my left hand and pushed on the shift selector with my right.

Something made me pause for a moment and gaze at the beautiful Christmas lights that were strung haphazardly over a young maple's branches on the front lawn. In front of the lit tree, stood a brightly-illuminated, four-foot, plastic Santa Claus. The caricature had a wavy gray beard, a red and white suit, and silvery buckles that shined in contrast with his black belt and boots.

"What a nice dinner," I said softly, shaking off the cold. "I'm stuffed, how about you?" My dinner date started to answer before we were both startled by a fist of knuckles wrapping loudly on the frosted window on my driver's door. As a dark figure stood beyond my vision, I put the van in park and pushed down hard on the window button. It was my daughter Lauren's boyfriend, Scott. He stood with hands in pockets and his knees bent in an effort to keep warm in the night's crisp and cold air.

"Scott!" I said, with surprise in my voice. "What's up? Where's your jacket? It's freezing out here!"

He looked at me with eyes wide open and that "deer in the head-light" look on his face.

"Um," he paused briefly, before slowly speaking again a few seconds later.

"I didn't get a chance to speak to you tonight," he said, while stepping back and bending forward, without taking his eyes off mine. "Well, um..." he continued. "I wanted to ask you..., if it was okay with you..., and, do I have your permission... to ask Lauren... to marry me. Tomorrow? On Christmas morning?"

I stared back at Scott, frozen and in total shock! He continued to lock in to my eyes, still bending his knees but shifting his cold hands to his armpits while waiting for my answer. I felt my throat close and my eyes start to water.

"Answer him!" my date hollered, as she whacked me on my right shoulder and arm, shaking me from my dazed stupor. Holding back an eruption of bubbling emotions, I slowly began to speak.

"Scott...," I answered, as I leaned through the open window,

With Ricky at Cousin Kim's wedding after the accident.

feeling the night's air sting the tips of my ears. "I would be honored..., truly honored to have you as my son-in-law." I put my hand out and tightly grabbed his. "And, of course, you have my permission," I announced proudly, pulling his hand through the window as his arm and body followed.

"Come here!" I commanded with a smile, and hugged him through the opened window without letting him go. He laughed and said, "Okay..., okay thank you," but I still wouldn't let go.

I drove home that night with a lump in my throat and joy in my heart. *How will I walk her down the aisle on her wedding day?* I asked myself. It was dark in the car, so I think I got away with wiping the tears from my eyes on the drive home.

75

THE TIME FINALLY came for me to face my fears. It was Lauren's wedding day. I hadn't slept a wink the night before—worrying about walking, well, rolling her down the aisle.

I worried about it all. My rented pant legs didn't cover my ankles while sitting in the wheelchair. I worried about that. My tuxedo's jacket sides kept getting caught and tangled in the wheel spokes. I worried about that. I was going to be shorter than everyone else, especially in the wedding pictures—and I worried about that. I worried about everything!

Then it hit me as I was putting my cufflinks on.

This is Lauren's wedding day, not my day. If I blow it today and can't do something quite right, I know that my daughter will still have the best day of her entire life. Just don't fall out of the chair in front of everyone.

I finished dressing, threw my wheelchair in the van, and drove to the wedding with my date. A few years ago, Derek bought an online license to become a minister, so Lauren asked her brother to marry her and Scott. Derek was in the wedding party too. The magnificent church that I imagined while lying under that tree never materialized. They just didn't want a Catholic church wedding but the venue was beautiful just the same.

The wedding planner positioned me in the doorway where I could see Lauren standing behind me, waiting for her signal. When our eyes locked, it tugged at my heartstrings. Her dress was beautiful. *She* was beautiful. And she looked so happy.

Before she appeared, the guests' eyes were all on me and I could sense that. When signaled, the flower girls, my two granddaughters, Nevaeh Angelina and Olivia Lauren, started the procession down the aisle while throwing red rose pedals onto the white runway before them.

My thoughts were on the moment but I also couldn't help thinking of that day under the oak tree. *This is the moment I've been worrying about since my accident. I can't believe it is finally here.*

Lauren leaned down and kissed me as I whispered in her ear. *You look beautiful,* I said, quietly and calmly.

"Thank you, Daddy, you look handsome too. Are you ready for this?"

"I am," I answered, looking out to the crowd of guests on both sides of the isle.

"Let's go then, try not to roll on my gown, okay?" she giggled. As I pushed my wheelchair forward, I kept my left hand opened wide to push her wedding dress away from my wheel and spokes with my stiffened fingers. If it became tangled in my spokes, it would have been ugly. It was hard to roll straight with my hand half off my wheel, so I rolled a little sporadically. I tried to remember that all eyes were on her and not me.

"You're doing good, Daddy," she whispered. I looked up to her face for a split second and I could see the happiness in her eyes. Right then, my worries turned to love, and I didn't care what people thought. I also realized that my daughter wasn't disappointed that I couldn't walk her down the aisle. The worry that consumed me from the time I hit the ground on that cold morning in November and continued all those years, was all for nothing. She didn't seem to care in the least.

We made it to the podium where Scott was waiting. I hugged him and put her hand in his. Derek looked so sharp and handsome in his tuxedo, as he made the most amazing speech about his little sister. He then praised Scott, commenced with the ceremony, and pronounced them husband and wife. It was beautiful. There wasn't a dry eye in the room, including my own. When rolling in a wheelchair, you cannot take your hand off a wheel to wipe your eyes, because the chair quickly turns in half circles and goes off course. *That* was hard, but I kept adjusting.

We took pictures which I hated, then headed to the ballroom for the reception. That is where the father-daughter dance would be held. I couldn't get it out of my mind. I couldn't even stop thinking of it while people spoke to me. I was only half listening to them and I think it showed. I couldn't help it; it worried me so much. *How am I going to dance with my daughter? Will I embarrass her in front of all these people?* I headed to the ballroom with butterflies in my stomach.

76

THE ROOM WAS decorated like the palace of a princess. Soft blue lighting blended with the white..., um..., everything. Lauren always dreamed of white. The setting that Lauren had coordinated was truly elegant. I couldn't believe the detail.

A square-shaped dance floor was in the middle of the room with guests surrounding it on all sides. I couldn't help noticing that a bothersome lump formed in my throat.

The disc jockey played soothing music during the delicious dinner, and I tried to keep busy with small talk, but the "dance" still loomed in the back of my mind. The "father-daughter" dance.

When the dinner portion ended, the emcee made some announcements and introduced the wedding party. I kept looking over to Lauren. Then, he asked my daughter to come to the middle of the dance floor. Just my daughter. The emcee handed her the microphone and she accepted it gracefully. I could not believe my eyes! You see, Lauren was a stutterer when she was a child. Not severe, but just enough to keep her from speaking in public. Hard work and lots of speech therapy made it hardly noticeable, but she remained deathly afraid to speak in front of even a small group, never mind a roomful of people.

What is she going to do with that mic? I wondered. I felt nervous for her. As she cleared her throat, as I empathically cleared mine, and tested the mic, I couldn't help but feel so much love and pride for my little girl.

"Hello," she started, with a smile on her glowing face. "On behalf of Scott and myself, I want to thank everyone for coming." The silence was deafening. "I would like to take this opportunity to thank you, Mom and Dad, for the guidance that you've given me and the love you've shown me through the years." Emotions began to bung up, so she took a deep breath and slowly continued. The palms of my hands were soaking wet.

"I'd also like to share a quick story about my dad and me if it's okay." My throat started to close and my heart began to pound. Pins and needles devoured my legs and it felt as though my feet were on fire. I rubbed the tops of my thighs to calm them down but it was no use. The nerves were in hyperactive mode.

Lauren went on. "Well, when I was a little girl, about three or four, I obviously adored my dad as all daughters do. He was my everything. I even asked my mom if I could marry him when I grew up and when she said no, I cried. I reminded her that she said I would marry someone that I loved, so I asked her, "then why not, Daddy?" The guests quietly chuckled.

"When the Bette Midler song, *Wind Beneath My Wings* came out, I used to climb into bed with my daddy and sing it to him; only I couldn't say the word "hero" correctly. Instead, I would say 'heo', instead of 'hero'. I'd snuggle up to my daddy and sing, "Did you ever know that you're my 'heo!'"

The room burst into laughter and I had never been more proud of my daughter,—and she didn't stutter at all! If she did, I didn't notice it.

Then she continued. "I think that many of you now know that when my dad had his accident, he laid in the woods that day worrying about how he was going to walk me down the aisle on my wedding day. And, I know that it has bothered him throughout these years. "But Dad," she said, as she turned to look right at me, "we did it! *You* did it. You walked me down the aisle, just in a different way, as you tell the kids, your own way!"

———

MY HEART POUNDED HARDER. "NOW, it's time for the father-daughter dance, and I'm not sure how we are going to do it, but we'll figure it out. Come on, Daddy," she said, while waving me over as she walked to the dance floor.

Just then, the DJ began playing the song, '*Wind Beneath my Wings*, by Bette Midler.' On the far side of the dance floor sat a huge flat-screen monitor, which ran a looped video showing still slides of Lauren and me doing things together when she was a little girl. There were pictures of us fishing and camping together, followed by stills of me holding my little girl as a baby and a toddler. I looked a lot different back then with legs under me rather than wheels, which made me a little sad, but only for a second.

I unlocked my brakes and pushed myself to the dance floor. As I got to the middle of the floor, I locked my wheels and looked up at my little girl. She was beaming with happiness. She gathered up her gown and sat gently down across my lap, one leg across my legs and

Lauren with Dad at Galilee.

her other one atop my wheel. I struggled a little to turn my body sideways to hug and to hold her, and then to keep that position, but it wasn't bad. It wasn't bad at all.

"I love you so much, Lauren." I whispered to her, with a very shaky voice.

"I love you too, Daddy."

"Lauren, I..." At that moment, Bette Midler belted out that verse and choked me up so much that I couldn't say another word. "Did you ever know that you're my hero," Bette Midler sang. It was heart-wrenching. Lauren sang along quietly in my ear. "Did you ever know that you're my heo," she sang softly, with a giggle that reminded me of days gone by. My heart rate lowered and the pounding in my chest slowed.

To mimic dancing of some kind, I pushed and pulled my wheel-chair wheels back and forth and made ever so small turns. It felt nice.

Suddenly, both of my shoes slipped off the footplate and almost dumped Lauren off my lap and onto the dance floor. The bottoms of the rented tuxedo shoes were so smooth, they slid off the footplate

Father-daughter dance.

with just her weight on my legs. I began to panic! But, Lauren laughed, hopped off, waited for me to reposition my feet back onto the footplate and gathered up her dress again and hopped back on. I began my little dance once more when my legs buckled again and she almost fell off my lap this time.

"It's okay, Dad. Let's try again." After lifting my legs and planting my feet back on the plate again, I asked her to get back on slowly and I wouldn't push the chair to dance this time. "It's fine," she said, and just held me and I held her. We stayed perfectly still while Bette Midler continued to sing her amazing song. Our song.

Over Lauren's shoulder, I watched the slide show of me and my little girl, as I held her tight. I kissed her face about ten times and tried to tell her how much I loved her. Then I couldn't speak at all. I just broke down crying, buried my face in her neck and soaked her smooth skin with my river of tears. It was just she and I, and like an ostrich with his head buried in the sand, I remained there, thinking, holding, hugging, squeezing, gently kissing, thinking some more and above all, loving my little girl and appreciating all that I have. Finally, it all came out.

"Dad," Lauren said laughingly, through tears of her own. "You need to let go of me now. The dance is over," she giggled. "You're going to ruin my makeup." Again, giggling softly.

Back to reality and somewhat embarrassed, I covered my eyes with one hand and caressed her warm cheek which I'd made sloppily moist. I couldn't stop crying!

I found Derek's exceptionally long-lashed eyes, blinking like mine, among the muted crowds, and I locked on, loving him from afar. Not because I couldn't dance,—but because I could, and because I did. I am a very, very lucky man.

Blinking with long, slow, and deliberate blinks, the entire room came into view. I hadn't noticed they'd been standing, standing by their chairs—some hand-in-hand, some clutching crumpled tissues, and some with wide-spread fingers over hearts in awe of my beautiful daughter. My mom looked on, as streams of "hope" leapt from her body, as if endless flocks of birds raced to be first with their message, then enveloping us in a veil of calmness. Silently, reciting the poem, I thought of Cousin Carolyn. "Hope is the thing with feathers that perches in the soul and sings the tune without the words and never stops at all."

—Bobby

Made in United States
North Haven, CT
27 December 2022

30226696R00192